# Under A Mackerel Sky

# RICK STEIN

## Under A Mackerel Sky

### A MEMOIR

EBURY
PRESS

9 10

This edition published 2014
First published in 2013 by Ebury Press, an imprint of Ebury Publishing
A Random House Group company

Copyright © Rick Stein 2013

All photographs © Rick Stein unless otherwise stated

The Random House Group Limited Reg. No. 954009

Addresses for companies within the Random House Group can be found at
www.randomhouse.co.uk

A CIP catalogue record for this book is available from the British Library

**Penguin Random House is committed to a sustainable future for
our business, our readers and our planet. This book is made from
Forest Stewardship Council® certified paper.**

Designed and set by seagulls.net

Printed and bound in Great Britain by Clays Ltd, Elcograf S.p.A.

ISBN 9780091949914

To buy books by your favourite authors and register for offers visit
www.randomhouse.co.uk

*For Sas, Ed, Jack, Charles, Zach,*
*Olivia, Jeremy, John and Henrietta*

*And in memory of Janey*

# CONTENTS

PART ONE

Rikki-Tikki-Tavi – *page 1*

PART TWO

Rites of Passage – *page 59*

PART THREE

Early Days – *page 149*

PART FOUR

Giddy Times – *page 221*

PART FIVE

Back to Australia – *page 291*

Afterword – *page 309*

Acknowledgements – *page 311*

*All men should strive to learn before they die,*
*what they are running from, and to, and why*
**James Thurber**

PART ONE

# Rikki-Tikki-Tavi

# I

I loved fishing off the rocks with my dad. There weren't a lot of things I loved doing with him; I was a bit scared of him because he shouted a lot. But fishing was a time when the tying of knots in nylon line and the threading of ragworms on hooks involved us with practicalities and I forgot my reserve. He kept his wooden reels in a green canvas bag flecked with fish scales and he always took with him a little wire folding stool with an orange cloth seat which he also used when painting watercolours of the medieval bridge at Wadebridge or the view of the Camel estuary towards Stepper and Pentire Point. We had a house in Cornwall on Trevose Head and my dad knew a lot of local fishermen, mostly from going to pubs: the Cornish Arms and Farmers Arms in St Merryn and several of the half a dozen or so pubs in Padstow, particularly the London Inn, the Golden Lion and the Caledonian.

A strong memory of childhood is sitting in the back of our Jaguar with my sister Henrietta drinking St Austell ginger beer and eating crisps with a little blue paper twist of salt, waiting while my mum and dad had a drink on a dull day. We were never allowed inside the pub but the smell of beer and tobacco smoke and the sound of good-humoured conversation billowing out as people came and went was tantalising, particularly in the warm summer drizzle, when the dampness of the air seemed to hold in those aromas, infused with the scent of wild fennel from hedges nearby.

Henrietta remembers interminable hours in one boat or another with Bill Cullum fishing for mackerel, garfish and pollack, or with Johnnie Murt hauling lobster pots. Most of the time she would sit and read. Occasionally, we'd both be sick. Once, alone with my father in a small boat, we narrowly missed being turned over in the surf at Polzeath. In our excitement at catching so many bass we had let our lines become tangled, snagging the propeller and stopping the engine. I remember the panic then, as we drifted towards the breaking waves. Years later two local boys, Bronco Bate and Arnold Murt, out salmon netting on the Doom Bar drowned because the same thing happened; the atmosphere in Padstow the next morning was as dark as I can recall.

The downstairs bedroom next to the kitchen in our house, Polventon, would often be used for storing live lobsters, crab or crayfish which crawled over the floor, bubbling and making cracking noises. I loved the crab meat and quite liked the crayfish, but the lobster was too intense. Its firm, white, sweet-salty flesh was too strong for a child and the bright yellow mayonnaise too pungent with the olive oil that my mother always used. How special now are those flavours that I couldn't take then; the beer tasted horribly bitter, particularly the Whitbread Pale Ale which some of the workers on our farm drank. I can still recall the black, heavy screw stoppers with red rubber seals, and the men sitting with their glasses on the just-filled barley sacks at lunch break during harvest time.

Fishing off the rocks we never caught much more than wrasse and pollack. The wrasse were gorgeously coloured; deep red, orange, yellow and sometimes green or golden-hued, but tasted of nothing. The pollack were always the same colour, a silver belly and brown back and large dark blue eyes. My dad and I would take the fish back to the house where the wrasse were treated with little enthusiasm by my mother. She left them till they were starting to smell, I think to make me feel better about it, then threw them out onto the springy cliff grass for the gulls. The pollack she made into fish cakes, often with mackerel, which were ever-present due to the almost daily boat-fishing trips. All the cooking I've ever done since is in some way an attempt to recapture some of the flavours of the cooking at home when I was a boy. Those pollack fish cakes with mashed potatoes, parsley, salt, pepper and dazzlingly fresh mackerel, just put under the grill with a sprig of fennel, are still the best I've ever eaten.

One summer we went to stay on the south coast of Cornwall, at Church Cove on the Lizard peninsula with some friends of my parents, the composer Richard Arnell and his wife Colette. They had a daughter, Claudine, whom my brother John admired even more urgently than I did, he being some years older, but I was fascinated by her: she was far and away the most beautiful girl I had ever met, and with the longest legs. She was like a real-life version of Brigitte Bardot, whom we then thought the ultimate in sexiness. Church Cove seemed very dishevelled, the thatch on the cottages patchy and full of holes, and a large pile of smelly cattle bedding straw right next to one of the houses. I may be recalling wrongly, but I think that some of the local boys of my age had no shoes. The holiday house had been the old fish cellars. Below it, at the top of the pebble beach, there was a capstan house for hauling up the pilchard boats, and Henrietta and I would spin round on it while Claudine played cool.

One evening, after an afternoon's fishing, I returned in triumph with about 11 wrasse and a couple of pollack and Colette cooked a bouillabaisse. My mother had a well stocked cupboard but it baffles me now where Colette could have got the ingredients for that fabulous fish stew. Not in Cornwall, for sure. The olive oil perhaps from the chemist. There would have been plenty of well-flavoured tomatoes. Maybe the saffron was bought locally too, that would have been available for Cornish saffron cake. Garlic – green and moist – grew in the hedgerows, but I suspect that Colette had a whole box of things like bulbs of garlic and tomato purée from London because, being French, these were essential for her.

Colette's bouillabaisse – with its dark orange colour and the saltiness of it and the way it made those wrasse really taste of something – really stays with me. I must have been 11 or 12 but I still remember the glorious crunch of cornflakes with full-cream milk, brown sugar and clotted cream for breakfast. And the perfection of my mum's spaghetti in the kitchen of Polventon, with the view from the window of the Merrope rocks jutting out into the sea below with Cataclews Point across Mother Ivey's Bay in the near distance and, beyond, Trevone and Stepper and Pentire Point.

# II

I was born in Chipping Norton on 4 January 1947. My parents, Eric and Dorothy Stein, owned a farm in Oxfordshire, and I was the fourth of five children. The youngest, Henrietta, was my childhood playmate on the farm and on the beach; we are still incredibly close. John is six years older than me; he was idolised by my mother for his good looks and his brilliance at exams. Janey, nine years older than me, was idolised by both Henrietta and myself for her trendy clothes and cheerful don't-care attitude; she had countless boyfriends, most of whom were disapproved of by our parents. Jeremy is my half-brother, my mother's son from a previous marriage. He is 12 years older than me, and soon after I was born he went to the Royal Naval College in Dartmouth. After that Jeremy was away at sea so I didn't see much of him. He had built a model railway at the bottom of the garden and had large model yachts and other grown-up toys which I vandalised with clumsy wonder as most much younger brothers do.

My father had a manager – Harry Watson – at the farm, helped by a young woman called Joyce Unwin who had come to work on the farm as a land girl in the Second World War. My father spent most of the week in London, where he and my mother had a flat in Bloomsbury. My dad ran the family firm – Stein Brothers, whose main business was distilling – with his brother Rolf. By the time I was born it had been taken over by the Distillers Company and, in time, my father became managing director. The Steins, including my father's sisters Zoe and Muriel, had connections in North Cornwall, where my father and Rolf built Polventon, an Art Deco house on Trevose Head where we all spent our summer holidays. Many people thought it was eccentric and experimental in the 1960s and 70s – but today the architecture is much admired and, indeed, the house is now listed.

On Sunday nights at the farm in Oxfordshire, my dad made tomato and onion soup. It was probably little more than onions – or more likely shallots, because he adored them – sliced and softened in butter to which he'd then add some chopped tomatoes from the garden and simply simmer it all together with stock made from the leftovers of the Sunday roast chicken, with lots of salt and pepper. His soup was so clear you could see the pieces of shallot and tomato in it. No wonder I am drawn to simple dishes.

My father used to say with some pride at Sunday lunch that everything we were eating had come from the farm. Vegetables from the vegetable garden, which was surrounded by sheep netting near the Dutch barn where he also grew sweet peas (I can't think of those delicate shades of creamy-white, pink, blue and mauve and the sweet fragrance of them without a sense of comfort). The beef, if not immediately from our own Herefordshire bullocks, would certainly have come from a neighbour's. The pudding, too, would have been ours: in summer, strawberries from the fruit garden near the house and cream from the dairy in Chipping Norton, or a blackcurrant or gooseberry fool. In autumn, an apple charlotte from our apples or a damson tart from the tree by our house. When I was little I found my mum's pastry too rich but now I always use her recipe. It wasn't really delicate, not like the sort of pastries I've relished since in French patisseries. It was a mixture of lard and butter, 5oz of each to a pound of flour, but it had a rich crumbliness. She never altered it by putting in sugar for puddings, and I have always found that a nice contrast. I used to scrape out the mixing bowl, but raw pastry doesn't taste as good as it smells, unlike raw sponge mix which is so more-ish that it's frustrating.

My earliest memories of the farm are to do with food. A few years ago I made a television series called *Rick Stein's Food Heroes* in which I went round the British Isles and Ireland. 'There's a whole band of people out there producing small quantities of food with passionate commitment,' I wrote, 'who look after their land properly, treat their flocks or herds with affection and respect and take their time to grow or rear crops or animals.' Only after some time did I stop to think that I was actually writing about our family farm.

The farm was 150 acres, down a long yellow bumpy lane just outside Churchill, on the road to Chipping Norton. It was called a mixed farm, which I later came to realise was a farm where there were lots of animals being reared and lots of crops being grown but you didn't actually make money out of any of it. I don't think it lost a lot of money, but my father was always blaming Harry, who ran the farm. Basically, it was never going to be profitable. It was not big enough, and not efficiently managed. I'm saying this only with the benefit of hindsight and having run – or tried to run – restaurants.

It was called Conduit Farm because it had a spring that fed the village of Churchill. One English summer, my father decided to build a swimming pool, which was rare in those days, especially in rural Oxfordshire. That year, there was a drought and the spring dried up and the locals had very little water. The *Daily Telegraph* reported that Distillers Company director, Eric Stein, had filled his pool while the villagers were queuing at the standpipes. In fact my father had fallen into the empty pool shortly before it was due to be filled and had broken his leg. He lost interest in it after that. It remained about a quarter filled with increasingly muddy rainwater. When it was finally full of clean water and we children got to swim in it, we were stung by the nettles which grew out of the mud near the edge because the paving slabs were never laid. The water always went green because the filter was never plumbed in. This was an early indicator to me how newspapers don't tell the truth. I was too young and naive to read the signs, but it was also an early indicator of my dad's state of mind. After the manic phase of building the pool came the depressive stage of the man who had used up all the water. It really upset him.

Much of what my dad did bewildered me. He came back from Japan with tons of gadgets – early transistor radios, cameras, tape recorders. I had never seen anything like it. Nowadays, I know that crazy shopping is a common manifestation of the manic phase of bipolar behaviour. As a child, I was embarrassed by my dad's effusive episodes; I honestly don't think I had much awareness of his depressed episodes. He was just terribly low, and I suppose I got used to living with someone who was intermittently sad.

Each year in November we killed a pig. I wasn't allowed to see the actual killing or the bleeding. The blood was collected for black pudding. Mr Nurdin, the local slaughterman, came over from Chippy (Chipping Norton) to do the killing and, as soon as the pig was dead and bled, I could watch the burning off of the hair with straw. The belly was slit open, and all the guts spilled out and were loaded into buckets. Then came the sorting out of various organs and the cleaning-out of the guts by attaching them to a tap or hosepipe and watching as all the shit and a few white worms ran out. When they were clean, Harry used to tie them up into bundles and make chitlins which we ate fried. He'd make brawn by boiling the pig's head and pressing the meat. He'd make sausages and hang bacon and gammons in our larder. I don't say it was carried out with the finesse of an Andalucian *matanza* but it familiarised me with the realities of slaughter and created my enjoyment of offal. A few years ago at Brasserie Bofinger in Paris, my lifelong friend Johnny Walter and I both ordered *andouillettes*, the speciality of the house. Realising we were English, the waiter laughed. 'I think maybe you don't like these,' he said. 'It's French speciality. No for English. Maybe you like *Choucroute Alsacienne* instead.'

'We absolutely want the *andouilletes*,' I said.

He shrugged, as they do, and blew a little from the corner of his mouth and shortly returned with two plates of the stumpy sausages which I can only describe as honking, in the sense of a strong blaring smell. They were very powerful – the same order of unsettling aroma as ripe Camembert but also sharp tasting in their intestinal taint. To the uninitiated they smelt of pig shit, but not to me. These were the intestines of my youth, albeit with a little extra maturity.

I can't honestly say I totally enjoyed them, but I was definitely not going to leave them unfinished.

As a child, I took pig evisceration as normal so there was no surprise when my mother pulled the guts out of a chicken on the kitchen table and occasionally let me have a go. I would marvel at the whole eggs in there, flecked with blood but without the shell, getting ready to be laid. I remember, too, a type of cottage cheese known as cherry curds, so-called because it was made from the first milk after a cow had newly calved and contained traces of blood. The facts of life were all around us: boars and sows, collie dogs, pet rabbits. On one occasion Mr Hutchinson, the owner of Sarsden Farm across the valley from ours, walked over a number of cows to be crossed with our bull. My friend Les and I sat on the wall of the yard watching. Mr Hutchinson, something of a gentleman farmer like my dad, told us to get off because it was not appropriate. I remember feeling embarrassed but also a bit bewildered because neither Les nor I could see why it was so wrong because we didn't really understand that there was a connection between what we were seeing and what humans did.

Shortly after they bought the farm, my parents joined the two original cottages into a rather well-proportioned limestone house, creating a large room between the houses and a floor above with two bedrooms. We called the room the Hall. It had an open fireplace, the wrought-iron grate was made by Rathbones, the blacksmiths in Kingham, and had two posts at the front topped with two heavy steel balls which were smooth and warm when you held them. We burned huge beech logs on the fire and it smoked incessantly. There was a large comfortable sofa facing the fire and, under the windows, which stretched the length of the hall, a bench seat with cushions, under which we kept games and jigsaw puzzles. These had all spilled out of their broken boxes because it was damp, so there was a confusion of jigsaw pieces and Monopoly money, all smelling of spiders. My dad had installed two 12-inch speakers at either end of the Hall, and he would play Beethoven, Wagner and Tchaikovsky as well as the musicals *My Fair Lady*, *Carousel*, *South Pacific* and *Oklahoma*. Later my mother told me how much she hated Brahms because my father always played it when he was depressed, but I can't listen to the last movement of the First Symphony without reliving the comfort of those days as a child, those safe Sundays and the smell of roast beef and bubbles of Veuve Cliquot in wide shallow glasses which my mother would sometimes let me have a small sip out of.

The Hall was always filled on Sundays with my parents' friends. Many were artists, writers, painters and colleagues of my dad's, including the Ifoulds and the Vernons from Sydney and Karl Finsterbusch from New York. England was rather grey in the 1950s, and Henrietta and I were impressed by the worldly confidence of these rich businessmen with their suntanned wives from California, Australia and South Africa.

Sometimes there would be German relatives: Tanta Brunhilda, who looked about a hundred to me; Walter Flender, who looked like a bear, but apparently this was only when he came for the last time and was dying; Tanta Alla, who complained to my mother that I was fat and lazy and did nothing but listen to Elvis Presley songs. Some of her nephews came too, Fritz-Eric, Martin and Alexander Schmitt, who were a bit older than me. My dad asked the teenage Alexander to mow the lawns. He spent the rest of the day doing it, mowing even under the copse of beech trees that surrounded the house. 'No wonder the Nazis took over,' my dad said. 'Give the Germans a command and they'll carry it out without question.' Not the greatest fun, having the young German second cousins to stay. They came from big houses in Dusseldorf and didn't quite 'get' our simple country life, though when I was older I met them again and found them unexpectedly humorous.

There was a rather unnerving formality about the German relatives; decent people, but a bit stiff. My ancestor, August Stein, expanded the family wine and spirit business in the nineteenth century. He bought vineyards on the Rhine and took the business into mining and shipping. He was clearly successful and sensible. His cousin, Siegfried Stein, joined the family wine business but didn't like it and gave it up in favour of an academic life. There is a book about the Stein family published in 1921 which says, 'Siegfried was a good academic but couldn't translate his knowledge into practical industry. Bad in maths, he was far too trusting of people.'

A bit worthy and correct they may have been, but after a successful expansion of the production of gin and vodka, the family opened the first hostel for alcoholics in Europe. Boring, maybe, but also good people with a conscience.

The German relatives might have found our farm a long way from home but, to me, the view from the farmhouse window was the frame of my early life. In the far distance was the tower of Churchill Church, modelled on the tower of Magdalen College chapel in Oxford. In the centre, our fields sloped down to Kingham brook, which was the boundary of the farm. Across the stream the land rose to the village of Sarsden and, to the left, the view was the dark green mass of Sarsgrove Wood. My earliest memory relates to that wood – a gate and two large pigs on the other side of it. I can recall the pink pigs, the grey of the gate, the green of the grass and the darker green of the trees. I must have been carried by my mother because I was looking over the gate down at the pigs. I was two at the time. Just a bubble of memory, but it's that road and those woods whenever I read Kipling's poetry:

> They shut the road through the woods
> Seventy years ago.
> Weather and rain have undone it again,
> And now you would never know
> There was once a road through the woods.

Kipling was much in evidence in my childhood. My mother used to read *Puck of Pook's Hill* to me; she particularly liked the story of the Romans on Hadrian's Wall. Kipling's tales made British history come alive for children before TV and video. My mother used to wonder how cold the native Romans must have felt in their tunics.

She went to Italy often with my dad; looking through the photo albums recently, Henrietta and I were filled with a sense of how many holidays they had. Boarding schools were very convenient for them with five children.

We were lucky in that our parents were unconventional. They both loved pubs – indeed my dad went to the pub every night, and he always favoured the public bar over the saloon bar. He enjoyed chatting to fishermen, farmers and builders and found their conversation a refreshing change from people from his own background. Perhaps because he had experienced anti-German taunts as a child, he didn't fit into the British Establishment. He relished the company of artists, composers and writers, and he didn't like the 'County Set'. He was a magnetic presence, very attractive to women, and very difficult to live up to. My father instinctively knew how the world worked and what was important about humanity: he always went straight to the truth of stuff.

# III

My mother married a fellow undergraduate called Alan Stewart in her last year at Cambridge, in a desperate bid to get away from her Dulwich home where my grandfather and grandmother were living in some disharmony. She became pregnant with her first child, Jeremy, but her marriage to Alan turned out to be as unhappy as the home she had fled. I came to know Alan quite well because later he lived near my school, Uppingham, and took me out on the occasional weekend. He was kind but there was nothing to do at his house except listen to his collection of humorous records by a singer called Paddy Roberts. This didn't appeal to a soon-to-be-rebellious teenager. One refrain I recall ran 'He went quite white and sloshed her right in the middle of a cha-cha-cha'. I didn't enjoy it very much.

My mother met my father while on holiday in Cornwall with her brother Charlie. My father was tall, about six foot four, and extremely good-looking, with dark hair and pale blue eyes. He was one of four children. His parents, Julius William and Clara, were Anglo-Germans, originally from Dusseldorf. His grandfather, Julius Otto, had come to London in 1870 to open a branch of the Stein Brothers firm which by then also had a branch in Bordeaux. The Steins had once been grain farmers but had branched into distilling alcohol and selling vodka and gin. As the business grew they moved to Dusseldorf and built large cellars, and then bought Fuchsberg vineyard at Geisenheim. They appear to have been markedly commercially-minded since their interest in the vineyard was not so much the fine Rheingau wines, but in selling a mass-market sparkling wine called Stein Trocken, which they marketed in a champagne bottle with a French-looking label.

In London they lived first in Baker Street, then moved to Walton-on-Thames in Surrey and built an imposing house called Rhinelands. But the First World War found them in a hostile country with a German name and a big house that was an obvious target. My father's sister, my aunt Zoe, who would have been four or five at the outbreak of the war, never forgot bricks being thrown through the windows. My father, too, was traumatised by the animosity. My grandparents bought a house in Constantine Bay in north Cornwall called Treglos, now a hotel. Cornwall at that time was somewhat remote from the rest of England and, at least early on in the war, the anti-German fervour was less pronounced. I can't find proof of it, but I believe my grandmother, Clara, was a friend of D. H. Lawrence's wife, Frieda, who was also German, and it may not be a coincidence that when Lawrence and Frieda first arrived in Cornwall they rented Porthcuthan House near my grandparents. Later, they bought a house in Zennor where Lawrence wrote *Women in Love*. I also believe that Clara was a friend of Emily Pankhurst and a member of the suffragette movement.

The Stein connection with Cornwall continued after the war and by the time my mother met my father, the family had been having summer vacations there for years. My memories of my father have been distorted by his bipolar disorder. The bouts of mania followed by depressions became more frequent as I grew up, so now I find it difficult to imagine how he must have seemed to my mother, on holiday in Cornwall, long ago in the 1920s, but I guess he was irresistible – intelligent, keen on art, architecture and music, and a good painter too. In any event, she parted from Alan. My dad's charms must have been considerable; it took a lot of courage in those days for a woman to break up her marriage. Mum lived for the rest of her life with the stigma of being a divorcee. As was the convention of the time, she was the 'guilty' party, and she had to suffer the misery of not seeing her first-born child for several years.

Eventually, Alan was forced to admit that his own household wasn't suitable for a little boy, and mother and son were reunited. Jeremy always said that the day that his life began was the day that he arrived at Conduit Farm. He was seven.

Despite my father's precarious mental state – or perhaps because of it – our parents gave us a secure childhood, and surrounded us with love, culture and friendship. The farm was our world. There was nothing there that failed to delight. We felt safe.

My maternal grandfather was a farmer's son from Stourport in Worcestershire who made his fortune in London manufacturing telephones. He ran a company called Telephone Rentals. I have a picture of him wearing spats and a wide-brimmed hat, one foot on the running board of a white Lagonda coupé. They called him Fred T. Jackson. My grandmother, Marie Henrietta, whose father was a missionary in China where she was born, suffered in her marriage, I guess, from neglect. My grandfather was ambitious and successful and, almost true to type, had a mistress called Margaret whom I remember as being rather plain. My grandmother, as they say, took to the bottle. But not uncontrollably – she always appeared well-dressed and when she wanted to go to *thé dansants* in Kent, she paid a good-looking man to accompany her. Indeed, many years after her death this man – his name was Robin – appeared in my life. He came to live in a cottage in Swinbrook, just down the road from Burford in Oxfordshire where my mother spent the last 25 years of her life. He was magnificently queenie by then, portly and often dressed in a kaftan or a vast mauve Kashmir sweater with a large gold medallion. He referred to my grandmother as Mrs J. We all loved his outrageousness, except my mother, who got cross with him from time to time, particularly on one occasion when he invited me to his house for dinner. I must have been about 25 and should have been more sophisticated. He plied me with whisky, then said, 'You remind me of a young lion. Can I come and lie down between your paws?' I was so pissed by then that I said yes. And then realised more was expected of me and fled laughing from the house, leaving a large purple walrus lying on the carpet.

Henrietta and I occasionally went to The Philippines, the estate my grandparents bought near Sevenoaks in Kent. It was a bit boring, but my grandfather had a room in the attic where he made 12-bore cartridges, which was fascinating to me. Equally fascinating to me now is the memory of being taken into the kitchen for a glass of milk and realising from the taste that it was really weak. Only later did I wake up to the fact it had been watered down. Why, I wonder, did the maid do that? Perhaps she thought that strong milk was too much for a child. Maybe she was playing a joke, or stealing milk from my grandparents. I remember that, and walks in the woods of the estate with my mother in autumn with brightly coloured mushrooms everywhere, particularly the red-and-white spotted *Amanita muscaria* or fly agaric. Mushrooms, watered-down milk and a gun room – oh, and a horse on wheels that you could sit on when you were very little.

My brother Jeremy is responsible for why I'm called Rick rather than Christopher, which my mother really wanted. My mother had been reading aloud *Rikki-Tikki-Tavi* from Kipling's *Jungle Book*, and Jeremy dubbed me Rikki. I would have been three or four at the time and was as inquisitive as any mongoose. I had dark red hair and freckles and perhaps he thought I looked like a mongoose too. I can see how the name would have stuck. My son Jack also has dark red hair. When he was little I thought he was not unlike his pet chipmunk Dave – always nosing into things.

I re-read *Rikki-Tikki-Tavi* recently and decided that, after the visceral humour of Roald Dahl's writing for children, it suffers from a dated sort of decency, but it does describe the natural world of an Indian garden with charming attention to detail. The story also has a dark side, in the shape of the venomous cobra Nag and his mate Nagaina. Does every idyllic garden have a dark side, I wonder? Mine certainly did, in the shape of my father, or more correctly my father's manic depression.

My mother spent much of my childhood trying to hide the worst from me. I merely knew that my father was someone I was scared of. Most of the time I was uneasy in his presence. Years later I did a television programme on manic depression with Stephen Fry. Stephen, who is himself bipolar, said in that programme that in his depressive stage he felt completely useless. I think that's how my father must have felt. Most of my life I have had to fight against a creeping conviction that I might be completely useless, too, and at such times I can understand that my father wouldn't have wanted me to be like him. But the result was that he could be very tough on me.

Naturally, as a little boy, I did lots of wrong things. I had a friend on the farm called Les who was the son of the farm manager, Harry. Les and I were inseparable. We constructed a sort of tractor and cart from what was called an Allen Scythe, a petrol-powered finger-bar mower. We simply tied its handlebars to a metal wheeled cart that had been part of a water pump. We used it to travel round the farm, and were shouted into abandoning the really sharp mower at the front. We were skilful at removing nuts and bolts from an early age; you just are on a farm. Eventually, the throttle jammed and we careered down a steep bank – and the scythe, the truck, me and Les turned over. After that we gave the scythe a miss, but there were always things like climbing on high roofs then falling off, and a fabulous game of building a network of tunnels and rooms in the hay bales in our Dutch barn. Our tunnels ran up to the roof and down over the edges with drops; we made pits and stuffed everything with spare straw so that it was totally dark. Then we'd invite neighbours' children into the hay to scare them, and quite often Henrietta too. I'm sure we always had boxes of Swan Vesta matches in our pockets. Leaving aside the danger of conflagration, the tunnels and rooms could have easily collapsed.

The day after 5 November, we were playing with firework cases, fascinated by the brightly coloured boxes and the smell of exploded gunpowder in the damp morning air. Les struck a Swan Vesta and dropped it into a rectangular jumping jack case with green and blue snakes painted on it, just to see what would happen. There was a hiss of smoke … and the next thing I saw was his yellow jersey, blackened at the top, and him screaming, and then going with Joyce and Harry to see him in hospital in Chipping Norton and getting really ticked off by my mum who told me he could have been blinded. Les's father, Harry, used to say (in his Oxfordshire accent), 'You boys are so naughty it just makes me cry.' I don't know if we were any more mischievous than other boys. Some of the things my sons did at that age make me blanch now just thinking about them. They poured petrol into an old pram, lit it and pushed it down our drive into the main road and the path of their mother, Jill, driving home from the restaurant. Another time a neighbour reported being overtaken by my son Edward on a go-cart with another boy on the back doing 65 miles an hour on the road into Padstow.

My dad didn't just shout: he created an atmosphere which went on for days. I think he must have been in his London flat in Mecklenburgh Square with my mother when Les was hospitalised after the fireworks, otherwise I would remember a low moment being even lower. Once, when I was really small but old enough to wield an axe, I chopped down a beech sapling in the copse of trees which surrounded our house. It must have been during harvesting because afterwards I was sitting on sacks by the combine harvester, in the field we called the Hollerback, when I told Harry and Charlie who worked on the farm. They laughed and part of the joke seemed to be how angry my father would be with me. Then I realised they weren't joking. He never, ever, hit me but on this occasion brandished a hazel switch at me which was completely shocking.

It must have been a little after then that I really overstepped the mark. My father had created a garden, lovely but simple – which is still, for me, the way all gardens should be planned. He used plenty of the glorious assets available to everyone in the Cotswolds, the local lemon-coloured limestone. Right in front of the house was a terrace where we would congregate before lunch in the summer and at Easter with glasses of champagne or Gewürztraminer, and ginger beer for me and Henrietta. In front of the terrace was a walled flower bed in which he grew celandines. These have slightly oily green leaves and their yellow flowers at Easter smelled of woodlands, as if he had captured something wild. Below the terrace was a large lawn with wide herbaceous borders; particularly wide was the one at the back, beyond which was a limestone wall which he had built over the years during his manic phases, and beyond that the fields and the Cotswold hills that surrounded us. In that wide border I made my camp. I created a little tunnel so that I could crawl from the lawn through the flowers, then I flattened a large area behind, squashing down the sweet williams at the front and the lupins and hollyhocks and foxgloves behind. Of course he saw the damage and of course he found the camp. It took a while, but he did. His rage was awful. It wasn't just the discovery, but the days that went on after that. This episode was made much worse because he decided that I was so naughty I would have to board at the school I was then attending, Brandons in Oddington.

I had problems with Brandons, anyway. The head teachers and owners, Mr and Mrs Lyons, were perfectly nice, though they seemed to me to be very old, but Mr Lyons had a terrible cough and kept spitting yellow phlegm into his handkerchief. And the food was awful. Every Monday we had cold roast lamb and mashed potato. I could only eat the lamb fat if I could swallow it with lots of water. I'm sure everyone can remember that horrible feeling when trying to eat something so noxious to you that it makes you retch. I managed to board at the school one weekend but was so distraught that my mother insisted it was too much and brought me home.

# IV

I was nine when I was packed off to 'proper' boarding school. I spent a year at a prep school near Tewkesbury called Wells Court, and then three years at The Wells House in Malvern Wells, where all the Wells Court boys went, and finally five years at Uppingham, a public school in Rutland. I imagine everyone who has been sent away to boarding school can remember their first day. I can all too easily visualise the afternoon I turned up with my school trunk in the boot of my dad's pale blue Jaguar Mark 7, and I got out to meet Mr and Mrs Finlay at the door of what was something between a large country house and a stately home. My son Edward later described his arrival at boarding school as like having albatrosses in his stomach. I also recall my youngest son Charles on his first day of weekly boarding panicking when he realised we were going to leave him behind.

My first term happened to be the summer term and wasn't too bad. I felt most homesick and did most of my crying in the second term. The hardest thing was trying to eat and dry retching. One night I vomited all over my bed and the surrounding floor. I had to put up with the impatience of matron, who was woken to deal with it, and the irritation and taunts of the other members of my dormitory. That same matron – I have a feeling she was called Miss Semen Adams but maybe I'm making that up – on another occasion sent me to stand in a corner in the sick bay. Two hours later I was still there. She then blamed me for not coming to get her, as she'd forgotten me. I cried, of course. Another long-forgotten infringement had me disciplined by having to change in the corridor outside the dormitory. This punishment meant scrambling out of school clothes into sports clothes, then back again. In between the changes I was naked, which was the precise moment that one of the only three girls at the school came round the corner, saw me and laughed. I can still recall my embarrassment, the shame of having a girl see my penis. It wasn't, in retrospect, a laugh of ridicule but at the time it was easily the worst thing that had ever happened to me.

I remember going back to school on the train in my second term from Kingham in Oxfordshire and worrying that if my mother's dachshund, Rupert, had boarded the train by mistake I'd have to take him into school. Although I tortured myself with ridiculous imaginings, I wasn't, I guess, any different from most of the other boys. They just got on with it and so did I. My pre-prep school and The Wells House were both run by a man called Alan Darvel. His nickname was Beak. Beak was probably in his early fifties though anyone over 30 would have seemed old to me then. He was balding and rather red-faced but otherwise quite fit, if a little overweight. I know this because he was very keen on swimming naked at the pool in our playing fields at the foot of the Malvern Hills. Not having any guidelines to go on, none of us thought there was anything odd about this, though a naked middle-aged man with large hairy testicles striding around a pool surrounded by ten- to thirteen-year-olds would not perhaps pass muster these days. Beak was unmarried and we were all a little scared of him. He was keen on beating us regularly. I managed to avoid it generally, but others were not so fortunate. He ran things autocratically and sometimes would punish the whole school with detentions, runs and changing exercises if culprits didn't come forward and own up to some misdemeanour.

On one occasion the punishments went on for weeks when no one admitted to snipping the bristles off all the nylon hairbrushes in the lavatories. Finally, it was discovered the bristles had shrivelled up in basins of hot water. On another occasion he called us all into the 'big school' for an assembly where he lamented our appalling behaviour. He announced that he would turn his back to us and ask all those who thought he should go to raise their hands. The deputy head would then count the show of hands. We were appalled. Poor Beak. Of course no one raised his hand.

When I got home and told my parents about it, they said he was a silly old histrionic queen, and we all should have raised our hands just to call his bluff. I was shocked but rather pleased to be included in the joke, though I didn't quite realise what was being implied. It was one of those occasions when a child begins to realise that his parents know things he doesn't know. I didn't particularly like Beak – I was a bit nervous of him – but he lived for his boys. He used to spend several weekends each term visiting us in all the schools we had gone on to, so we would see him once every couple of years. He would arrive, blue-blazered and grey-flannelled, in his dark green Jaguar and take us out to lunch. This was a bit weird. I was at Uppingham by then and did not really know any of the other boys there who had been at The Wells House. They were certainly not the sort I wanted to be associated with in the teenager world of public school. I have to confess that the last time Beak came I was enjoying a liaison with a girl who worked in the kitchen at my school house. I made an excuse, and stood him up for lunch, but felt guilty about it and still do to this day.

Interestingly, Beak never touched or spoke to any of us inappropriately and was a thoroughly good headmaster. He was very keen on all outdoor activities, not just swimming but hiking too and, perhaps more importantly, set great store in boys spending as much time as possible outside – so much so that we were very much left to our own devices to explore the Worcestershire countryside. The degree of independence we had then seems staggering today. There's no chance of going back to those freedoms – it would be too frightening and risky for today's teachers and parents. We spent lots of time building camps in the grounds of The Wells Court and, when we got older, roaming the hills, building huts and swinging from trees. The huts were mostly made from branches and walled with hay, though in the Malvern Hills acquiring sheets of corrugated iron or the odd bed-base or rusty car suspension was a bonus. Some of the more ambitious huts had two storeys. One in particular, the Alamo, had a palisade round it. I took part in a raid of the Alamo. The physical skirmishes were fought with ferocity and involved a couple of the more daring of my band defecating into pages torn out of exercise books, which they then threw over the walls. It's all there in *Lord of the Flies*.

When I finally got to build my own hut, I borrowed a pickaxe, a shovel and a wheelbarrow and dug a significant pit in the rough granite soil of the Malverns. I found some rusty corrugated iron and sheep netting, made beams from some old bedrails, tied everything together with bailer twine, then shovelled earth on to the roof, and hung a grain sack over the entrance. I built a fireplace from some house bricks I found behind Cuff's lemonade factory – which is now Schweppes Malvern Water – and made a chimney from an old earthenware pipe. I would slump down into my stony covered pit, lie on the damp ground and light a twig fire (drawing up the chimney, though with plenty of smoke coming my way) and 'smoke' an old man's beard. I felt like king of my damp humpy. Old man's beard, a wild clematis, hanging down in grey fluffy swathes over the leaves of autumn in Worcestershire, is to me the background in every image in Keats's 'Ode to Autumn'. On darkening foggy winter afternoons when I walked back to school with my friend Hector Blackhurst along the narrow sheep paths through the trees, the old man's beard would be a shroud of grey all around us. I felt very close to Hector, and we were so serious when we were walking along the paths, pulling up the occasional bracken frond and talking earnestly about life and love. We both read a great deal, lying on the floor in the school library. He was very keen on Henry Rider Haggard. I had read *King Solomon's Mines* and thought it was good, but I liked novels about people and their emotions much more than stories of discovery of lost worlds. Hector was obsessed with Ayesha, 'She-who-must-be-obeyed'. I read *She* and its sequel *Ayesha*, became equally absorbed, and so our deep conversations involved much talk of a sorceress whose beauty was so intense that she had to remain veiled and keep behind a partition away from ordinary men because otherwise she'd send them mad with desire. This was a theme of enormous power to someone on the cusp of puberty, and was all we needed to discuss matters of the heart. We were filled with a sense of entering a world of physical love, of deep and meaningful wonder.

Hector was a huge fan of Lonnie Donegan and his skiffle band and 'Rock Island Line', 'The Battle of New Orleans', 'The Grand Coulee Dam', 'Sweet Sixteen' and, above all, 'Does Your Chewing Gum Lose Its Flavour On the Bed Post Overnight?' Ah! And to think that we were listening to Lonnie Donegan while Elvis was waiting just around the corner. I built a crystal radio set from parts I bought in a component shop in Soho. All my friends were making their own and were into popular music. We got the plans from *Practical Wireless* magazine: a crystal diode, a tuning coil, a resistor, a variable coil and a set of Second World War headphones. We made the sets in tobacco tins or cigar boxes or just on a piece of wood, and had to keep them hidden because we weren't allowed radios. You needed an aerial and an earth, so you could only set it up if your bed was by the central-heating pipes. The aerial was no problem – we just used the bed springs. The joy of slipping on your headphones in bed at night! In would come Radio Luxembourg: Buddy Holly and the Crickets' 'Not Fade Away', 'Yakety Yak' by The Coasters and, the most fabulous memory for me, The Everly Brothers' 'All I Have to Do is Dream'. There's a song by Van Morrison which recalls those far-off days for us prep school boys. It's called 'In the Days Before Rock 'n' Roll' and remembers the excitement of tuning in Radio Luxembourg. It was a delicate task as there were loads of other stations in the medium wave band at night around 208 metres.

By the time I was tuning into Radio Luxembourg, sex was still distant, though fast-approaching. I wonder what it's like for a child these days to become aware of sex? I only say this because my growing realisation of the realities of sex occurred to me in such a natural manner, if not necessarily comfortably, that I wouldn't, in the words of William Holden in *The Wild Bunch*, have had it any other way. Will the constant stream of information from television and the Internet change the utter bafflement of it, I wonder? I struggled in semi-ignorance. This was when I still kept my teddy bear, Blue Ears, hidden under the sheets in the dormitory. We boys spent some time trying to figure it out and then we heard that if you went and asked Beak for what was known as a sex lecture he'd tell you all about it. The idea of doing this was shameful, but we egged each other on and finally a group of about ten of us knocked on his study door and asked him. He seemed perfectly at ease and agreed to talk to us all. The information that he imparted was completely astounding to me. The idea that I had little seeds in my penis, which would fertilise eggs in girls' wombs; it was frightful. Beak's little lecture went on for about an hour and I was late for gym which was being taken by the assistant headmaster, Mr Hall, whom we all knew as Stubbs. I revered Stubbs. He was our games master and was almost as wide as he was tall, but it was all solid muscle. He epitomised health, vigour and clean living. I had begun to show some promise as a rugger player. Stubbs coached the first XV and I really wanted to be in the team.

'You're late. Where have you been?'

'With Beak. Sir.'

'Oh yes? What have you been up to?'

'Lecture, sir.'

'A lecture? What sort of lecture?'

'Sex lecture, sir.'

I used the letters S-E-X in a Scrabble game at home with John, my dad and an artist friend, Enslin Du Plessis.

'Ah,' said my dad.

'Sex rears its ugly head,' said Enslin.

Enslin used to chain-smoke. I can still hear the intake of breath through the corner of his mouth with the smoking cigarette firmly clasped in his lips as he painted. It was as if he was slapping the smell of cigarette smoke and turpentine on to his canvases. He painted Henrietta and me sitting on the lawn in front of our farmhouse. Another work by him is hanging above the kitchen table in my house in Padstow. It's a painting of the mantelpiece in the flat which my parents shared with him in Mecklenburgh Square. There's a mirror at the back, a bottle of sherry, a bottle of VAT 69 and a tall green bottle of Gewürztraminer. Whenever I look at it I remember Enslin's bald head and the gas boiler in the flat and the interminable time between turning on the water, the smell of gas and then the explosion as it fired up. That, and the comforting smell of his cigarettes.

# V

I went to Uppingham because my father and Uncle Rolf had been there before me. My father hoped I would go to Winchester like John, my brother, but I went for a tour of both schools and discovered that when the Winchester boys got up in the morning they had to wash using a jug of water and a bowl whereas Uppingham had baths and showers. I was – more importantly – also nervous because Winchester had a much higher academic standard than Uppingham, and I didn't think I had any chance of passing the entrance exam. My work at prep school had improved over the years, but I was a bit B division.

Public schools in the early 1960s were not the friendly places they are now with lots of girls around and a pastoral emphasis on the care of young minds and bodies. Years later, travelling through California with a couple of Englishmen on what would nowadays be called my gap year, I had them spellbound with tales of the fagging system, permitted beatings by other boys and the use of whips along the touchlines during rugby games.

There were 12 houses at Uppingham and the house prefects could beat younger boys with permission from the housemasters. The housemasters also did a bit of beating; the school prefects, called pollies, also carried out beatings, as did the headmaster. At house level it started with a walloping with a gym shoe, then progressed to flogging by the entire complement of house prefects, with the head of house having the privilege of two strokes. In this case they used what was known as a corps beam, a leather-covered stick carried by the teacher officers in the Combined Cadet Force. The same instrument was used for school floggings by all the school prefects. These, mercifully, were rare. The headmaster used a thick cane; again these beatings were rare but they were accompanied by the sort of collective atmosphere of slightly enjoyable jittery tension that I imagine would attend an execution. I can only recall one multiple flogging by the headmaster when all 600 of the school had to walk to a halt station on the main London to York railway line. Easter was early that year and we had been made to stay on at school. There was a collective anger at this which led to a lot of equipment at the station being vandalised. A box of detonators used to halt trains in an emergency was stolen and exploded on a return walk, while a track-maintenance trolley, propelled by a push-and-pull handle, was left on the main track (fortunately it was discovered before another train came down the line). It was like the aftermath of the recent riots in London. The atmosphere at the railway had been similarly anarchic.

Afterwards, everyone was questioned by the headmaster. At the time I felt that the fact that I didn't vandalise anything was pretty lame. I have, I now realise, a vein of cautiousness running through me which I have come to dislike because it prevents me from being the hero I would like to be.

Even at 17, I was completely opposed to older boys being encouraged to beat younger boys. Tim Dale, one of my closest friends in our house, West Deyne, shared my view. He also shared my view of rock and roll, blues music, Elvis Presley, Tamla Motown and Fats Domino. Both Tim and I were house prefects, but neither of us was actually prefect material, or so we thought at the time. By then, we were counting the days until we could leave the school, and it was with intense distaste that we witnessed the occasional beatings carried out by the other prefects. Two of the first-year boys were constantly in trouble for various misdemeanours as fags. Fagging was the system by which the junior boys were made to clean washrooms, changing rooms, dining rooms and corridors, but were also expected to fetch and carry for the prefects. For a while you were the personal fag of a prefect, which meant you had to tidy his study and run errands for him, including going to the buttery for snacks. I was Godfrey's fag. Not only can I not remember his Christian name but I probably never knew it, as we called everyone by their surnames. Godfrey was a short, dark-haired person of serious demeanour who was impeccably dressed. My daily routine included brushing his jacket and hanging it on the back of his chair and shining his shoes. I remember he used a pocket watch slipped into his top pocket with a black leather strap attached to his buttonhole. His desk had to be exact and he had a large number of ornaments, lacquer boxes and family photos, all of which had to be at 90- and 180-degree orientation with each other. He was not ever of an inclination to praise me for keeping his glass poodles, Mount Fuji boxes and fountain-pen holders in alignment, but I lived in fear of getting more than the occasional black dot for sloppy work.

The dot system ruled our lives as fags: if you got six in a term you were automatically beaten. Tim Dale and I were indefatigable in our efforts to keep boys who were on five dots out of trouble. I think in the process we must have impressed on the other house prefects that beating was barbaric. The term ended, and no one was beaten by us.

⌐⌐⌐

I've dwelt on the downside of life at Uppingham too long. The upside was considerable. For a start, the town is in a particularly beautiful part of rural England. The local building stone, ironstone, is similar to Cotswold limestone but the rusty presence of iron ore near the deposits of sedimentary rock means it's not so much yellow but as the colour of dark honey. Uppingham is surrounded by the prettiest villages: Ridlington, Lyddington, Cotesmore. During my last summer term after A levels I spent a couple of weeks with friends bicycling out to local pubs like the White Horse in Morcott and the Gate Inn at Bisbrook. At the Cuckoo in Wing we drank pints of bitter, ordered cheese sandwiches made with Cheddar and thick slices of local bread, and smoked Players tipped. I have never tasted bitterer beer or so much enjoyed the farmyard aroma of a good cheese sandwich and the light-headed euphoria of a cigarette. This was mightily to do with the fact that what we were doing was completely illegal.

Bicycling along the country roads of Rutland is a happy memory. Another friend, Christopher Arnott, came from a family near Otterburn in Northumberland which was very keen on shooting and fishing. I spent many a weekend with him fishing for trout on the Eye Brook or the Welland. He was a really good fisherman who would set out to stalk a trout, whereas I only managed to catch two- or three-inch ones, but my inability didn't matter because whenever I think back I am right there on those sunny stretches of river, the overhanging trees, the smell of cow pats and cows in the river, the gnats, the elderflowers and nettles and the wet mud. Christopher Arnott was nicknamed Nose at school. I was called Cat. If you go to a school where no one uses Christian names, then nicknames stick.

Arnott and I had similar tastes in music, except that he liked Cliff Richard and I liked Elvis. We shared a great enthusiasm for Buddy Holly. Buddy Holly looked like an office clerk in his thick-rimmed rectangular glasses but The Crickets' 'Not Fade Away' is still one of my favourite songs. I can't hear the syncopated rhythm of it without wanting to get up and throw myself about. It's straight out of the blues. That's why I love the USA.

One evening, Arnott asked me to go to his study to listen to something. He had a really smart record player. I don't think it was a Dansette, it was even smarter, maybe an HMV, but more importantly it was an automatic, which we all coveted. That night, though, there was only one single at the top of the spindle that could hold ten 45s. It was a red and yellow 45, Pye International with R&B stamped on the centre. The song was Howlin' Wolf's 'Smokestack Lightning'.

*Ah, oh, smokestack lightning*
*Shinin', just like gold*

Chester Burnett, known as Howlin' Wolf, sang with such swagger in his voice. Coming out of the darkness, so assured, so gravelly, so lived-in – and the harmonica-playing was like the wail of that train.

Recently I presented a TV film on the Mississippi blues in which I described that moment as an epiphany. Buddy Holly and Elvis were my bread and butter but early blues was the very heart of all the great American music which defined my generation, or certainly my side of it. The influence of everything American to me was almost as important as having been born in Oxfordshire and going for my holidays to Cornwall every single year.

But it wasn't just the music. There was TV too. My dad wouldn't buy a television, he thought it was all drivel. But Harry bought one early on. By then he and Joyce were married and lived in a bungalow on the farm, so Henrietta and I would go and watch theirs. They were our surrogate parents while ours were away and we adored them. Westerns were my myths and legends. *The Range Rider*, *The Cisco*

*Kid*, *The Lone Ranger* and later *Laramie* and *Bonanza*, *Tenderfoot* and *Rawhide*. These simple tales of right and wrong were my great love. My parents visited America and brought me a real hide double holster with two cap guns and red wooden bullets. The farm over which I roamed was my ranch; the way the trees followed the bends of the brook at the bottom of the fields was the Rio Grande; the view from the front window of our house was not the rolling green Cotswold hills, but the shimmering distance of Texas. The Big Country. John took me to the Odeon in Leicester Square to see *The Big Country*. It is still the best cinema moment in my life. I can't hear the theme music by Jerome Moross without becoming misty-eyed about Gregory Peck and Charlton Heston. Jean Simmons was, for me, the most beautiful woman in the world.

I'm fond of saying I belong to the rock and roll generation. People like me were so influenced by everything American that our lives are defined by it. I'm definitely English, but there's a big difference between me and the English characters of the Second World War and post-war generation described in novels such as Anthony Powell's *A Dance to the Music of Time* series as I find myself at home in places like Australia and America. The power of rock and roll liberated me from the restrictions of being a middle-class Englishman. Buddy Holly and Elvis and Howlin' Wolf, The Beatles and the Rolling Stones were all my world. Before The Beatles and the Stones, British pop always seemed to be poor imitations of the real sex, which was USA. Cliff Richard almost broke out in his hits 'Living Doll' and 'Move It', but there was almost no one else; records like Acker Bilk's 'Stranger on the Shore' dominated the charts for months. Then along came The Beatles. They sang about their own lives and the real people they knew and, for all its grey drizzle, the real place called Liverpool, England. In their first album *Please Please Me*, they were largely covering blues songs but we hadn't heard 'Twist and Shout' and 'Money' before, so the music seemed to be ours. Blues music was powerful. The Beatles, the Stones and The Yardbirds found in those rural songs with African rhythms a language with which to speak of the reality of the frustrating urban lives that they were living – and we schoolboys went right along with it because, privileged though we were, we could see that this was a language we could understand and communicate with. We speedily got Beatle haircuts and took to wearing black turtle-neck T-shirts and elastic-sided boots. Speedily, too, the authorities at school began to oppose what we were doing, but the cat was out of the bag. Rebellion was in the air. Tim Dale and I formed a band. We started The Spartans, which then became The Screaming Ab Jabs, which morphed into Lightning Strikes. We suffered the perennial problem of young, noisy and out-of-tune bands: trying to find somewhere to play where we wouldn't disturb too many people. Our welcome in the school boarding house was short-lived, and we moved to a social club in London Road. We left there because they wanted money for rent and finally we hit on the idea of borrowing the local cinema, the Rutland, outside screening times.

In the early days our equipment was rudimentary. My bass guitar had cost £24; I'd bought the amp from a company advertising in *Practical Electronics*. Tim had a 30-watt valve amp, also from the ad pages of the same magazine. He kept the speaker that went with it in a cardboard box, meaning to house it in some sort of cabinet when he got home for the holidays. The caretaker, Mrs Flood, had a couple of cats in the cinema to keep down the mouse population so it stank of cats' pee behind the screen. She was remarkably kind to let us use the cinema and actually we didn't abuse the trust much … well, at least, not until our one and only concert. We used to leave the equipment there and unfortunately one of Mrs Flood's cats took to sleeping in

Tim's 18-inch speaker and destroyed the cardboard. We discovered this when he opened with the first bars of 'Apache' by The Shadows and only a buzz came out. We were due to play a couple of numbers before the school's Saturday afternoon screening of *The Great Escape*. Being of a practical bent, Tim wired his amplifier to the cinema sound system which included two 15-inch speakers and tweeters. The noise was electrifying – much louder than The Beatles in 1963 at Finsbury Park Astoria, where you couldn't hear anything because of the screaming from all the girls in the audience. Sadly, however, at our own rather more modest cinema extravaganza, all you could hear was Tim's lead guitar on 'Saturday Nite at the Duck Pond', a rather vulgar take on *Swan Lake* which we opened with. You couldn't hear any of the other instruments at all, including my bass guitar.

Mrs Flood not unnaturally got a little aerated and that was that. Lightning Strikes did a mini tour of some Christmas parties of our friends and that, as is so often the case with school bands, was about it. We were dogged by the appalling ineffectiveness of our equipment. A Donovan-inspired folk singer called Jake Walton and some other boys from Uppingham tried to resurrect us as a band in Cornwall in the summer of 1964. Our last booking was at Wadebridge Town Hall. Our sound was so bad that the manager of a local band called The Vigilantes actually loaned us two Vox AC30s, changing over the amps as we were playing. The improvement in sound was what we had needed all along, but I'm afraid it merely showed up how bad a bass guitarist I really was. Jake went on to become a well-known folk singer and dulcimer player. I was only in it to pick up girls. I recently found a picture of me playing the bass in Uppingham. I guess I felt I looked rugged and cool because, I see, I had several prints made at the time.

Awful school food is legendary, but not true in my case. My memory of Uppingham is of standing outside the dining hall counting the seconds till the bell for supper, so hungry – so deliciously hungry – and then steaming in for roast pork with plenty of crackling, sprouts, apple sauce and thick brown gravy; or fish pie with mash topping and indifferent cod flakes made wonderful by a white cheese sauce with sliced boiled eggs and parsley in it and always soaked, boiled marrowfat peas. (If there is any legume more succulent I can't think of it.) The roast beef was always over-done, not like at home, but with plenty of horseradish and really good roast potatoes it didn't matter. Perhaps the most loved school dish was mince and potatoes. I wonder if anyone does this in a British pub somewhere? Maybe it's just too simple, but writing this gives me the thought of putting it on in my pub in Cornwall. As far as I can remember it was just minced beef, fried with chopped onions and carrots, then stewed with beef stock, salt and pepper. It was always served with cabbage and plainly boiled potatoes slightly falling apart. It was the sort of food that foreigners like to cite as an example of terrible British cooking. Try convincing a 15-year-old teenager that it was anything less than splendid. Of course we ate cottage pie (minced beef) and shepherd's pie (minced roast lamb left over from Sunday lunch). We also had steak and kidney pie from time to time, as well as kidneys and fried liver – and nobody complained about them. The puddings were the stuff of the Great British food revival, crisp-topped apple or rhubarb crumble, steamed treacle pudding with white plastic jugs of Bird's custard. Treacle tart wasn't as good as my mum's – too many breadcrumbs – but I wolfed it down. In summer we ate strawberries and cream, and raspberries often, and large summer puddings. For reasons I can't recall we were not allowed to drink tea after lunch or dinner in the houses. We just had water.

At breakfast there was a dish which I've never seen since – bread fried in lard, then smeared with Marmite or Bovril with hot tinned tomatoes on top. Scrambled eggs were always overcooked and a bit tough, like most hotel breakfasts. We brought our own jams, honey, spreads and sauces into breakfast. At home I'd never been allowed brown sauce, and I took to it with gusto. Even as a teenager, I could taste and identify subtle differences. A1 Steak Sauce a bit thin; OK sauce rather sweet; Fardon's Flag sauce both hot and sweet. An ad for this in the 1950s was 'What's the sauciest sauce?' 'It's new Flag, of course'. HP was sharper, Daddies peppery. Daddies had extra allure because it was the sauce served at the school buttery. The buttery sold the best cream slices I have ever eaten anywhere. The chef was an ex-Army baker called Sandy who made them every day. He used fresh whipped cream – not pastry cream – and his delicacy with puff pastry was peerless. On rugby match days Sandy cooked the fry-up against which all others were judged – eggs, bacon, sausages, fried bread, grilled tomatoes and baked beans with Daddies Sauce and mugs of hot sweet tea. You've had the communal bath in the pavilion. You're aching and bruised. You smell of wintergreen liniment and carbolic soap, you're warm and relaxed after the game which, though scary, you've won, and you and the whole Uppingham first XV and the XV from Rugby, Oundle, Tonbridge descend on the buttery for a ravening feast. Those are fond memories.

I was reasonably good at rugby. We public schoolboys called it rugger, but after two or three years playing the game with a bunch of farmers in Wadebridge in Cornwall some ten years later, I found that I could never call it that again. Being good at sport in a school like Uppingham gave you a sort of protection. If you played in the front five of the pack (I was a prop) you were decent, honest, a bit fiery and also jolly nice, but a bit thick. There was almost an understanding from the teachers – we called them masters – that you couldn't be expected to excel academically because you were sporty. This gave me an opportunity not to have to do too well in the subjects I chose to do at A level – English, History and Geography. Actually, thanks to my mother, I'd been reading serious books ever since I learned to read, so O level English had been a labour of love. The dark poetry of the Jacobean dramatists particularly appealed to me because it was violent and emotional. But it wasn't enough. I wanted to be the tough rugby star. The prospect of studying for a higher academic standard was daunting. And, indeed, I failed at it. At A level I was eventually awarded just two O level passes.

Two students in my year were what my friends might have called 'a bit spastic'. One was fat and stuttered, and the other spoke too much in a high-pitched voice and was 'weedy'. Both tried to avoid sport and endured sneers all round. But they excelled at English and both took part in school plays and were transformed by acting and drama. Looking back, I regret not having thrown myself into something cultural, but having made my rugby bed I sort of had to lie in it. The net result was that I became more and more disenchanted with school the older I got because I wasn't prepared to use what Uppingham had to offer – excellent music, drama and English. I had learned the cello at my previous school and continued in the first couple of years at Uppingham, but in my rugby role I felt that playing the cello was uncool. My father loved the warm sound of the cello, but I thought classical music (apart from the guitar and trumpet) was nerdy. I hated having to lug the cello back to school on the train: it was cumbersome and so not me. I imagined that boys on the train joked about the cello, but if I'd had a guitar it would have been a different matter.

I gave up the cello, and allowed my academic career to drift into the B division. All me and my friends wanted to do was listen to rock and roll, get in a band, learn to drive, smoke cigarettes, drink beer and pick up girls.

Girls were becoming a bit of a problem. There's no doubt that spending most of the year in an all-boys boarding school disadvantaged you in terms of behaving naturally in the company of the opposite sex. Which only made the earnest desire to remove their clothes even more disturbing. We all bought a magazine called *Parade* which had centrefold pin-ups of topless girls in knickers. My parents still had a flat in London – they'd moved to Kensington – and sometimes I took friends to stay there. We used to drink espresso coffee in The 2i's in Old Compton Street and another coffee bar called The Heaven and Hell Lounge. The Soho strip clubs were places of enormous tension. Total nudity was banned, so the strippers finished their acts with strategically placed plasters. They were not allowed to move, either.

When I was 15 I took a local girl into the sand dunes at Constantine Bay near our house on Trevose Head. It was in early September, a season of poignant tension in Cornwall with the summer just over and most of my friends gone. There was a melancholic sense of change; there seemed to be just me and Sally on the beach but, as is so often the case in early autumn, the weather was blue skies with a chill in the air. We kissed lots and I put my hand down her jeans and into her knickers and played with her vagina. It was unbearably exciting and I was aroused and the inevitable happened. We walked back to the golf club in silence, me feeling overwhelmed by the closeness and power of it and a dark patch on my jeans. She was quiet too. I think I was in shock. I had a strong desire to get away from her and to meet up with local lads in the Farmers Arms to talk about cars and beer, and to forget the physical reality of my first serious sexual encounter.

I didn't progress the relationship with Sally, but once intimacy had occurred it became quite regular with other girls, but there was never an opportunity to go the whole way. Indeed, I didn't lose my virginity till I was 17 when, in desperation at never being able to do it, I picked up a rather tarty girl in a pub – or rather she picked me up. I took her to the grounds of Dartmouth Royal Naval College where I was doing a diving course. I thought anxiously about my brother Jeremy who had been a midshipman there, and I had her in a completely shambolic manner against a tree trunk. I was appalled for weeks afterwards and formed the opinion that I had caught a venereal disease. I forced myself to go to a clinic in London where, needless to say, they told me there was nothing whatsoever wrong with me.

The enormously complex issue of, as the Americans say, getting laid as a teenager caused me anxiety and terrible feelings of inadequacy. Towards the end of my time at Uppingham, I befriended a girl from Liverpool who had a job helping in the kitchen and cleaning dormitories. Her name was Maureen and she was best friends with another maid from Gateshead called Isabel. Isabel was, I discovered, having a seriously dangerous liaison with my friend Arnott, and it was Arnott who suggested I might take up with Maureen. My natural caution was very much working overtime. But it was a long hot summer term, and Isabel and Maureen walked up and down the street outside my dormitory on many a night when thoughts of leaving that oh-too-restrictive school were strong. The warm breezes of an English June caused me to succumb. We four would meet in a barn outside town, smoke a number of low-grade cigarettes called Olympic tipped, listen to a transistor radio and indulge in lots of kissing and quite a lot of removal of underwear. Me and Maureen were screened from Arnott and Isabel by a couple of bales of hay. But Maureen was a Roman Catholic, and I was petrified of getting her pregnant and having to marry a serving maid from Liverpool. I was a horrid little snob, really. But when – years later, in London – I found Maureen in bed with one of my friends, I was mortified.

The trips to the barn had me squirming with tension. Then a little joke appeared in the school satirical magazine edited by Piers Gough, now a famous architect, which said, 'When out on your bike riding around Uppingham is a bell necessary?' We had imagined we were carrying on our trysts unobserved. That was unlikely. But I think the masters were in a bit of a pickle with Isabel and Arnott. It had gone on for a couple of years unnoticed and the prospect of informing Arnott's parents that their son had become entangled with a working-class woman was tricky one. The school, after all, was *in loco parentis*.

Nothing happened. But I was never promoted from house prefect to school prefect, and any other responsible roles for my final year evaporated. I stayed on one extra Christmas term to play rugby, and I renounced Maureen. Arnott didn't renounce Isabel. He stayed with her, and married her a few years later. They were very happy indeed.

# VI

I was required to re-take my A levels, in the hope of getting higher grades. I convinced my parents that I would be better off going to what was called a crammer, the theory being that if you had intensive lessons you could concentrate on improving your results. I chose a crammer in Brighton. I had read *Brighton Rock*, the first of a lifetime's fascination with the works of Graham Greene. Looking back on it, there was no chance of me doing better in my exams at a Brighton crammer than at Uppingham. The teaching was not nearly as good and the distractions were magnified by a factor of at least ten. Academically, it was a disaster. But socially it was wonderful. For a start there were girls in the crammer – lots of them – and access to pubs, and to clubs too. I had digs in a house with a bunch of youths who had similarly got frustrated with the monastic conditions at their public schools. We had a ball. It was 1965. 'Satisfaction' and 'Substitute' were on the radio. One of my flatmates, Clive Rowland, was also very in to folk and country music – Joan Baez, Phil Ochs, Tom Paxton. We both went to London to see Johnny Cash and the Carter Family at the Albert Hall, but the star of all those stars was Bob Dylan. The following year we went to the Albert Hall to see him too. The first half of the concert was marvellous – he did his latest songs 'To Ramona', 'Desolation Row' and 'Mr Tamborine Man'. Then the backing band, called The Hawks, came on. Dylan reappeared in a black suit and didn't look at all like the folky guy in jeans and a leather jacket huddled together with his girl against the cold as on the cover of *The Freewheelin'*. With the famously loud opening of 'Tombstone Blues', all the way to 'Like a Rolling Stone', decibels ruled. Within minutes loads of people were getting up and walking out. Someone famously yelled out 'Judas'. Clive was massively pissed off. But we stayed. I wouldn't say I loved it, the shock of the new is always a shock, but I sort of liked being shocked.

This was the time that mods and rockers descended on Brighton. Gangs on Lambrettas and Vespas rode up and down the seafront every weekend, all wearing identical parkas with fake fur collars, all with identical short haircuts and all with a fake aerial on the back with a squirrel tail tied to it. I wasn't attracted to them. I found their neat, cheap suits and button-down collared Carnaby shirts alien, except that The Who were wearing exactly those sort of clothes and I surely liked The Who. And I certainly wanted a scooter. Good reason to explore the warren of little streets just below the station called North Laine. To me, this area was much more atmospheric than the Lanes near the seafront. The tiny grocery shops and ironmongers and pubs were like front rooms, as were the antique and bric-à-brac shops. The sheer minuteness of them was a source of great pleasure. I was growing up, enjoying a seedy ambience that my parents just wouldn't 'get'.

Needless to say my A level grades were pitiful – two E passes – but it was summer again and Cornwall beckoned.

Julian Vere was a couple of years older than me but light years ahead in coolness. He wore tight jeans, moccasins and blue denim shirts, and drove a souped-up Ford Anglia at a ferocious speed. Riding with him was completely scary; he took on the Cornish lanes like Dean Moriarty. He smoked Embassy cigarettes and when he'd finished a packet threw it nonchalantly into the boot, intending to pick out the gift coupons when he'd got the time. The boot was always half-filled with empty packets. He wore tight leather driving gloves – the ones that don't cover your finger tips and have sweat holes on the backs. My mother said they made him look sinister. She disapproved of Julian and my other friend Chris Ghazillian. He arrived at the golf club in a three-wheeler called a Reliant Robin which had been given an extra carburettor and was really dangerous because it would spin with even a modest touch on the accelerator. Chris's dad had a garage in Macclesfield. His father plainly had plenty of cash because he owned a Bentley with a boot filled with diving gear and wet suits, and would drive it illegally over private land to good diving spots on the headlands around Constantine and Treyarnon. Chris had great Beatles-influenced clothes including a pair of soft leather Anello & Davide elastic-sided Chelsea boots. He also had an Epiphone lead guitar. Not only that, but he knew most of the repertoire of The Beatles and most of the songs sung by everyone in vogue in Liverpool and Manchester: Gerry and the Pacemakers, The Hollies, Billy J. Kramer and the Dakotas. He knew both words and chords. Naturally, I told him of my attempts at bass playing. Then it transpired that Julian occasionally played drums. We got talking about forming a little band, and I mentioned that at the back of my parents' house there was an old slate barn where we could practise.

My parents had moved from the Art Deco holiday house, Polventon, out on Trevose Head, and had bought a rather plain Victorian house called Redlands, built on the isthmus of land between Booby's Bay and Mother Ivey's Bay. The barn was actually a coach house, a building that had previously housed a horse and a carriage with a loft upstairs for hay for the horse. No electricity, but I bought a hundred feet of twin-core lighting cable. I had my bass and amplifier from school, Chris had a small practice amp and Julian just had a bucket to start with. Within a couple of practices, the atmospheric qualities of the coach house started to fill us with ideas. Why not have a party there and invite the six girls we had just met at the golf club? We were a bit stumped by Julian's bucket but then we heard about Roger Hawke from St Merryn village who had drums. We hoped to borrow his kit, but we could not avoid having Roger too. He arrived with a little sticker on the face of the bass drum which said 'The Astronorts'.

Preparation for the party went on for some days. I helped myself to my parents' account at the off-licence, Henwoods, in Padstow. Cans of Long Life beer and gallon jars of Merrydown cider. We didn't bother with any food apart from crisps. I managed to get hold of a couple of red fire-glow bulbs and we borrowed two table lamps from the house and covered the shades with red crêpe paper. I persuaded my sister Henrietta to lend us her pale blue Dansette record player. On the walls I hung a load of bark paintings, brought back by my parents from a trip to Fiji on the P&O ship *Orsova*, and I also stuck up a devil mask from the same trip and put a light behind it. And stuck up some LP covers too. We acquired a bed from the house and took some car seats out of a couple of cars which some local boys had pushed over Trevose Head. It all looked very sexy. In a blanket box in the house I had found some thick green curtains which we tacked up.

We'd gone out and pinned handwritten notes in the Farmers Arms and the golf club to say I was having a party. Imagine doing that as a 17-year-old today! Loads of people came – Australian life guards, Dave and Ray from the chippie in St Merryn, some of the locals from St Merryn, a few farmers, some fishermen's sons from

Padstow. Euphoria was in the air, as we all tried to get off with girls, one hand leaning against a beam above empty glasses and bottles and drinks piling up on the top of the sandy walls under the eaves. At about midnight my father made an appearance and said he thought it would be a good idea if we stopped and we did.

My dad liked a good party as much as I did. I have very fond memories of the parties he threw every Christmas at Conduit Farm. I recently met the daughter of one of my parents' friends, Elizabeth Archibald, now a professor of Medieval Literature, who described these parties as perhaps the most memorable thing about her childhood in Oxfordshire. I think it was a combination of the house, which was friendly and comfortable, and my parents, who were sociable and interesting and interested in their friends. My father made a point of always serving really good drink. I once found a bill from Berry Brothers in an old filing cabinet: red and white burgundy, Gewürztraminer, Veuve Cliquot and Rheingau. For their parties, my mother prepared boiled then roasted ham with mustard, cloves and brown sugar, roast beef and two salads (a chunky potato salad with homemade mayonnaise and finely chopped shallots, and a salad of beetroot, apple and celery). I remember how jolly my parents were – and how welcoming. The centre of my comfort zone, in retrospect, is my mother a bit tight with a gin and tonic in one hand and a cigarette in the other, smiling at me, full of pleasure in having me there.

No wonder I loved that party in the coach house. Actually, it wasn't just one party – we went on having them all that summer and the summer after. The wire that ran from the house was always a problem; it was lighting flex and on rainy nights was lit up with blue sparks all the way. We finally bought a heavy-duty cable but it wasn't the only safety concern – the loft floor used to sag alarmingly.

We never thought that the whole floor, weighed down by maybe 60 people, might crash down on another 30 or 40 below, we just fixed it by dragging a couple of driftwood logs up from the beach and propping it up. As the parties grew in popularity we started doing food, mainly just bread and cheese, but on one occasion we tried roasting a pig. It was raw in the middle, so most of it was eaten by Claud Holman's Alsatian, Porky. Claud had a garage in Lostwithiel. I bought a diesel Land Rover from him with some of the money I had inherited from my grandfather's brother, great-uncle Otto. Claud himself bought one too and so did my sister Janey. Claud became a leading light in the party organisation – not least because he had an uncle in Lerryn who made cider.

I see now that all this activity was an early foray into the world of restaurants. I realise that I really enjoyed setting the scene and making other people animated, whether in conversation or dancing or eating and drinking.

Living vicariously – that's where success as a restaurateur lies. Our farm home was isolated, and school had been all boys. I was subdued by my father and suffered from the feeling that I wasn't very good at anything. As a result, I was constantly trying to please others, so they wouldn't notice how ordinary I was. I *had* to run the parties, I *had* to run the disco, I *had* to get satisfaction from other people enjoying themselves. Now, I had lots of friends and something to offer – my barn, Rick's barn.

I'm not always criticising myself. I know I'm good at cooking, that I can pick just the right tune to urge people to get up and dance, and that I can find the words to express myself in writing. I love nostalgia. I used to listen over and over again to 'Theme from a

Summer Place' by Percy Faith at my aunt Zoe's house at Treyarnon. At school there was 'Sealed with a Kiss' by Brian Hyland and the Shangri-Las' 'Remember (Walking in the Sand)'. But my two favourites are 'The Boys of Summer' by Don Henley and 'Night Moves' by Bob Seger. They both play on the sweet tension we all feel as effortless summer days move into an almost imperceptible chill in the air with autumn arriving.

'Time's winged chariot' as Andrew Marvell puts it.

But it wasn't just the parties, the girls and the songs that made Cornwall my summer place. I loved the ruggedness of north Cornwall; high cliffs, endless beaches, gales in the winter so that the trees all leaned one way, the romantic bleakness of the headlands. Short tough grass, pink thrift, yellow gorse. I loved the gnarled endurance of the fishermen, the dangerousness of the pubs in Padstow. I adored the Cornish accent. I tried to copy it but I was no good. In the Farmers Arms in St Merryn, there was a landlord called Derek Cripps who you just couldn't understand. He was the originator of the word 'directly' meaning 'very slowly'. He told tales of life as a farm labourer in the era of steam-driven threshing machines and horse-drawn corn binders, when the corn fields were filled with poppies and butterflies. It gave you some idea of what story-telling was like before there were books. Derek used to have his own beer mug which held two pints. He was a very large man with rather a red face and white hair and a large stomach. He always wore a white shirt rolled up to the elbows and a wide leather belt with a big buckle, which he wore tightly round his trousers, but there were no loops on the waistband so the belt was slung so low it seemed to prop up his stomach. He had a well-dressed and slim wife called Edie who came from the East End of London and who probably gave Derek a hard time when the pub was shut. But during opening hours it was Derek's show.

He would shout greetings as you walked in. There was a garden at the back with a few barrels sawn in half as tables and St Austell Brewery beer crates as seats. There were chickens in the garden and a damp all-slate gents which had moss growing out of the walls. My parents described Derek as a reprobate but that was almost a term of endearment. To me he was a total hero. To have Derek notice me was a warm glow. The pub had a favoured table near the fireplace with high-backed settles on either side so that you were cut off. I came in once to see Rod Stewart sitting there dressed in a suit. He was with a beautiful girlfriend. I was there with the composer Malcolm Arnold.

There used to be singing nights. A contingent would often come from Padstow, including Johnnie Murt whose tenor voice was clear and tugged at the heart. His repertoire included 'Pleasant and Delightful'. Henrietta was always enchanted by the way he sang the word 'melodious' – it sounded like 'melodieuse' – 'the larks they sang melodious at the dawning of the day'. He also sang 'The Nightingale', which was my father's favourite.

> For to hear the fond tale of the sweet nightingale
> As she sings in the valley below?

I tried to learn that on a mouth organ some years later. I was working in an abattoir in Roma in Queensland, so lonely and so homesick, and that song made me feel better. It made me feel that one day I would get back to my beloved Cornwall, where my father helped Johnnie Murt financially when he needed to buy a fishing boat, where you knew everyone and everyone was your friend. Where Johnnie Murt sang 'The Wild Rover', 'The White Rose', 'Little Eyes', 'Lamorna', 'Goin' up Camborne Hill, coming down' and 'Trelawny'.

Derek used to sit in the settle and sing what was definitely my favourite Cornish song:

*Eating and drinking is so charming*
*Piping and smoking there's no harm in*
*All such things we take delight in*
*When we meet together*
*Whack for the leero, leero, liro*
*Whack for the leero, leero, liro*
*All such things we take delight in*
*When we meet together*

On each whack he'd thump the settle with his elbow. Lots of things look better in retrospect but those were glory days.

# VII

My A level results came in July. I had squeezed passes in only two, History and English. I was entirely uninterested in going to university. My father made me attend a vocational guidance test which came up with the answer, 'There is no doubt that you are best suited to working in the Sales Division of a large manufacturing or retail firm.' The report said that my emotional stability was average, self-sufficiency very low, extroversion (whatever that was) average, dominance low, confidence low, sociability above average. Armed with this personality profile, my dad persuaded me to go for a sales job at British Petroleum. He had friends in BP because his company, The Distillers, at that time not only produced whiskies, such as Johnnie Walker and Haig, and gin, including Gordon's, but also made chemicals whose production was closely linked with BP. I went for an interview and did embarrassingly badly. Finally, in a sort of desperate bid to please my dad, I suggested maybe a job in hotel management would sort me out. Without the cocoon of Cornwall and the parties in the barn, my confidence was very low and at the time I felt a failure in everything. Catering seemed to me to be just about what I was capable of, bearing in mind that catering was not the sort of job that the careers master at my public school would have advised. Fifteen years later, a friend of mine, Philip Minty, asked me what I was doing in a third-rate job like catering. The joke was that he was in catering, too. We came to the joint conclusion that it was because we hadn't done well at school.

I went for an interview with Trust Houses whose flagship was Brown's Hotel in Albemarle Street, London and with British Transport Hotels, which ran all the railway hotels at the main stations, including the Midland in Manchester and some hotels near stations at popular Edwardian holiday destinations such as Gleneagles, Turnberry and the Tregenna Castle in St Ives. Trust Houses was a bit fusty – all wood panelling and afternoon teas – but I landed a job at the Great Western Royal Hotel in Paddington station, as a management trainee, to start in early January the next year, 1966.

I was sharing a flat in Finborough Road with my two best friends from school, Tim Dale and Christopher Arnott, and another chap from the Hong Kong and Shanghai Bank, which he called the Honkers and Shankers. It was a long wait for the Great Western job, and I didn't do anything much for month after month and got steadily more despondent. Finally, in a fit of bravado, I took a job as a road sweeper.

I'd just read Orwell's masterpiece *Down and Out in Paris and London*, and had wanted to present myself with something unfamiliar, to get away from the ethos of public school. In point of fact, the experience of sweeping roads was less than life-enhancing. I was appalled by the odour of most of my fellow-sweepers. I'd never known such a smell of stale alcohol – that and damp leaves and unwashed crotches and dog shit. No pitying thoughts of how these people came to be doing what they were doing – just plain boy-from-a-privileged-comfortable-home aversion. I was depressed by their dimness.

I was sweeping the road outside the Natural History Museum when my flatmate Tim drove up in his Land Rover. 'I think you should get in,' he said in a tight voice. He then told me that my father had died.

I often think I have no memory for detail but I can remember every colour, every hue of that moment. The greyness of the sky, the blue-green of the Land Rover, the darker green of its seats, the coat I was wearing, a brown raincoat, short and, I thought, Italian-looking, which I had worn with such swagger at school with the blue scarf which meant I had been awarded my colours for rugby. The coat was showing its age and I had tied it round with a bit of parcel twine to keep out the wind on London's streets.

Tim told me in the Land Rover that my dad had been blown off a cliff. I'd actually heard it on the radio that morning – an incident in autumnal gales – but had made nothing of it.

Quite soon I discovered he'd dived off the cliff.

I'd had an argument with Tim only six months earlier about suicide. His father had just shot himself in some woods at his farm in Cheshire, driven to despair by memories of what he'd done as a soldier in France in the Second World War. I had said that it was cowardice to kill yourself. Tim had said that it was brave. I was horribly insensitive. But, curiously enough, I don't look back on that with shame. There's something reassuring about the callousness of youth; you haven't yet learnt about the dark side of life. I see that swagger today in my own sons, but also see their innocence and their hope. Today, I can feel sorry for the memory of myself at 17 having to deal with my dad who leapt off a cliff at Trevose Head.

I don't remember much about the funeral, just his coffin in St Merryn church and then a slow car journey to the crematorium in Truro. I don't even remember if there was a wake. My mother received masses and masses of letters about what a great person he was. She was just broken. So sad, but angry too. She spoke of being furious and let down. I thought it was a little hard to be angry with someone who had just killed himself. Only later did I realise what an enormous strain it is living with someone with mental illness.

# PART TWO

Rites of Passage

# I

I started at the Great Western a couple of days after my eighteenth birthday. First I had to go to Denny's in Soho to buy three chef's jackets – white and double-breasted – check trousers; white scarves to be worn with a small knot at the front with one of the corners hanging down your back, and of course chef's hats. Having worn nothing but jeans ever since I left school it seemed archaic to force myself into this old-fashioned uniform, particularly the hat, which flopped over: I knew nothing about starch at the time.

I had been given a case of Prestige knives by my brother Jeremy. They never made it out of the box. Within the first week I had been lent a 12-inch cook's knife and a 3-inch knife by the demi chef de partie, Ricky Richards, and had gone to Leon Jaeggi in Shaftesbury Avenue and bought my own Sabatier steel knives and a 6-inch cook's knife.

For the first three months I worked as a larder chef and learnt how to make mayonnaise by the gallon. In those days, we had few labour-saving mechanical devices and I learnt how to finely chop onions and parsley, dice potatoes and swedes for Russian Salads and mix up vinaigrette with salad oil, white wine vinegar, mayonnaise, white pepper and salt. I washed hundreds of lettuces and dried them, and sliced cucumbers. I made thousands of sandwiches using triple-length white tin loaves. My main job was to look after the hors d'oeuvres: about 30 dishes, called raviers, on a tableclothed trolley. There had to be two of everything, so every day I made up 15 different hors d'oeuvres. The dishes included egg mayonnaise, potato salad, beetroot vinaigrette, salted rollmops, tomato and onion salad, anchovies, cocktail onions, smoked herring, sweetcorn and diced red peppers, sliced tongue with persillade sauce, and stuffed olives. After a month, I was given free rein to put new dishes on the trolley but I didn't know what. I went to Foyles and bought a book on hors d'oeuvres but I didn't really go for its rather luridly photographed ideas. Actually, I was happy turning out the regular things. I enjoyed making the mayonnaise. My mother had only ever made it with olive oil and Orleans white wine vinegar. I liked tasting and testing the new flavours. I was experimental with groundnut oil, English mustard, malt vinegar from an oak barrel in the store room, salt and white pepper. I took great care to cook the ingredients for the Russian Salad perfectly. Green beans had to be cut into quarter-inch pieces and cooked for four minutes in salted water, then refreshed in iced water, then strained. Swede, carrot and potato had to be cut into quarter-inch dice. Each had to be briefly boiled separately; the potato needed especially careful watching so that it was cooked but not gone too soft. I combined all these, plus peas, with some mayonnaise but not so much as to make it too rich. Most of the ingredients for the trolley came from tins or jars but the quality of everything was good. I was being introduced to stuff I hadn't tried at home. I was always sneaking a rollmop out of the jar in the cold room. I grew to love the smoked herring in oil too and formed a passion for tongue. It was my job to cook the tongues in salted water and skin them, leave them to cool, then slice them for the hors d'oeuvres trolley where I served them with a parsley vinaigrette. Once I'd got used to the sight of the lolloping look of whole raw tongue with all the muscle below the tongue itself, I became very attached to the taste of the pink flesh and its texture which was slightly resistant. Apart from the hors d'oeuvres, the tongue was used by the sauce section for Sauce Reform which went with grilled lamb chops, the sauce being a beef stock, port and mushroom mixture with julienne strips of tongue, egg white and gherkin.

The kitchen was organised traditionally, that is, there were five sections (each called a partie): larder, veg, sauce, roasts and pastry. The larder prepared all the fish and meat. It also made the salads and any other cold first courses as well as the many sandwiches for drinks parties, and canapés. The sauce section made all the sauces and cooked the fish. The roasts did all the roasting and grilling of the meat but not the fish. The veg section prepared all the veg and made the soups and looked after the stockpots, which were vast and constantly simmering. The pastry section was not part of the main kitchen and was quite different from the rest. It was presided over by an Irish pastry cook called Pat who wore his apron very short and on the diagonal so it gave him a swagger. He kept asking me if I was 'getting any' and thought it hilarious when I didn't understand what he meant. The daily running of the kitchen was, as is normal, down to the sous chef, Jeffrey Taylor, who shouted a lot, as is normal. In charge of the larder was a 'Garde Manger' called Harry who had smoked so much he had difficulty breathing and used to gulp in air rather like a fish expiring at the bottom of a boat. He and Ricky, his demi chef de partie, did all the fish filleting and butchery. A lot of the fish came in whole. I wish now I had concentrated then on what Harry and Ricky were doing because both had skills which most chefs would not be taught these days.

I was transferred from the larder section to sauce after about three months. The great thing about British Transport Hotels in those days was that the training scheme was very thorough and included a period in the kitchen cooking classic French cuisine. On the sauce section, I learnt how to make béchamel and velouté sauces, how to grill and pan-fry Dover soles, and how to put together cod and parsley sauce. The other superb thing about BTH was that it had a really good wine cellar. Shamefully, I wasn't into wine when I worked there, although I was overly interested in beer.

My problem was I didn't really like being at the Great Western Hotel. Looking back I can see why. My father had died, I was in turmoil, I couldn't work out who I was. I just didn't know how to feel at ease with these chefs who lived in what seemed to me to be far-away working-class places like Walthamstow or Acton or Balham. Many of them came to work in suits which was weird when all my friends were wearing jeans. In truth, you couldn't meet a nicer bunch of people. Ricky Richards was endlessly patient with me, a perfect foil for Harry, the boss in the larder, who was apt to get bad tempered from time to time but who was underneath soft hearted too. It was a kind kitchen. The head chef was not a bastard; the sous chef was noisy but not sadistic. I can still remember him yelling at the pass when I was taking my time delivering a salad, 'Dépêchez-vous, Mr Stein, if you *please*!' His voice was fierce but his words were polite, and the laughable mix of kitchen French and East London English was ironic and formal. Quite often we'd all go to the pub, the Pride of Paddington, in Praed Street for a couple of pints. They welcomed me into their chefs' lives. But I just couldn't reciprocate. Around them, I felt even more of a failure than usual, confused and with nothing to say.

Part of the problem was my extreme love of Cornwall. I worked one weekend on, one weekend off, and every Friday I longed to go home on the sleeper to be where I really wanted to be. The hotel kitchens were below Praed Street. On the weekend of Easter when I was stuck down in this basement I was almost panicking with frustration, knowing that all my friends would be streaming into Cornwall for a glorious holiday week. It was a bright Easter Saturday and I saw a little ray of sunlight on the floor and looked up at the bright day through a window high on the wall. The feeling of imprisonment was almost unbearable. I had just bought an LP by The Who called *My Generation*, and one of the tracks, 'The Kids Are Alright', was me:

> *Sometimes I feel I've got to get away*
> *Sometimes I know I've got to get away*

The longing to get back to Cornwall was what I read into the words.

I had felt like this a couple of years earlier when I went to Majorca during the holidays with a schoolfriend, Martin Robinson. We stayed with David Moorehouse, a friend of Martin's family, in Moorehouse's villa in Calle Major. He was much older than we schoolboys. We intended to work there for most of the summer. I got two jobs, one washing up in a cafe in the main street during the day, and the other in the evening in a nightclub called Haimat which had an Egyptian theme so we all had to wear fezzes. My job included refilling the Gordon's and Smirnoff, Johnny Walker and Bacardi bottles with very cheap imitations from large basket-covered glass flagons kept in the cellar. I was massively hung up about only meeting nice girls who you couldn't have sex with, and David, in his role as laid-back mentor, suggested a visit to a prostitute. I went to the red-light part of Palma in my prized torn jeans and the blue leather jacket I had saved up to buy with my cafe and nightclub earnings. The assignation did not go well. I was so nervous that I picked up the first girl on the street. She was a bit plump and had quite bad underarm BO. She took me to her little rented room and made me wear a condom, probably because I looked so rough in my jeans. It lasted all of 20 seconds, and I returned to David's house full of remorse. I then suddenly realised I was dying to get back to Cornwall, driven by The Animals' 'We've Gotta Get Out of This Place'.

I abandoned Martin and fled to Cornwall, where I went directly to Trevose golf club to be met at the front door by the owner, Peter Gammon, who said, 'You're not coming in here in that blue leather jacket.'

I had decided to go to Australia because of the lifeguards on Cornish beaches. These Australians were charismatic characters, young, mostly blond, fit and good surfers. They were exceptionally attractive to the local girls and we all loved their accents and their openness. They came from a young sunny world altogether more optimistic than ours. I almost got the feeling that people didn't die suddenly in Australia, let alone throw themselves off cliffs.

By this time I was sharing another flat, this time in Aynhoe Road in Hammersmith, with Christopher Arnott and Clive Rowland and a couple of others. Everything had started to come together. I'd escaped from the hotel basement, and Christopher had got me a job with the Clerical Medical and General insurance company in St James's Square, right opposite my father's former offices. The job involved updating records manually, then delivering them to the computer room where people converted them into holes punched into cards to be fed through an early computer. I had started cooking for myself and my flatmates. Nothing too adventurous, spaghetti Bolognese like my mother cooked.

Clive Rowland argued incessantly about how I was making a big mistake taking off for Australia; how I had a great future in the Clerical Medical and General; how, if I left and came back two or three years later, all my friends would have advanced up the ladder and I would be at square one. I certainly wasn't unaffected by this train of thought, and it would be wrong to think that the prospect of warm weather, surfing and the company of those trouble-free lifeguards and their blonde female friends was more tempting than a career in insurance. But what really stiffened my resolve was a letter from David Moorehouse who had looked after me in Majorca. He was twenty years older than me. He had a refreshing amorality and a loveable Spanish lobo dog called Yogi. Moorehouse told risqué stories about his upbringing in India. I looked up to him.

I wrote to him and told him my father had died and that I was thinking of travelling to Australia and that all my friends had said it was a bad idea. This was his reply:

*'No one ever regretted running away to sea.'*

I applied to Australia House for an assisted passage which cost £10 but my mother decided she would pay the fare which cost £195. Perhaps she hoped I would come home sooner than the two years you had to stay if you were a 'Ten pound Pom'. I was in such a muddle about myself, running away from my emotions, that I didn't at the time appreciate the sacrifice she was making in letting me go. Heaven only knows what she was going through herself – grief, guilt, regret, rage. And loneliness. Having mental illness in a family puts enormous strain on everyone. In our case, this was mostly on my mother because she hid the reality from us all as best she could. Only after my dad died did she reveal that twice she had intervened to stop him killing himself – once at our farm she took a kitchen knife from him and once she caught him trying to climb out of a train window.

All through her life my mum had a soft spot for the underdog and I think she saw me as that person in our family. My father thought I was like him – and this similarity made him very uncomfortable. I'm no psychiatrist, but it seems to me now that during the depressive stage of being bipolar he would have been full of self-loathing, so that everyone who reminded him of himself would have been part of his dark world. It wasn't as if he was particularly hard on me; it was more that he deprived me of confidence in myself. I passionately believe now that the best thing you can do for your children is make them feel loved and make them feel special. To live the first five years of your life feeling that you are valuable is a wonderful thing and, if you don't have it, then you spend the rest of your life trying to find it. I think my mother realised this and tried to compensate for my father's extreme preoccupation with himself.

The day I left for Australia, I went to the Old Swan in Notting Hill Gate for a last pint with my schoolfriend Tim Dale before we set off for Southampton in his Land Rover. As we emerged from the pub in the September afternoon sun we were under a high mackerel sky.

In Cornwall a mackerel sky is associated with stormy weather to come, and now it only increased the butterflies in my stomach. This feeling was magnified as the ship, the RHMS *Ellinis*, edged away from the dock leaving my friends waving on the quay. Ship departures were so much more heartfelt than going through the departure gate at an airport. There were your friends, getting smaller as the gap between you widened, and in my case the enormity of what I had done was given physical reality.

~

My parents had often talked about the pleasures of travelling by sea – to New York on the *Queen Mary*, to Sydney on the P&O's *Orsova* and to Cape Town on the Union Castle Line, all first class. Here was I – with two leather suitcases that had belonged to my dad with ES embossed on them, and a nice Daks blue suit and pink shirt bought from Simpson's in Piccadilly with my mother a couple of weeks earlier – in a cabin full of working-class immigrants. Even after the months in the Great Western, my ability to get on with my cabin mates was limited and their willingness to get on with me was the same. We shared a six-berth cabin on one of the lower decks with no porthole. My companions included two painters from the north of England who spray-painted factories and had brought their equipment with them. There was a forestry ranger from Devon and two fat dark-haired brothers from London called Pierre and Eugene, half-French, half-English, who were not keen on me at all. They had short dark hair, brown eyes and puffy white skin, and both were prone to sweating. They wore rather old-fashioned clothes – big vests and underpants, and suits. As it got hotter out came the short-sleeved nylon shirts and baggy slacks and the shorts with turn-ups. They sort of reminded me of the Kray twins. They clearly came from a very close family and their conversation was always about father and mother and relatives. It was almost as if not much existed for them outside their world, certainly not a nineteen-year-old with a posh accent. They dominated the conversation in the cabin and the others were almost only given leave to speak if they did so as the character that the brothers had ascribed to them. I like to be liked and will do much to ingratiate myself, but Pierre and Eugene weren't interested. I was simply ignored.

Outside the cabin things were a whole lot better. The *Ellinis*, run by a Greek company called Chandris Lines, was a pleasingly proportioned liner. She had been built in 1932 for voyages between San Francisco and Hawaii so all the public rooms had names and decor like the Outrigger Bar and the Waikiki Dining Room. About two-thirds of the passengers were Greek immigrants. The food was not great: overcooked roasts and steaks and hard pieces of breadcrumbed fish, but I certainly enjoyed the Outrigger Bar and particularly a beer in a green and silver can called Victoria Bitter. I retain great affection for that beer to this day. The company in the bar was generally rather good. There were a group of nurses from Exeter emigrating to Melbourne, a young good-looking, half-American, half-English youth of my age called Guy and another boy, Tom, of 17 or 18 who was on his way to a job at a bauxite mine in northern Queensland. Most importantly there was a girl from Toorak in Melbourne called Kaye. Kaye is still the occasional subject of my dreams. She was very tall, probably six foot, slim and blonde with light blue eyes and an air of exclusivity about her. She dressed fabulously. She was just not part of that ship of fools: she was *la belle dame sans merci*, she was Ayesha. She was, I knew, unattainable for me but that didn't stop me trying. For some reason I have kept my diary of 1966. Frustratingly, there are only three entries in it. One of them says, '*I want her and I find myself delighting in her presence but not daring to speak to her. I can't help but get the feeling that she is patronising me.*' Looking back, I see she was not patronising, she was just older. On the last night before we docked in Melbourne she dined with Guy. Did they do it? How I hoped not. Eighteen months later I rang her from a hotel. Even though I announced my name clearly on the phone, she said, 'Who are you?' Our evening together was strained. '*She was beautiful I was lost,*' I wrote, with all the immaturity of callow youth.

I grew up a little on the *Ellinis*. I realised that my cabin mates, the spray painters from Manchester, were funny and that the forester from Devon was salt of the earth, and I guess I became a bit of an alternative because the brothers steadily increased their antagonism towards me. They discovered a way of upsetting me by treating the cabin steward as little more than a slave and using plenty of language like 'wops' and 'wogs'. In the end the worm turned. Pierre addressed the steward as 'a little dago c\*\*t', and I lost it, but with no real power behind what I was saying.

'You shouldn't behave like that.'

'Like what?' shouted Pierre.

'Don't speak to him like that,' I squeaked.

'Don't you talk to me like that, you little runt.'

He didn't attack me, just let it be known that I was going to be thrown overboard later. I was petrified for 24 hours, then mysteriously he started talking to me again as if nothing had happened, which I must have found acutely embarrassing because the note in the diary says, '*I think my new friendship with Pierre is a dubious pleasure.*'

Only since reading *Rites of Passage* by William Golding have I begun to realise what a spoiled prig I was then. It's the story in three books of a voyage by a British frigate to Australia during the Napoleonic wars, seen through the eyes of an 18-year-old boy called Edmund Talbot. The novel is related in the form of letters from Edmund to his godfather. The reader is made very aware of the grim realities on board, but Edmund doesn't grasp what is going on because of his youth and upper-class upbringing. Gradually he grows up and, though his arrogance and insensitivity irritate, his innocence engages our sympathy.

My rites of passage started on the *Ellinis* and continued for the two years I spent in Australia.

# II

I arrived in Sydney on 6 October and spent a few months on the North Shore at Warrawee, living with a family whose father, Lister Ifould, was in the same business as my father. I remembered him and his wife Mary from their visits to Conduit Farm.

The night I arrived Lister said to me, 'One thing you've got to understand about Australia is we're an outdoor country. We don't spend time sitting by the fire reading books and poetry. We play lots of sport and swim.'

I was suffering another bout of insecurity. Having got used to the ship, here I was again in a strange environment, feeling acutely homesick. I found most things about Sydney unfamiliar and hostile, even little things like the grass: though there was plenty of grass everywhere, it wasn't the same as the grass at home, which was soft. In Sydney it was almost abrasive. Far from revelling in the hot sunshine, I got heat rash. I was bitten by mosquitoes. All the colours were too bright, not like the pastel shades of Cornwall. I stood out because the clothes I'd bought were entirely out of style with what all the young people were wearing in Sydney.

There were four children in the Ifould family – three girls, Pam, Marion and Frances, and one boy, Edward, who was the same age as me. Ed was welcoming to me but I found it difficult to reciprocate. The Australians have directness, possibly only shared in my country by some Yorkshire men and women, and some Geordies. For me in those far-off days it was purgatory. I'd always found it difficult to say what I wanted, and I shared with many inhibited English people the slightly irritating way of expressing myself – almost a language of self-effacement, understatement and indecision. Ed Ifould's personality was like a hot knife cutting through the butter of mine.

Ed: 'I'm going to Newport for a surf. Want to come?'

Me: (thinks) Does he really want me to come or is he just saying it because his parents have been telling him: be nice to Rick, he's over here, his father just died.

Me: 'Well … if you don't mind …'

Ed: 'It's fine.'

Me: (thinks) Does he really mean that? Wouldn't he prefer to be with his friends rather than with me? I'm so boring to him because I don't act in any way like them. I'm just the irritating Pom staying in his house …

Me: 'Look, I really don't mind if you'd prefer just to be with your friends because …'

Ed: 'Look, do you want to come or not?'

Me: 'OK.'

Needless to say, I hero-worshipped Ed. He was very fit, a brilliant surfer, an amusing raconteur and unfailingly popular with the girls. On the way out to Newport in his beige VW Beetle, when it was wet he would always swing round the bends through Ku-ring-gai Chase in a controlled tailspin just for the pleasure of it. Wherever we went everyone was delighted to see him, so why would he bother to spend time with me? What I didn't understand was that he was in his element, he was just being Ed. I, on the other hand, was floundering.

When my father died, his sister Zoe was with him. He'd been in a state of agitation all morning, and she had persuaded him to go for a walk to calm him down. They left our home, Redlands, and walked up the small road towards the lighthouse on Trevose Head. Three-quarters of the way up, they turned right, into the grey bumpy drive of Polventon, intending to walk along the cliff path. At the narrowest point, beyond a herring-bone slate wall with a tamarisk growing out of it, where the track runs very close to the edge, my father turned to Zoe and said, 'I told you I'd do it,' and dived on to the rocks beneath.

The Ifoulds had two houses. One was at Bay View which is on Pittwater, a stretch of calm water which lies behind the ocean beaches of Palm Beach, Whale Beach, Avalon, Bilgola and Newport. Their main home, at Warrawee, was in a smart suburb not dissimilar to where my sister Janey and brother-in-law Shaun lived in Highgate in London. Nice people, good schools. Children going off to them every day in similar uniforms, albeit with bigger hats. Tidy streets, good cars. But the northern beaches were different. It was there that I had discovered the burger shop in Newport. Its hamburgers were like nothing I'd ever tasted. Back in the UK we just had Wimpys. A Wimpy burger was probably three ounces of overcooked minced beef with lots of onions and shoestring chips. The only accompaniment was tomato ketchup. We teenagers loved a Wimpy. But here, a burger meant a much bigger piece of meat in a bun with cheese, sliced tomato, sliced beetroot, onions, lettuce, bacon, a fried egg and ketchup. On top of that, and almost more memorable, was a chocolate malted milk shake. It was this hamburger and this milk shake that made me realise that Australia was a good place to be. Food has always been a comfort to me and an inspiration, and as I became enthusiastic about Australian food I became more enthusiastic about Australian life. It suddenly dawned on me that these people were enjoying extraordinarily good times. Every weekend there was a party. The Newport Arms was the best pub in the world. My own experience of beer gardens had been the Farmers Arms in St Merryn, sitting on a beer crate with a few chickens clucking around. Newport was open-air drinking on a scale and sophistication that I could never have dreamed of. For a start the pub was enormous, with two or three outdoor bars and parts of its garden overlooking Pittwater. What intrigued me above all was the pouring of the beer from what looked like petrol pumps. For some time I was nervous about asking for a schooner or a midi, because the punters used to call out, 'a schooner and you,' which I took to be some sort of compliment to the always-pretty barmaids, in other words, 'a drink for you, too.' Only subsequently did I find that what they were actually saying was, 'a schooner of new,' new being Tooheys new as opposed to Tooheys old which was dark beer and not to my taste. I loved the lagers of Australia.

Lister Ifould got me a job on the newly formed TV Channel Ten, scenery-shifting in the studio. The main show was a weekly variety programme called *The Barry Crocker Show*. Barry, or Bazza as he became known, went on to star in two films based on Barry Humphries' strip cartoon in *Private Eye* called *Barry McKenzie*. Crocker is a legend in Australia, as one of the last of the great variety performers. Also his name has slipped into the vernacular in rhyming slang – a Barry Crocker is 'a shocker' but also barking, as in 'off your rocker'. The show was hard work for us scenery-shifters because it had a lot of different sets and none of it was pre-recorded, so there was a lot of rapid moving of stages, pianos, people and, on one occasion, donkeys. The main part of the job was putting up the stage walls which they call flats and which we had to join with cord and brace with sandbags. Our boss was a tough and wiry man called Harry Miller, who was scary. He had a difficult job to do and he didn't take slip-ups well. He shouted at everyone except me. The more he didn't shout at me, the harder I worked to avoid being shouted at. We all wore green cotton boiler suits and nothing on underneath except underpants because it was very hot. None of us looked good in them except Harry who wore pointed, light brown leather brogues with thin soles and walked across the studio floor with a swagger. He was consistent in his bollockings and I found myself very eager to please him. It's actually bliss to be working under someone who knows what he wants. Harry had jaundiced views on politics, the Channel Ten management, and virtually everything else outside stagecraft. He'd been working in theatres all his life; he was probably gay but no one would have dared to ask him any personal questions.

In addition to the Barry Crocker show, we had daily promotional scenes to set, often for local furniture shops which exhibited five or six different bedroom or living room combinations of cheap and very nasty furniture. We also went on outside broadcasts, mostly to wrestling or boxing matches in RSLs (Returned Servicemen's Leagues) in areas like Redfern, Manly or Parramatta. I'd never been in a working men's club in the north of England, but I imagined these would be similar if a little more modern – i.e. lots of drinking and lots of shouting at the wrestlers who, it didn't take me long to realise, were mostly not wrestling, just good at looking like it.

I've kept the best part of the job till last. Every week a young married couple would drive right into the studio in their pale blue Karmann Ghia car and take out pots, pans, plates, a refrigerated box of food and two or three bottles of wine. Looking after their set was an easy job because the small studio was permanently set up as a smart, wood-panelled kitchen. This cook was an Englishman called

Graham Kerr, and his wife was Treena. I was aware at the time of Fanny Cradock, but wasn't interested in TV cookery programmes. Graham's show, *Entertaining with Kerr*, however, was fun. He cooked lovely food and he let us finish off the wine. If he was making something like scrambled egg, you just had the feeling it would taste better than any egg you had eaten before. It goes without saying that there was lots of butter and cream in his recipes, but who cared? He'd make a red-wine stew with a bottle of Penfolds and help himself to a glass while he was doing it. The programmes were engaging because he was so clearly enjoying himself. Two years after I left the channel, he moved to Canada and re-emerged as the 'Galloping Gourmet', a name which he and the late and much-lamented Australian wine maker Len Evans had come up with.

Shortly before I started working at Channel Ten, I had moved into digs near the station in Roseville, a few stops down the North Shore line into Sydney. My room, a tiny bedroom with communal cooking and washing facilities, was at 28 Archer Street. It was a pleasant federation house with a big garden at the back. I don't remember many of the other residents except a woman in her thirties. She was slightly overweight and a bit too theatrical for my liking. And yet there was something about the peachy softness of her lightly dimpled thighs which made me wish I could join her in her bedroom. I think now that she wouldn't have minded, but then, I had absolutely no experience in making such a suggestion. I had retreated into myself. I read Joseph Conrad's *Lord Jim*, Ernest Hemingway's *Death in the Afternoon*, Evelyn Waugh's *The Loved One* and *Scoop* and, most notably, Dostoyevsky's *Crime and Punishment*. I had been influenced into reading Dostoyevsky after a glass or two with my mum in our big upstairs sitting room at Redlands which had picture windows looking over Booby's and Constantine Bays. It was the room where my mother spent a lot of time after my father's death. She'd ask Henrietta and me to join her for a sherry in the late morning so she could share her sadness with us. She described marriage as a huddling together in the dark, and recommended Dostoyevsky for his unwavering clarity of the realities of human existence, made more stark by his time spent as a political prisoner in Siberia and his addiction to gambling. I could hardly claim that 28 Archer Street was like the tenement building in St Petersburg where Raskolnikov, the penniless student, murders his landlady. In *Crime and Punishment* this is a building of tiny apartments inhabited by 'tailors, locksmiths, cooks, Germans of every description, prostitutes, petty clerks and the like'. But lying on my narrow bed in my little room in Roseville with a landlady who was to me as foreign as St Petersburg, I didn't feel too chipper.

Of course, I wasn't depressed all the time. I went out with Ed – lots of schooners of new and Marlboro reds, and on one occasion at the Greengate pub in Killara, the Supremes on a very loud jukebox singing, 'You Can't Hurry Love'. I liked the job too. If I'd stuck with Harry and scenery-shifting, I would have probably ended up as a TV director. But I wanted to write. I coveted the journalists' jobs on the channel but didn't know how to manipulate this. I was censorious about most of the girls at Ten who seemed to spend their time flirting with the producers, directors and presenters, but I know now that to get on in TV, that's how it works. God, I was serious in those days.

It was shortly after he retired that my father killed himself. He was only 58. I don't know whether he was made to retire, or whether he did so of his own volition. His firm, Distillers, had been involved in the marketing of thalidomide, the drug prescribed for pregnant women suffering from morning sickness. It had the side-effect that many children were born with deformities. I don't know if the shame and horror of this scandal had anything to do with either his retirement or his depression. But I do know that he was not cut out for a life of idleness. He found retirement difficult. After he died, I discovered a filing cabinet in which he had carefully labelled everything in his own hand. I imagine that in his heyday as a successful businessman, Miss Screech, his secretary, would have done such things for him. Sitting in his room at home obsessively labelling his own files, his life had become devoid of meaning and empty of decision-making.

# III

Jobs were easy to come by at this time. Before I began at Channel Ten, I had worked in one of the Colonial Sugar Refining Company's chemical factories sweeping up powder which would become polythene by some complicated chemical process. But young people always think the grass might be greener and now I wanted to travel.

I spent the holiday at Bay View with the Ifoulds surfing, listening to The Monkees interminably singing 'I'm a Believer', the song of that Christmas, 1966, and eating hamburgers and chocolate malted milkshakes from the takeaway in Newport. Three days after my twentieth birthday on 4 January 1967, I set off for far north Queensland.

I latched on to two schoolfriends, Jake Walton, who had played in my bands, and his chum Bill Heath. In those days everybody hitch-hiked. Today most people are too scared, or they discover that flying is cheaper. I speedily learned, when I got out on the road and stuck up my thumb, that Australia is overwhelmingly large. Hitch-hiking was like some big lottery. I never knew who would stop. There was an instrumental single at the time called 'Cast Your Fate to the Wind'. That's what it was like. And it was also like that for the drivers who gave me lifts, too.

One hot day, a pale blue VW Beetle stopped. Its driver, Steve, was a printer from Newcastle, New South Wales, who had decided to quit his job and go travelling. He didn't know where he was going any more than I did. He was in his early twenties, wearing shorts and a short-sleeved shirt, a sort of uniform for most youths in those days but within that were myriad nuances in style. Steve's shirts were just a little too patterned, the shorts just a little too tight. I looked frightful too. I wore an over-tight blue-and-white shirt in blocks of colour, with a little button on the narrow turn of the sleeves, and unfortunate pale blue shorts. At least nothing could be read into the flip-flops we were both wearing. They're called thongs in Australia, which means g-string to us, which can be confusing of course, but in those days everyone wore flip-flops. Except, that is, Jake and Bill. Jake had cowboy boots. Bill's summer clothes were conservative: brimmed hat, Viyella shirt, khaki trousers and desert boots. I know this because I have a picture of us in Brisbane taken for the local paper, the *Courier-Mail*, the story being three Englishmen hitching around Australia. News must have been thin on the ground that week, even for Brisbane. The caption reveals that, by then, I so wanted to be an Australian I had started trying to talk like an Aussie.

My diary starts then. I come over as cautious, irritable, critical, sometimes sorry for myself, occasionally funny, but at least it's the real me at 20. I begin by asking the question: what is the point of a diary?

*The main reason is surely to record my actions for the purpose of pondering over my youthful incompleteness at a later date. I would think that a record of my actions at this most interesting time in my life will be of great interest to me later. Writing a diary is a mental exercise providing it is regularly kept up at a time when mental exercises are pretty inactive. This might prove invaluable and of course a diary should perhaps clarify mental problems, so to conclude a diary must contain a factual account plus emotion plus problems.*

So, ponderous too! I had been reading *Voss* by Patrick White, a beautifully written and very literary account of a doomed Victorian expedition into the outback. My English companions pushed off, while Steve and I continued on.

> *I must say it is rather depressing to see them go. Jake made me extremely homesick for Cornwall. Ah well one has to be firm of intention and I must stick to my plans but I would certainly like to go with them.*

Surfers Paradise, south of Brisbane, was then absolutely the place to go to if you were young and liked beach life. The fact that you could pay to be sprayed with coconut oil to improve your tan was enormously indicative to a young man keen to meet blonde Aussie girls that here it would all happen. I haven't been back since but, from the air, Surfers looks like Rio with high-rise hotel and apartment blocks lining the beach. In 1967 it was empty. Pubs were called hotels, and life revolved around the pubs. There was live music and lots of noise. I note that the Surfers Paradise Hotel is now called The Surfers Paradise Tavern. Taverns in Australia don't rock my boat.

On my first night in Surfers I wrote,

> *Steve and I went to the Chevron Hotel looking for women and grog. We got the grog but the women angle was bad. It must have been my lack of technique in chatting up. Last night I was asking too many important questions, many of which probably passed right over the dear ladies' heads. I was asking about jobs and their opinions of tourists. I don't think even I was too interested in the answers any more than they were about the questions. Still how does one chat up rather clueless girls. If I*

*knew I would be a champion rooter. I will try flattery next time
and a lack of questions.*

My eventual success was down to Steve. Four girls were renting
the caravan next to the one we booked for $15 a week, on a road
going into Surfers from the south. They turned out to be anything
but clueless. We suggested going into the town together and it was,
I'm sure, the fact that one of them, Helen, took a shine to Steve
that another one, Karen, started talking to me. That's always how
it happens – they start talking to you. Karen was a lovely-looking
girl, not so much pretty as statuesque; she had long, very curly, light
brown hair and brown eyes. Her friends all called her Affie because of
her hair but also because she had a big nose which did indeed make
her look a bit like an Afghan hound. Whenever I hear of women
having plastic surgery to decrease the size of their noses, I think of
Karen: beauty is definitely not about trying to make yourself look
the same as everyone else. She had long legs and, as I discovered,
small breasts and long arms. She wore a dark blue skirt of some light
man-made material which clung to her brown stomach and bottom
and drove me wild.

Back in Cornwall, my last girlfriend had been a slim blonde
called Gill Richards, who was the darling of the Australian surfers
but who was not keen to have sex with anyone at that time. She
was very attractive and I found I could revel in a chaste relationship
and concentrate on treating a graceful female with correct respect.
From Australia, I wrote dutifully to Gill – long letters full of
manly adventures. I left out all the adventures with women. One
particularly hung-over Sunday in Surfers I went into the camp
shop and bought a tin of ice-cold Golden Circle pineapple juice.
I remember marvelling at the civilisation of a hot country which

had such life-saving drinks for sale, chilled, in somewhere as humble as a small shop on a campsite. My time with Karen was similarly charmed: trips to see the dolphins jump (plain boring) and the sharks (fascinating, really evil-looking, sleek and beautifully dangerous when viewed from above), a floor show in a place called the Cha-Cha and lots of swimming in the sea. One diary entry is suggestive, *'Another great night but the bed collapsed'*.

Steve and I left Surfers to travel north because our new girlfriends were going back to work in Brisbane. We drove 400 miles to Gladstone with a feeling of adventure. I suppose we expected to find another Surfers Paradise and we chose Gladstone because we could get a ferry to Heron Island which is at the southern end of the Great Barrier Reef. We thought it would be where the action was. Gladstone was where the reality of most of rural Australia began to dawn on me. There wasn't much going on. We arrived in the evening, tired from the long journey. We went into a couple of pubs and discovered the town was full of construction workers building an aluminium smelting plant. There was nowhere to stay. We slept in the car and woke at 6.30 feeling dusty and demoralised. We couldn't get a ferry to Heron Island so we took one to Curtis Island. It seemed to be inhabited by about 30 people. I was made even gloomier by the ramshackle nature of the houses and the sight of a couple of trucks dating back to the 1940s parked on the beach. In another life everything there would have seemed quaint and charming but then it made me feel like I was suffocating with depression. In the diary I recorded a lot of drinking sessions so I was probably hung over and Steve was no help. He was bright and cheerful, but I found myself getting irritated by his laugh, his always clean and pressed shirts and shorts, the neatness of his little car. The more he irritated me, the more pissed off I was with myself for being such a bastard. I wanted to be drinking XXXX beer with the construction workers in the Gladstone Hotel, not travelling around with a nice guy like Steve.

He and I parted company at Maryborough. He was going home to Newcastle and I was carrying on to Cairns. I was not looking forward to loneliness in the outback and, as I grew more experienced, I realised the handicaps of travelling solo. I was constantly reduced by lack of companionship. No wonder I read so much and wrote so frequently to my mother. Every time I arrived in a new town I would head straight for the post office Poste Restante, to see if there was mail from her. Once I even planned my route based on a Poste Restante which I would get to in ten days' time.

I gradually got better at getting what I wanted on the road. I soon learned that starting to hitch-hike in a town was waste of time. Better to walk to the outskirts, also to choose an open stretch of road with somewhere where a car could pull in. I figured that I should always look as clean and tidy as possible and smile as much as I could. Part of the deal was that I should talk as much as the person who picked me up wanted to, and soon I began to enjoy it. I travelled with a professional boxer who told me about Sydney's underworld and Long Bay prison, with the Italian owner of a sawmill who was also the president of soccer for Queensland, with a guy in a singlet smelling of sweat who drove an 'artic' (articulated lorry) loaded with railway sleepers. I made it to Cairns only to hit the rainy season. Depression started to set in, and I alleviated it by reading *On the Beach* by Nevil Shute and going to see *Ship of Fools* with Vivien Leigh, Simone Signoret and Lee Marvin in a cinema where all the seating was deckchairs. I returned from the cinema to find my 65p a night room was full of cockroaches. That was when I decided to go back to Karen.

By then, I was getting really quite sharp at hitch-hiking: south of Cairns the car I was in joined a queue to wait for a creek which had flooded the road to subside so I thanked the driver, got out with my stuff, and walked down the queue of cars asking politely at each window where they were going, till I found a driver who was heading for Brisbane. When I got there, I phoned Karen. She put me up but things didn't go too well, and soon I was on my way again.

I was running out of money so I went to the employment exchange in Toowoomba. They found me a job in an abattoir in Roma, about 200 miles further west. I must say I was apprehensive about working in a slaughterhouse – which they referred to as a meat works – but I was still imbued with the Hemingway-esque idea of proving myself as a man by doing tough things. It took me five lifts to get there and I was tempted to take a job offered by a very pleasant farmer on his farm near the turn-off to Condamine. When I got to Roma I checked in to the Hotel Grande, and recorded that in the next room was 'an attractive chaste looking barmaid. The prospects are promising'. Only later did I realise that she was a prostitute in town for the slaughtering season. So naive was I, and so lustful, that I lay in bed the first night thinking of going to her room and asking to sleep with her but deciding not to as she seemed to be rather restless, constantly opening and closing her door and walking around the room and getting in and out of bed.

I've never been in a war zone and only occasionally have been in serious danger, so I can't claim to have seen it all ... but that slaughterhouse really shocked me. Even the night I arrived I could smell it and hear the disturbing bellowing from the cattle in the field into which a brown effluent was pouring from a large pipe. I was distinctly uneasy as I arrived for work at 6.45 a.m. I can remember exactly what I was wearing: jeans and a dark blue work shirt. I was given the job of sweeping up blood and guts in the killing section. In my diary I wrote,

> *When I first looked round I thought that I would faint. I panicked with a feeling that I couldn't stand it but I didn't and felt it was going to be alright, maybe just a slight twinge when I first saw the beheaded cows swinging along on hooks attached to rollers. The smell was rather odd I think it must be the smell of warm blood.*

Each cow was forced up a ramp from the stockyard on to a weighing platform. Just beside the platform stood the big death man, with a contraption that looked like a sawn-off rifle. This had a rod about one foot long which shot out of the barrel when fired into the head. The cow fell down a chute, legs still twitching, and was hoisted up by its back legs. First the throat was cut and bleeding induced by a man in black oilskins and sou'wester who stuck a rod up an artery. The blood ran into a trough. The cow was beheaded and then let down on to a ramp where it was cut open and the guts and hide removed. Then it was hoisted back on to the rails and taken to be sawn in two and chilled for boning.

My day of sweeping blood down drains was long, and I sweated a great deal. I also discovered that the pay wasn't great, so I moved into what I called a no-hopers home which cost £2 per week. On my second day at the abattoir a bullock broke loose after having been shot. It slipped in the blood trough, got up and started galloping round the factory knocking over buckets and bins. Men were scrambling up ladders to get out of the way. Finally they got the fear-crazed animal cornered, and the slaughterman took another shot and the bullock took off for another lap of the abattoir. Finally everybody grabbed it and it was shot at the blood trough. The whole killing department roared with laughter. I found it distinctly unfunny. I was hoping in earnest that the animal would do some real damage, perhaps knock the place down so that we could all go home.

*I hate it. I start in the morning indifferent. By first smoko I'm wishing the death man would kill faster so that the 165 quota can be over quicker. By breakfast I'm thirsty and covered in blood and hair. By lunchtime I'm bored stiff and fed up. By the last smoko of the day I'm so depressed and wish so much to get out of that smelly blood hole that I'm half mad.*

Nowadays, I can see myself as I was then and quote my hero Dylan:

*Now, little boy lost, he takes himself so seriously*
*He brags of his misery, he likes to live dangerously*

Next thing I'm going to the pub with half the residents of the flophouse. My diary records a drinking session that lasts from midday till two the following morning, during which I had an argument with Pedro who is a boner in the meat works. By about 4 p.m. we were all pissed and he flatly refused to buy a round of drinks, which the Aussies call a shout. There was no way I was going to buy them. We were about the same size, and the conversation went something like this:

'Do you want a fight?'

'Do *you* want a fight?'

'No, I'm saying do *you* want to step outside?'

'Look, mate, I asked you first. Do you want a fight?'

'I don't care. Do you want a fight?'

He got up and bought the drinks.

I kept this photo of me aged about five on my chest of drawers in a picture holder I made in a carpentry lesson at prep school.

My father and mother at Polventon on a flaming July day in the late 1950s. Behind are the Merope Rocks where the Padstow lifeboat slipway is now located.

Me, my mother and my sister Henrietta on holiday in Ireland in the fifties.

The whole family except Jeremy in the 1950s. Janey, me, my dad, my mum, Henrietta and John. This is Sas's favourite picture of us. Happy days in Cornwall.

My brother John and me at my sister Janey's
wedding to Shaun O'Riordan in London 1959.
I wasn't happy about wearing a suit.

Me, my sisters Janey and Henrietta, and my mother outside the pub I now run in St Merryn, Cornwall.

Me, Henrietta and my father at Castiglione della Pescaia in Tuscany in 1960.

My father in
1964, a year
before his death.

I never met Great Uncle
Otto but the money he
left me helped buy the
building that was to
become The Seafood
Restaurant, so I owe
him a lot.

I must have loved this picture of me on the bass guitar at The Lodge House in Uppingham in 1964 because I had two copies printed.

*Below and right:*
A fettler's life. Me at Deepwell camp working in a track maintenance gang on the old Ghan railway near Alice Springs in 1967.

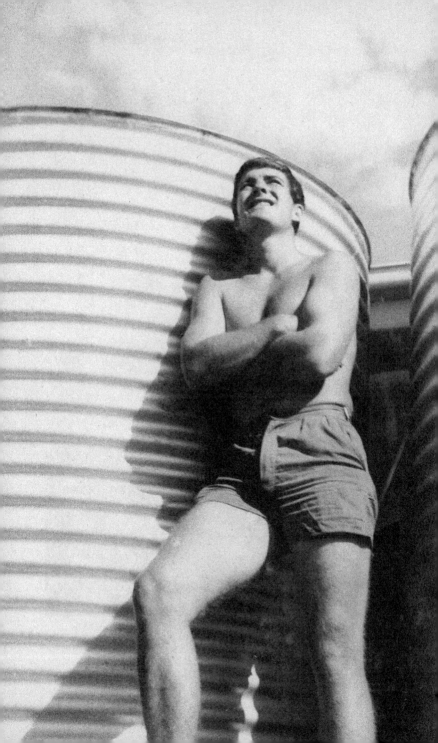

On holiday in Kos, Greece, after the first truly busy
summer season at The Seafood Restaurant in 1977.

The fearless Wadebridge Camels on tour in the
mid-seventies. I'm in the front row, third from the
left – exactly where I played as a prop. Cornish
comedian Jethro is third from left in the top row.
I still see most of them at Camels games.

One final note is from the margins of the diary after a weekend drinking session in the pub. I crashed what is called a B&S or Bachelor and Spinster Ball. I chatted to two girls and was beginning to think how intelligent they were, and how nice, when one of them said, 'You're far too pissed. You'd better go home.'

I had become used to sleeping in my sleeping bag under the stars. I had my radio and my camera, an Emi K which I'd bought in Aden on my way over. I had a couple of T-shirts, two shirts, two pairs of shorts, underpants, my flip-flops, boots, razor, toothbrush. The books that I had read become a problem, as I was loath to leave them behind, *The Grapes of Wrath, Voss, Lord Jim, South by Java Head, My Uncle Silas, The Carpetbaggers*. All of them had a serious physical presence for me and eventually I hit on the idea of sending them all back to Sydney by post. Apart from the diary and biro, I had my Avia watch and a Dunhill cigarette lighter which my brother-in-law Shaun had given me as going-away present, and that was it.

The hotels I stayed in were pubs with rooms, rough but atmospheric. The rooms often had a wide communal veranda and swinging from a hook in the roof there'd be a canvas water bag which delivered quite cool water by a process of evaporation. One of my enduring memories was a hotel in a tiny place called Augathella, between Charleville and Longreach: a few beers in the evening with the locals, sleeping with the fly-screen door shut on to the veranda, getting up early in the morning for breakfast of lamb chops in thick gravy and strong tea and the smell of wood smoke in the air from the breakfast stove as I shouldered my backpack and set off down the road in my R. M. Williams riding boots that I'd bought in Brisbane.

Looking back, the abattoir had been another rite of passage. It had toughened me up and made me happy with my lot. I began to love the dry, fiercely hot country I was passing through and the sparseness of the towns.

# IV

In the fettlers' camp at Deepwell they called Alice Springs 'Callous Springs'. The reason, they said, was that when you were working in one of the camps and you had time off, you went to Alice to get pissed and 'pick up gins'. Not many of the locals wanted you around and they made it clear. I was told that gins – old aboriginal women, – were mostly alcoholics and you'd go off to the dry bed of the Todd River with a gin and flagon of red wine and fuck her, then leave her with the wine.

Arriving at Alice Springs in the rain in a caravan towed by road grader and driven by a Yugoslavian called Bruno, I had been rather disoriented because in the mist and drizzle it felt a bit like Cornwall. I hung around for a couple of days, staying at the Country Women's Association for 10 shillings [50p] a night, then got a job as a railway track maintenance workman also known as a fettler.

It took about 12 hours to go the 50 miles from Alice to Deepwell on the train because much of the track had been weakened by having the ground washed away from under it. The last part of the journey was made by a motorised section car and at times we were going over track with nothing under it.

The morning after I arrived I was at work by 7 a.m., assisting a bulldozer to push the desert sand under the tracks and levelling the track by what was called lifting and packing. There was no ballast (crushed granite stones), under the tracks, just sand, which was why the track was always being washed away and why the passenger train, which ran from Alice Springs to Port Augusta, travelled on its narrow-gauge 3-foot 6-inch rails at speeds so low a boy could run faster. Lifting and packing simply meant jacking up the track with a hand jack till level, then packing sand under the sleepers, ramming it home with the handle of a shovel. We also replaced the wooden sleepers by digging out the old jarra timber ones, sliding the new ones under and securing the track by belting in a thick steel nail called a dog with a sledgehammer. Being able to hit the dog fair and square every time was what counted and took some learning. If you were off course you'd break off bits of steel which would fly everywhere. I've still got the scar on my chest where a white-hot piece of steel hit me.

When we worked the work was hard, but we spent a lot of time not working – lounging under gum trees in the heat of the day with a tin mug of billy tea or lying around the camp reading. We'd work from 7 till 9 a.m. and then have smoko, which was tea and a cigarette. Building fires was easy as there was always plenty of dry firewood. The billy was a two-pint can with a wire handle. You'd fill it from the canvas water bag hanging on the section car. The tea would be imbued with smoke from the fire. That smoky tea with a roll-up was heaven. Tobacco used to come in on the Ghan (the train) once a week at about nine in the evening, when it was deathly quiet with an intense canopy of stars. You'd hear the Ghan 20 minutes before it arrived. A distant hum, then you'd see a hue of light in the distance. A crackling in the rails and it would appear, in its giant red and silver magnificence, its light briefly illuminating the water tower. It rarely stopped, unless a rail boss was coming to see us – Mr Donlan in his sinister leather coat. The train simply slowed down and someone passed out the mail and the tobacco and any other parcels. Then it would be off through the black hills and the rumble would fade to silence. Out there in the bush, there was no sound. I used to think about the explosiveness of silence. My mother sent me a quote from George Eliot: 'If we had a keen vision of all that is ordinary in human life, it would be like hearing the grass grow or the squirrel's heart beat, and we should die of that roar which is the other side of silence.'

Roger the Bludger, the cook, snatched it (left in a hurry). Clem arrived and the relative harmony of our lives at Deepwell was made whole. Most mornings Clem would cook us steak with gravy for breakfast. Lunch would be just cheese or ham sandwiches. Tea, on the other hand, was splendid: we had roasts or fry-ups every night, all cooked in a wood-fired range, followed by tinned peaches, apricots or pineapple with evaporated milk. We had a fridge at the camp driven by paraffin, but no fresh vegetables, so it was roast potatoes, pumpkin and tinned peas. Most nights we'd play euchre after dinner.

Many of the fettlers had been in some sort of trouble with the police. They used to say that the Northern Territory was a bit like a prison anyway because there were loads of people there with some sort of criminal secret who were safe as long as they stayed there. Far from being a wilderness into which you could escape, it was an enormous swathe of land with a tiny population so that, unless you were an aboriginal and could survive in the bush, everyone knew where you were.

Deepwell was one of about 45 track maintenance camps on the line. There were usually five fettlers, a ganger and a cook. The fettlers were Billy, an Irishman called Mick, a Torres Strait Islander called Mike, and an aboriginal called Robert. Our ganger was called John Kopsandy, a magnificent boss who ruled by a certain enigmatic quality so you never knew whether he was pleased with your work or not. I wrote in my diary, 'Christ that bastard gives me the shits when he puts on the Julius Caesar/God act.'

*He bestrides the world like a colossus.*
*And we petty men run in and out of his legs and peep about.*

Not having access to a copy of Shakespeare I didn't get it quite right. But he was a bit of a role model for me. Probably about five years older than me, tall, dark and lean, he was of Hungarian origin. He perfected a style of showing his muscly arms right to the shoulders by ripping off the sleeves of the Bisley shirts we all wore, like team shirts of the Australian rules players. We all followed suit.

A month after I arrived at Deepwell John Kopsandy left and Billy took over. Billy was not a good boss. He was dangerous and paranoid but he was highly intelligent and I liked him. At long last I had found someone I could really talk to. On the strength of his history, ours was not a likely friendship. From Sydney, he had been living with two prostitutes and pimping them. He had spent time, much of his life, actually, in Goulburn and Long Bay prisons for robbery and violence. His father was dead and he didn't know where his mother was. He was quite short, about 5-feet 5-inches, but very well built, wide-shouldered and strong, with thick, short dark hair and a powerful nose. He had bright green eyes and a number of tattoos, a snake going up one arm and over his shoulder to his neck and two words on his index fingers: LOVE and HATE. He had personally tattooed DICK on his penis.

He described endless fights which he called 'battering people'. He occasionally hit his prostitutes. His life in jail was shocking. If these tales of sodomy, stand-over and random violence had been told by one of the slaughterhouse workers, I would have put them down as another example of why outback Australia was a depressing place. But Billy made his past come alive and – for all his vices – it was very entertaining. There was also a frisson of excitement in that, finally, this sheltered boy from middle-class England was learning some of the darkest secrets of real life. I existed in some fear of Billy because he was unpredictable, mostly when he was drinking. We were a 'dry' camp but that only meant we chose not to order beer, flagons of wine or rum. But once we found booze in the caravan of a digger driver who was repairing a bridge, and on another occasion, rum which one of the gangs had given to Clem the cook. Billy became menacing and started laying into me for being privileged and wet behind the ears. He called me Pom and patronised me at the best of times. In the camp there was a white cat called Snowy and a dog called Warregal. No one was quite sure where Warregal came from, he was just there and Clem quite happily fed him. The dog was black, with a wide head, said to be half dingo. For reasons that still escape me, Billy decided that Warregal was a bad thing. One night he said Warregal would have to go.

'I'm going to put Warregal down. He fucking irritates me.'

'Why on earth does he irritate you?' I asked.

'I don't fucking know, don't ask fucking stupid questions, he just does.'

I was terrified but also angry at what I took as his baiting of me. It was as if he was trying to shock me with his horrible intention and wanted me to react – to plead with him for Warregal's life – and I bloody well wasn't going to do it.

'I see,' I said. 'And how are you going to do that?'

'With a fucking axe.'

So he went off and killed Warregal with an axe and came back and told me. I said, 'OK, fine,' but I was quivering with rage and indignation, horror and fear that this lunatic might go for me next.

It passed. Most of the time life was peaceful and nothing like as dangerous. Robert, the aboriginal fettler at Deepwell, worked hard when he was there but quite often he wasn't. He'd literally go walkabout. I used to watch him just standing in the bush looking at things, a stone maybe, stock-still as if he were communicating with it. He was about my height but fatter. He never wore shorts, always jeans, and had the elastic-sided riding boots and the khaki shirt with the sleeves torn out. He smelt a bit of sweat but not unpleasantly. There was a calmness about him. You couldn't really talk to him, because, though he spoke English, he didn't really use it like we did. He lived in a parallel world. I think that's what really got to me about Deepwell, this extraordinary effect that the landscape of the outback has on you.

Mick was good-looking, Irish, tall, thin and very strong, probably in his mid-forties, with a slightly sarcastic demeanour. On good days, he reminded me of Patrick McGoohan in *Danger Man*. He never said much but what he did say was often confrontational. He was a real loner. What, I always wondered, had happened to him? Broken heart maybe, double-crossed and sent to prison for someone else? He viewed me as a tiresome youth. On one occasion, I said I didn't like Melbourne to which he replied, 'Ah, you stupid young bugger. You probably only stopped there three days in the rain, then pissed off because it was too fucking cold.' This happened to be the absolute truth. I'd got off the *Ellinis*, wandered around the docks on Port Philip Bay, bought a Big Ben pie, taken a taxi to Collins Street. It was freezing there and I went back to the ship.

On another occasion at Deepwell I rolled out of bed and went straight to the table, and Mick said, 'Don't you usually wash before you come to breakfast?' I was a large, fit, bolshie 20-year-old who hadn't washed his face. But I've washed before breakfast ever since.

Mick once found me killing redback spiders, which had webs all round the veranda that surrounded the house, and asked what the fuck I thought I was doing.

'There's redbacks everywhere.'

'Have you been bitten by one?'

'No.'

'Nor has anyone else. Leave the fuckers alone.'

He was a bit of a martyr. He was like Boxer in *Animal Farm*. He kept trying to work harder but it was not out of the goodness of his heart. He made us do things round the house. He organised the building of a stockade of sleepers round the camp to keep the dingoes out, then we did the same to make a vegetable garden. We all joined in but found his almost competitive work-hard ethic exasperating. Yet, at the same time, we all felt affection for Deepwell, we wanted to build the garden. We were proud we didn't drink and in spite of the fact that we didn't work as hard as we were supposed to, we probably worked harder than most of the other camps on the line.

It was very early one morning and I was still in bed when Mick strode through the house banging a shovel on the walls. He smacked it against my door shouting, 'I'm going to kill that fucking Pom.' Then he walked out of the house. In my diary, I wrote, 'I acquainted myself later with the fact that it would not be entirely ludicrous to consider an attempt to murder me by Mick.' Some months later I said goodbye to him. He looked me in the eyes, shook my hand, smiled and said, 'Good luck, you'll be all right.'

And I thrived, I grew up a little more, I guess. There were boundaries. At times, I was the young Pom who needed to be taught a thing or two, at others I was like Billy's mum or wife. I was the one who listened to his stories about low life in Sydney, his dark secrets like becoming some powerful tobacco baron's 'girl' in prison so that in return for sex he got protection. I was in awe of him but I also understood him and at times felt very sorry for him. I often thought about how in another life he would have been really quite something. He had a death wish. Why else would he have CUT HERE tattooed on his throat? I also felt that I mattered to him because our conversations were an intelligent connection. For all my youthful naivety, I was a breath of fresh air.

I also had a particular role in the camp which gave me great pleasure. I was in charge of the bore pump. The reason that the Ghan railway ran on the route it did from Alice Springs to Adelaide was because it followed a line of bore holes; without the bore water there could have been no steam engines. The Deepwell bore was pumped up from a long way down by a twin-cylinder diesel engine through a four-inch pipe and up to a water tower. Though the diesel engines which passed through no longer needed water, it was still used for watering the cattle who were mustered at Deepwell once a year and herded into cattle trucks, and it also supplied us with water for washing and for the garden. It was unpleasant to drink, as it was quite salty and sulphurous. Showering in it was not brilliant either, as you were always left with a feeling of scum on the skin, but it was a lot better than the dust of the day. The water was heated by wood chips which seemed even then to be a masterpiece of energy efficiency. Maintaining the diesel engine and pumping the water gave me a feeling of worth and happiness, and standing on the top of the water tower was the best view in Deepwell. In the cold clear air of an early morning I had a feeling of breath-taking distance, seeing the line stretching way off between some red flat-topped hills south towards the next camp at Rodinga. It was like being in a Western. Wandering through the cattle yards with all the redness of central Australia around me and standing on the hard dirt left by the cattle's hooves and thinking 'Those pens will be empty for a year, those cattle come from nowhere miles away, are briefly seen in a melee of movement and then are gone forever'. Walking through empty wadis, much deeper than me, seeing the washed-out roots of trees hanging down at the sides and big balls of a spiky weed called spinifex torn up and blown down into those instant gullies. Climbing out, all the effects of the rain still evident in the confusion of purple and yellow flowers everywhere, mingling with the deep green of paddy melons with the fruits already beginning to bloat and rot with the first frosts of winter, the stark spindly branches of dead trees and the foliage of the desert oaks hanging down in vision-blurring wisps. It's incredibly beautiful and I feel it belongs to me, to everyone. Almost as if I know how it feels to be Aboriginal. I sort of get it in that landscape. It influences me subliminally and there's such an ache in the emptiness. A song on the radio at the time, Slim Dusty's 'Mt Isa Rodeo'. There's a verse about wandering around the empty showground after it's all over for another year:

> *Now when the dust has settled, and the crowds have all gone home*
> *It's kind of sad to wander through the rodeo grounds alone.*

The day finally came when the Ghan was flagged down to stop for me. I got on as a passenger and did the trip to Adelaide.

# V

Adelaide was the last place in Australia where the pubs shut at 6 p.m, called the six o'clock swill. I joined in, ordering two glasses of beer like everyone else. I felt like I'd just been let out of prison. There were pretty girls everywhere. In the bush I'd switched off. Adelaide was waking me up but at the same time I found it daunting. Part of me wanted to be back in the camp at Deepwell with my books. I missed my room, listening to my radio – 'Hey Joe', 'Penny Lane', and 'A Whiter Shade of Pale' – with the collage I'd done over one wall mostly from pictures out of *Australasian Post* and Snowy the cat sleeping at the end of my bed. I moved on to Melbourne where I met a girl called Nonny at a party. The diary says it all,

> *Jesus was I rapt. I mean she wasn't exactly a knock out drop but I was so starved of female company after the bush that when we got round to close dancing I could have put her on a pedestal and worshipped her.*

By the time I arrived in Sydney I was ready for some fun. I got a job as a clerk working in the personnel department of the naval dockyard at Garden Island. Most of the staff were very attractive girls. I travelled to work every weekday on the ferry, made lots of friends and at the weekend went to wild parties. After one such party, I spent the night with a very pretty naked nurse from the

Royal North Shore Hospital but was too drunk to do anything. The next morning I rolled out of bed to answer the banging on the front door. It was Ed Ifould. The pretty nurse had gone and I told him what happened. He expressed the view that in my complete failure I had become a true Australian male.

Ed was the star in everyone's firmament. It's rare that you find someone so positive. He had a seemingly unending energy, so that he was always doing something – surfing, swimming, running, going to the pub, going to the football, going to dinner. I knew that he had a disagreement with his father, Lister, about his future, just as I'd had with mine. They both expected great things of their sons and neither Ed nor I wanted to toe the line. Indeed, Ed upset his by opening a sandwich bar soon after he left school. Thereafter he worked at things he wanted to do. He never seemed to doubt himself, unlike me. He just got up every day and got out of the house. He was, like many Australians, refreshingly outward-looking. He enjoyed other people and took pleasure in their company, so much so that he was always quietly the centre of attention – confident and interested in everyone. He died suddenly of a heart attack while out in his boat sailing in Pittwater. He was in his late forties. I miss him.

I started cooking again in Sydney, not expansively but occasionally. I did spaghetti Bolognese or pea and ham soup or tomato and onion salad, the things my mother used to prepare, but I noticed that whatever I cooked my flatmates seemed to like. The fish and chip shop up the road near the arches of the Harbour Bridge in Kirribilli was about as good as food got in Sydney, at least for us. They did battered Tasmanian scallops which I was particularly fond of. I had never tasted scallops before. I was inordinately fond of Chiko rolls which you could get there, too. A Chiko was a bit like a Chinese spring roll, but it had a thick flour wrap, which became crispy in the deep frying, and it was filled with cabbage, onion, green beans, soft barley and beef.

Judy Wheeler was stepping out with one of my flatmates. They were almost engaged. Nevertheless, she and I got on very well; in fact I'd go as far as to say she was the first girl I ever felt completely alive with. She was pretty and very funny and took the piss out of me. She was bright and illuminated my world. We never became intimate but that perhaps made it more memorable. We sought out each other's company and the fact that she was unavailable made her even more delicious. I remember sitting with her in a car listening on the radio to *Sgt. Pepper* before the LP was released. I can't hear a single track of it now without remembering that time and that place in Sydney.

Meanwhile, in personnel at the naval dockyard I filled in forms. They called it 'higher orders'. I had to work out the extra pay for dockyard workers when they temporarily took on a better paid job to fill in for holidays. I found it tiresomely complicated. Naval architects, electrical engineers, mechanical engineers, boiler-makers, painters – each had three or four grades of pay and the forms slid mercilessly into my in-tray, the pile getting ever higher. I'd drop the *Sydney Morning Herald* on to the toppling pile to hide it. Another job was checking who was registered for the draft to fight in Vietnam. Since I wasn't registered and had no intention of being so it was only a matter of time before the job would have to come to an end.

I left Australia before the draft could catch up with me. The pretty girls in the office threw a leaving party – such nice drinks in the Fortune of War in The Rocks – and they gave me *The Australians*, a lovely book of photographs with a picture of a gnarly Australian farmer in a battered hat on the cover. They all signed it: good luck, Rick, pleasure knowing you, etc. I felt bad about the mess I'd left behind.

# VI

In no time at all, I found myself parting from a country I had no wish to leave. As the ship drew away from Circular Quay heading for New Zealand the sight of Judy in a black and white dress waving furiously felt like leaving my mother at the station when I went off to boarding school.

The Wellington pubs smelt of disinfectant and the beer was weak. I was running out of money but discovered that there was plenty of work in Hawkes Bay on one of the fruit and vegetable farms owned by the tinned food company, Wattie's. Soon I was picking asparagus and thinning peaches.

What I needed – as always – was company. I hitch-hiked and stayed in youth hostels. New Zealand was convivial, but I missed Australia and Judy. The evening before my twenty-first birthday my lift dropped me about 40 miles out of Kaikora. It was getting dark and I was thinking wanly that I would have to spend the night of my coming-of-age under a bridge. Then miraculously, I was picked up by a farmer in an old Ford V8 Pilot. Our conversation was not about farming but about the price of cars in New Zealand. I could hear curious muffled thumps from the back. He dropped me right by the beach and let six sheepdogs out of his boot. Then I went into a restaurant and celebrated my birthday: I ordered crayfish (a spiny lobster) and sat in solitary splendour eating it. This was the first time

I'd deliberately treated myself to expensive food. These days I go to New Zealand once a year and adore it.

~

I got a job working my passage from Auckland to New York on a German freighter. The *Cap Finistere* took up to 12 passengers, and I was ensconced with an Irish carpenter called Jim in one of the passenger cabins. Another was occupied by a horse-trainer called Milton who had four racehorses housed in wooden stables on the deck. The cargo was wool and deep-frozen New Zealand lamb which, rather depressingly, was going to be used in the States as pet food.

The night before we sailed, Milton and I went to Ma Gleason's, a well-known maritime dive. We drank much but there were very few women there. I wandered into another bar: I could hear music and see that it was filled with girls. I asked one to dance and all was going swimmingly, except that I made the fatal mistake of thinking like a fox in a hen-house. A well-travelled backpacker once said to me, 'In any community, however rich or poor, find one girl you like and stick with her. If you flirt with lots of them you'll be without a girl in a bed.' And so it turned out. I was told to get lost.

Returning disconsolate to the *Cap Finistere*, I heard the sound of a party aft. It was filled with girls and soon, beer in hand, I was chatting to a Fijian nurse. I was enormously encouraged by the fact that she spoke to me first. She had a forceful animal quality. Sex was never discussed: it was a natural thing to take her back to my cabin. Awakened in the morning and having indulged a little more in the fun of it all, I suddenly realised that such frolicking in a guest cabin might not go down too well with the captain and chief engineer whose quarters were next door, so I asked her if she'd mind terribly if I asked her to go. She didn't. It was the sort of uncomplicated carnal experience every young man dreams of. The only thing that I regret is that Jim was in the bunk below all night and was not amused. I am appalled to this day to think of my insensitivity but at that time I never thought about him.

A friend of mine, Richard Blight, used to be an engineer on merchant ships. He had what I would call a sallow complexion and always looked like he was wearing a thin film of oil. I wouldn't have thought of this without my month in the engine room on the *Cap Finistere*. In another life I would choose to work in a big engine room. It was fearfully hot and oily but the engine room was rather like a kitchen. The crew were nice to me, and cheerful, and I love machinery. In Auckland harbour only two of the Deutz diesel generators were going, and various pumps, but as we prepared to leave the main engine roared into life with a thunderous power, heat and noise that was thrilling. There was a hiss of compressed air that used to start the pistons moving, then an explosion as the compressed fuel fired, then a rapid clatter as the engine started. Thick black smoke would pour out of the funnel, soon disappearing as it all warmed up.

My job was to help the first engineer strip one of the generators. At the same time the entire engine room was repainted and I had a second job of removing spare cylinder-head bolts from the propeller shaft tunnel. These were in brackets all along the tunnel. It was icy cold and damp with a narrow walkway between the sloping keel of the ship and the revolving shaft. I could hear the bilge water swishing below the steel plates on which I was walking. Not somewhere, I remember thinking, you'd want to be on the way to Murmansk in the Second World War with torpedoes around. I had to cradle each bolt in my arms and carry it to the lathe in the workshop, then the lathe operator would machine a tiny amount off each one till it became silver and like new. The ship was going back to Hamburg for a refit, so I couldn't quite understand why they were taking so much trouble to smarten everything up. But they were German, and one thing I learnt on that trip was they do things well. A couple of days into the voyage the whole crew shaved their heads. These days it's not surprising but at the time of the cult of The Beatles haircut it was weird. Lots of, yes let's face it, rather square-headed Germans with white scalps. They were good fun. We drank an awful lot of Holsten together. I liked their cigarettes, HB filters, which tasted Continental to me, as did their food – lots of sausages, smoked ham, sauerkraut and schnitzels.

It was early February and when we sailed into Norfolk, Virginia, it was freezing. The transition from summer in New Zealand caused me a lot of depression because I realised I would soon be leaving the warm certainty of the ship for the cold and uncertainty of the shore. *'Sitting on the dock of the bay wasting time…'* Otis Redding's song on a jukebox in a bar in the docks in Norfolk filled me with unease. It was even colder when we docked in Philadelphia. Finally we were sailing up the Hudson River into New York with dirty snow all round. I stood on the deck inside the black funnel of the *Cap Finistere* looking out at the Statue of Liberty on the left and planes landing at La Guardia airport in the distance and felt deeply uneasy. Music always seems to carry so much more meaning at such times. I can't listen to 'Love is Blue' by Paul Mauriat without recalling that panic. But it also gave me a sort of romantic objectiveness about my lonely situation, about to set foot on a strange, icy continent. This wasn't helped by the crew who told me that the New York docks were really dangerous. I walked down the gangway on to the quay with my new backpack bought in New Zealand, feeling sure I was going to be robbed as I trudged the half mile to the road and scuttled cravenly into a taxi.

New York, for me, turned out to be a bit like *Midnight Cowboy*: cold, not enough money and the YMCA, where the only men that you got to talk with seemed to want to share a room. I fled south where it was warm. I got on a Greyhound bus for Winston-Salem. I chose Winston-Salem only because the journey was long enough to give me a night's sleep. I'd been stunned by the price of accommodation and decided I'd be better off with my $99-for-99-days Greyhound ticket, sleeping on the buses. I worked out that I would need to travel 500 miles to get a full night's rest, so began to plan late departures from central city bus terminals. If I'd known about Edward Hopper's 'Nighthawks' I might have enjoyed the comparison – if I hadn't been so serious.

As I child, I'd hero-worshipped Americans. As a teenager, I'd felt that American culture ran in my veins; cowboys, Texas, Hollywood, singin' the blues, Elvis ... but the reality I experienced on this first visit was so bleak that my childish enthusiasm seemed like daydreams on another planet.

I spent the next fortnight in Florida, New Orleans and Texas trying to find company and succeeding only in attracting homosexuals and cursing myself for being so naive as to think that the naval officer I got talking to in Miami was just interested in casual conversation with a travelling Englishman or that the middle-aged man in Houston was not letting me sleep in his apartment just because I was tired and needed a shower. I talked myself into believing that Mexico was where I really wanted to be. America felt like one big highway; I was on buses all the time and I missed human contact and the homely conviviality of New Zealand. If you've got very little money, America is a scary place to be.

My experience of Mexico was better because I knew I was in a third-world country and had fewer expectations. The people understood poverty: one woman offered me money for the bus fare. I had started hitch-hiking again, and was grateful to meet people through doing it. The Mexican hotels were cheap and many were also used by prostitutes. Not that I realised this – I was always amazed by the amount of comings and goings in the night and the appalling state of the toilets next morning. I drank Carta Blanca beer and tequila with lime and salt in cantinas which were really rough places where the pissoir was part of the bar with just a little partition up to waist height. In Tampico, oppressed by loneliness, I went down to the docks and found a British Harrison Line freighter and was invited to come aboard. I spent a couple of days with the crew, drinking on board and in local bars. Needless to say there were lots of local girls who inflamed my lust but I couldn't conquer my caution. On the way back to my hotel, where I was in a room with no windows and barely enough space to walk between the bed and the wall, I was propositioned by a prostitute in a doorway. I was incandescent with desire but when she dropped her opening price of 25 pesos by half I was convinced it was dangerous and forced myself to go back to my foetid cell. I've never forgotten that encounter, the road not taken. When I'm feeling critical about myself, it epitomises my over-cautiousness. When I feel good, that refusal reinforces how fundamentally sensible I am.

I have to question what I thought I was up to at the time. Why was I doing this? What did I hope to get out of it? Certainly I had very little money, but I could very easily have cabled my mother for some to be sent to Western Union. I was trying to act like a manly Ernest Hemingway character, when all the time I was on the run from the memory of my father and the cliff.

After a very gloomy and solitary week things took a turn for the better. I was sitting in a cafe thinking about a third-class bus fare to Mexico City and listening over and over again to a song called 'The Disadvantages of You' by a band called The Brass Ring when a boy of about 18 started a conversation with me, practising his English. In my diary I wrote,

> *In any other situation I would have had very little to do with Arturo being in my opinion rather a loud mouthed little squirt. Small thin with a type of un-handsomeness of face which is not ugly but full of that type of arrogance which comes from being the only son in a family who's [sic] elevated position in the community is without question. But Arturo was very kind and liked me and you cannot but like that in a person.*

He looked after me for three days and took me to meet his parents who put me up in their hotel in the town. He even took me to the town brothel, but it was shut. We went shooting at a friend's ranchero where I marvelled at the simplicity of the farmhouse – just two adobe huts thatched with palm. I noticed a bedroom with handmade wooden beds covered by multicoloured Mexican blankets, hard dirt floors and the ochre plaster on the walls slightly crumbling around the wooden frames of the glassless windows. No ceiling, but the thatch tied down with leather straps to the crooked rafters and just a gun and cartridges propped up in the corner. We shot red and green parrots, taking turns with the one ancient 12-bore, and drank glasses of warm frothing milk straight from the cow. Needless to say, I was worried about getting TB from the milk. Many years later I read *Scenes from a Clerical Life*:

*'The golden moments in the stream of life rush past us – and we
see nothing but sand; the angels come to visit us – and we only
know them when they are gone'*

I bumped into two Englishmen, Derek Scott and Ian Stewart,
who were on their way to Acapulco. They had a car and asked
if I would like to share the costs – and my life lit up. I had
found companionship. Derek, Ian and I spent all day on the
Acapulco beach, only repairing to a restaurant called the Students
International in the early evening to eke out a beer or two. Our
diet consisted mainly of frankfurters and sweet American-style
sliced bread which we bought at the supermarket to save money.
Every day I sat on the beach near a restaurant where Americans
were being served whole grilled red snapper with sliced tomatoes,
chillies, spring onions and crispy thin chips. I had rarely felt so
hungry. The smell of fresh grilled fish skin, and chips cooked in
clean oil. It was enough to imprint on me a sense of the excitement
of eating right there by the waves.

I stayed in a cheap hotel in the old part of town. It was a brothel
too but I didn't realise that till I took back a French–Canadian called
Lise and the concierge demanded '15 pesos for the girl'.

I couldn't believe my luck to have begun a relationship with
Lise who was small, dark-haired and very pretty in a pouty sort of
Brigitte Bardot way. She was from Montreal; it was her Frenchness
that really attracted me, and of course her accent. It made me feel
very grown up to be stepping out with a French girl whose priorities
in life were looking elegant and finding good food. When we went
out to restaurants, she paid.

Lise talked about food all the time. She understood the difference
between corn and flour tortillas. She knew what guacamole was. She

taught me to love tamales. One night we met up with officers from a French Navy frigate anchored in Acapulco Bay and we went out to dinner with them. I ate enchiladas stuffed with chilli, tomato and beef with a salad with salsa rioja, and was transfixed. It wasn't just the food – it was the dazzling French officers in their blue and white uniforms, and it was Lise. All these worked together to position food a lot higher in my list of priorities.

The Students International, where I first met Lise, was run by a young American ex-student called Scotty. It was cheap and filled with young people, mostly Americans. It did indeed attract students, mostly well-educated ones, and the conversations ranged far and wide, including literature, Aztec history and the Mercedes that Jerry, not much older than me, had driven all the way from San Francisco. One of the Mexican managers introduced me to the Spanish poet Lorca and his poem 'A Las Cinco de la Tarde', and so taken was I that I actually went to a bullfight in Acapulco to experience the flavour of Lorca's Spain.

When Lise left, I accompanied her to the airport in the early morning. There were black vultures on all the telegraph poles along the road, which in retrospect seemed a harbinger of not such nice things to come. I decided to sleep on the beach. Derek and Ian had been doing that ever since we arrived. They had a large American car, a Dodge Dart convertible, with front seats that tipped so far back that they formed passable beds. There was no room for me, so I tied my backpack to the steering wheel and put my sleeping bag on the sand next to the car. It was my sense of caution – for which I have so often castigated myself – that made me tuck my diaries, my passport and my dollars into my sleeping bag. Next morning the backpack was gone. My whole trip gone: photos, camera, radio, clothes, letters, books. Gone.

In the Students International, Scotty said was I was very lucky.

'Lucky!'

'Yes. If you'd woken up and seen someone stealing it, you'd have gone for him and he'd have killed you.'

I left Acapulco with Derek and Ian. We were heading for Mazatlán in the state of Sinaloa, just opposite the tip of Baja California. We'd heard that there was good surf and good beer there. I was in a state of shock about the loss of my backpack. I bought a change of clothes and a small blue duffel bag to put it in. As the effects of the theft of the luggage began to wear off, a new and unfamiliar emotion began to take hold: liberation. Never before had I considered the implication of the Latin word for luggage – *impedimenta*.

# VII

After I said goodbye to Derek and Ian, I took buses through Oregon and Washington State all the way to Vancouver, and found myself in a basement flat with a bunch of dope smokers. There was a track on the stereo by a band called Love. It was clearly, I thought, written by someone on marijuana. The first line was, 'Oh, the snot has caked against my pants'.

I was shocked at the lyrics and all those drugs. It was one of those occasions – like first registering the blues at my school – when I was aware that my taste in music would never be the same again. Within six months, Love's album *Forever Changes* would be my most treasured LP, closely followed by The Doors. I would also be enjoying the occasional joint while listening to *Disraeli Gears*.

At the time, though, I didn't want to know. It was 1968, and I must have been one of the few 21-year-old boys in the whole of America who had never even experimented with dope.

I was heading to Montreal, where I spent a week in a flat belonging to a friend of Lise's. It had no furniture except a bed with no bedding so I laid my sleeping bag on it. There were no curtains either, but it was warm and I was back with Lise. Our love-making was a little compromised by the lack of sheets and the brightness of the room, but it was either that or a sofa in Lise's parents' tiny house and no sex. By then I hadn't enough money for any hotels at North American prices. I had come to Montreal out of love for Lise.

Now, my love for Cornwall was taking over. It wasn't Lise's fault. She couldn't have been more attentive and generous and, needless to say, the cooking at her parents' place was spectacular. I can still remember the daube her mother made. But the foghorn on Trevose Head was calling me to a misty summer day and I had to get back.

Coming home to Cornwall felt like Odysseus returning. My Penelope, Gill, was off with the suitors. The chaste idol, to whom I had written so many long, intense, carefully censored letters, had grown up. I was delighted for her. I was returning to where I was happiest. My mother was overjoyed. She had bought every LP by The Seekers while I was away; they had kept her closer to me. My sister Henrietta was back for the summer holidays, waiting to go to university. She had changed completely since I had last seen her. Then as a schoolgirl, shattered by our father's death, she had been dispatched to a school in Switzerland and had loathed it so much that my mother sent her to do her A levels in London where she'd grown up too. She looked fabulous, she wore great clothes and was very trendy. Shops such as Bus Stop and Biba were flourishing and girls were very chic. If she hadn't been my sister, I would have been too nervous to talk to her, but she was and she had lots of pretty friends and she loved me. The sun shone every day. I was the most interesting person at the pub.

At a little club called Rosehill, I met a pretty blonde called Teri, who introduced me to Jill Newstead. Terri was much more talkative than Jill but it was Jill I fancied. She wasn't tall, which appealed to me, and, as we used to say in those days if we were being polite, she was 'very well put together'. She had long dark hair and beautiful blue eyes. I asked both girls to my delayed twenty-first. It became a party of trying to get off with Jill. The evening was, as my mother would have said, 'an absolute riot'. We did indeed take to each other happily and Jill and I were inseparable for most of the summer.

The parties in the coach house were wonderful and my confidence and serenity unassailable. I went out with Jill virtually every night. Then at August bank holiday I asked her whether she was going to the Farmers Arms on the Saturday and she told me she was going with somebody else. To say that I didn't see that coming was an understatement. I had been massively intrigued by her enigmatic quality and completely overwhelmed by her beauty. When I discovered that she was going to the pub with someone whom she'd met before she met me, and who also proved to be an excellent piano player, my humiliation was extreme.

The scene in the Farmers Arms is forever etched in my mind: Jill next to the piano with him effortlessly playing a selection of Beatles songs. When he'd stopped there was 'Hey Jude' on the jukebox. I wrote a little two-line poem soon after:

*Perhaps it was the leisure of interminable days*
*That makes it seem so funny that it's gone*

When I 'ran away to sea' I had no desire to go to university. I'd flunked my A levels not once but twice and my father's suicide had left me lost and uncertain. But Australia and travelling on my own had helped me grow up. I returned with a sense of confidence in myself. When the latest lotus-eating summer of delights in Cornwall was over, and the nights were getting longer and autumn descending, I made up my mind to try for Oxford. It was a long shot, but I'd done a lot of reading while I was away and I was encouraged by various people saying that my experiences abroad and my age might help because mature students were favoured. I had lots of private coaching.

My English tutor John Hall was one of those people in their mid-twenties who find it hard to adjust from the gloriously sociable and valuable aesthetic life of university to the much more mundane business of finding a job. They maintain a connection with the golden era by teaching A levels and university entrance exams. With considerable entrepreneurial flair, John had also established a summer school in Venice, teaching fine art and visiting museums and churches. He staffed his operation with similar graduates, one of whom, Bill Baker, was to feature in my life as a restaurateur. John had a keen eye for what Oxford English dons would be looking for in a mature student. He taught me in a flat in Cheyne Walk, overlooking the Thames. Driving over in my brand new Hillman Imp, which my mother had given me as a late 21st birthday present, from my sister Janey's house in Crouch End, calling some days to Kensington for Latin or Belsize Park for French studies, I took to the prospect of life at Oxford with enthusiasm. At last I was discussing Thomas Wyatt's *They Flee From Me* with someone near my own age – noting the lurking danger in the poem of the illicit liaison at the court of Henry VIII. Was she perhaps Anne Boleyn we wondered, this delicious woman with the pale deer-like limbs? Drinking tea and eating buttered crumpets overlooking the Thames I felt I had moved back into a comfortable middle-class life.

My sister Janey had married an actor, Shaun O'Riordan. When she met him he also had a bric-à-brac stall in Portobello Road market. Challenging, keen on constructive arguments and twenty years older than me, he was at the height of his considerable success as a TV director at the time that I was trying for Oxford. He had style. His collection of shirts from shops in Jermyn Street included Harvey and Hudson big shirts with thick double cuffs which came in subtle shades of grey or mauve or yellow with white stripes. He had floral ties from Liberty and suits from Jaeger, and expensive colognes and aftershaves. He used Eau Sauvage and joked that savage water should be for young strutting men with big libidos but the only people who could afford it were over-paid TV directors and aging poofters. He scared the pants off most of my friends, particularly girls, as he demanded that everyone who came to his house gave an account of themselves and wouldn't let them get away with silence. He could usually be guaranteed to have a contradictory point of view about any opinion. His greater experience of life invariably won the day. I loved him to bits, still do. He had a workshop in the basement of his large house in Crouch End and let me have a corner of it, where I built two speakers to go with the Thorens GL68 turntable I had bought. I was saving up for an amplifier, in the meantime playing Love, The Doors and the Rockbuster through an old radio. He constantly pulled me up for failing to make the edges of the sides of my speaker boxes 100 per cent true. His attention to detail often made me frustrated at my own inability to get it right. He was completely thorough in everything he did, even the washing-up.

At that time specialist food shops were beginning to appear everywhere and Sainsbury's had the sort of cachet that Waitrose has today. All its packaging was plain – just one colour, orange, green or red, with a minimalist sans serif typeface on it – and it seemed to me to be very stylish. Janey patronised good food shops all over London: sausages from Baker Street, ice creams from Marine Ices opposite the Roundhouse in Haverstock Hill, Paxton & Whitfield for cheese. Janey followed Constance Spry because she was our mother's favourite, but she read cookbooks like novels.

Jane Grigson, Elizabeth David, Claudia Roden. The ability to flavour dishes with depth was something I learnt from Janey. She had the most beautiful handwriting. I tried to copy her precision with forming the letters, but could never get the satisfying roundness of her E. Everything she did – writing, organising her kitchen, labelling food for the deep freeze – was done with an attention to detail which affected her younger brother no end. Given that my father had made rather a mess of being a role model, I needed someone to look up to and aspire to – and they were Janey and Shaun.

I worked hard all that autumn and took my entrance exam in early December. I have a suspicion that what got me into Oxford was my answer to a general question about landscapes. I wrote about the outback in Australia, the red landscape of the Simpson desert and the rock formations rising out of the flat land where the balls of dry, spiky spinifex rolled around in circles in the wind and the little dust cones called willy-willies followed them.

Just after finishing my entrance exam I met – at a twenty-first birthday party in Kent – a friend of Henrietta's called Frances Pick. We rolled home to London in a train with no corridors and my behaviour was amorous and enormously confident. I just knew she would respond with equal fervour and she did. I was completely captivated by her, so much so that when I knew I had been accepted by New College, Oxford, I moved into a flat in Ditchling Road, Brighton, to be near her at art college in Worthing. I went to work for Robert McAlpine as a labourer building a bypass round Shoreham.

I wasn't much liked by the ganger, because I was not at all interested in working weekends or evenings because I wanted to be with Fanny. The best way to define our relationship would be tempestuous. I have described myself as lacking in confidence but that doesn't imply any lack of spirit underneath. Shy people are often also in something of a rage with themselves for being so unable to give account of what they are really like. What am I really like? Well, I think it takes a very close relationship to discover that, and also one that is over. I have kept all the letters from Fanny, in fact I've kept all the letters from all the women I've cared for. I like women. I find them much easier to talk to than men.

Fanny Pick's letters often say things like 'I was so happy you were in a good mood' or 'pleased you are feeling less depressed now'. It's hard to own up to being a moody person, hard to say that a lot of the time you see the skull beneath the skin, but she understood this and her letters illustrated it.

I loved the way Fanny dressed. She possessed an array of mini-skirts, some tweed, some pleated, some tartan. The shades of pastel in the tights she wore, her neat shoes and tight jumpers only just coming to the top of her skirts. Dresses in the summer of lightest pale cotton, tight and short. I don't think she possessed a pair of jeans. She had a rather languid way of speaking and a way of looking at men with a sort of secret smile if she liked them, as if she was saying, 'This is the conversation now but it could be so much more later.' She had warm brown eyes and she was very sexy and drove me wild. Looking back now, I just couldn't cope with her. It was doomed almost from the start but while it lasted it was so strong.

I remember once returning to my small but nice room in Brighton after an evening at the King and Queen just down the road. The company in the pub had been stimulating. Both my flatmates were students at Sussex University and there was lots of lively chat. Fanny and I got back full of joy and sat on the end of the bed in our coats and kissed. It was a moment of being as one. There were a couple of LP sleeves on the bed: *Sergio Mendes and Brasil 66*, memories for me of Sydney, or maybe *Also Sprach Zarathustra* because I'd just been to see *2001*, or maybe Jimi Hendrix's *Electric Ladyland* with the original cover with all the naked women looking a bit grey, or perhaps an Oscar Peterson album borrowed from Graham Knott across the hall who was reading maths at Sussex and was so bright he had plenty of time to get a 2.1 while listening to lots of Oscar.

I was so jealous, so possessive, that I hated being apart from Fanny. I got a sinking feeling in my stomach whenever I saw a girl wearing a dress like hers or smelt perfume like hers. The last time I saw her she came to my rooms in New College. She was dressed in yellow. But we couldn't go on, not at that age. I was just starting at Oxford, she lived miles away in Worthing.

The letters came as frequently as before, then they stopped. There was a reticence about her on the phone. I was in denial. Eventually I realised that she never telephoned me, and I was always ringing her. Finally, just after the autumn term ended and I was staying at Janey and Shaun's, I decided I would drive to Worthing and meet her walking from the art college back to her lodgings. I bought a bunch of blue paper flowers. When she saw me in my long black coat with the silly flowers she looked shocked and said, 'Oh Ricky, that's very sweet of you, but I want you to go.'

# VIII

Two sad songs were my companions that Christmas back in Cornwall: Jethro Tull's 'Reasons for Waiting' and Tim Hardin's, 'How Can We Hang On to a Dream?' But at that age things don't stay blue for long. I had made a new bunch of friends that summer in Cornwall. Word of my parties in the coach house had by then reached quite far afield and that included the Bude lot, who were lifeguards and ex-lifeguards from Widmouth Bay. One of these, Graham Walker, had become a student of landscape architecture in Cheltenham and he brought down a friend called John Thompson and his friend Francis Bowerbank. They were sleeping on a mattress in the back of a green Commer panel van in Constantine, and appeared at one of my parties.

The first thing John Thompson did was to help himself to Henrietta's cigarettes which were on the ledge under the roof.

I went up and said, 'Look, can you stop nicking my sister's cigarettes? She's very pissed off.'

To which he replied, 'Want one?'

And I said, 'Yes. OK.'

And so began a friendship.

I saw a lot of the three of them, zooming around London in the back of Francis's van, crashing other people's parties where you could always find us in the kitchen because most of the time we didn't know anyone. We crashed parties because in those days the pubs shut at 11 p.m. The form would always be the same: closing time, and you'd buy a couple of large cans of gruesome beer like Watney's Red Barrel. Someone, mostly Francis, would have heard of a party somewhere like Hendon or Acton. I can't remember a specific party because they were all the same. I don't think any of us – and we would normally be seven or eight – would strike up a conversation with anyone who was legitimately at the party, but we so enjoyed each other's company it didn't matter. I don't recall anyone getting stroppy: we always brought our own booze. We'd all tried hash but could leave it out. What we couldn't leave out was the alcohol. We all drank a great deal of beer. Even then, we were seeking out real ale pubs such as the Prince of Wales in Highgate which sold Courage Best and the Surprise in Chelsea which sold Bass. German Riesling wines such as Blue Nun and Three Crowns were still popular, as were blended wines like Hirondelle and Don Cortez but these were generally a bit on the sweet side. The wine of choice for us was a French brand, Nicolas, and the one I liked was Vieux Ceps which came in a litre bottle with a foil cap and with stars on the neck. It was the sort of wine you bought for a couple of francs in the corner shop in Paris. The fact that it cost ten times as much in Great Britain was not welcome.

I went up to Oxford in October 1969. My tutors were John Bayley and Christopher Tolkien, J. R. R. Tolkien's son, who took me in Anglo-Saxon and Old English. I was a rough diamond. I suppose I'd expected to feel somehow superior with my maturity, but I didn't, I just felt dumber. I was 22. My fellow undergraduates, all male at that time, were from public schools and all had just left them. This, I felt, put me at a disadvantage. I was distanced from quiet, scholarly, bookish work. My appreciation of English literature was as someone who had lived it. My brother John was a junior don at Magdalen while I was an undergraduate. I said to him at the time that it seemed impossible to me that someone aged 18 could write authoritatively about literature, having not had experience of most of the adult situations described. He answered simply, 'Some people just *do* understand, however young they are.' Looking back, I was partly wrong and partly right. People with the sensibility of a Mozart or a Shakespeare will always have instinctive understanding. People like me have to live it. I liked Robert Browning, whom I didn't discover till Oxford. He filled me with a sense of what the Victorians were really like. His dramatic monologues drop you into the middle of somewhere like the red-light zone of fifteenth-century Florence where a monk is discovered leaving a brothel, and you have to pick up what's going on and what the character is like from what he says to the police. I responded positively to these vignettes and John Bayley appeared to enjoy my enthusiasm. His tutorials took place in his pleasingly cluttered rooms in New College with pipes on the mantelpiece and books on a table behind the sofa. He smoked a highly aromatic Dutch tobacco called Amphora. I read *The Waste Land* with him and we got to the phase in the poem showing a slight colour to the grey land:

> Oh city. I can sometimes hear
> Beside a public bar in Lower Thames Street
> The pleasant whining of a mandolin
> And a clatter and a chatter from within
> Where fish men lounge at noon: where the walls
> Of Magnus Martyr hold
> Inexplicable splendour of Ionian white and gold.

I described walking past a bar in the City near the Thames on a sunny spring morning and the door of a pub opening. I could hear a piano playing. There was no church interior but the sun reflected off the water. I felt the reality of the piece and John Bayley said that my joy in the everyday was very infectious. It really heartened me, because mostly I felt like a fish out of water in the academic environment of Oxford.

John Bayley's wife was Iris Murdoch. I had actually read a lot of her books and loved the early ones especially *Under the Net* and *The Bell* but I couldn't think of anything to say to him about them that would be remotely interesting.

Being good at cooking changed this inhibition. Many years later I even dared to believe that my monarch might be interested in recipes. I had been asked to lunch with the Queen and Duke of Edinburgh. It was like a return to Oxford, but this time the company assembled for drinks beforehand were discussing Uganda, where the Queen was going for the twentieth Commonwealth Heads of Government meeting. Someone suggested it could be dangerous which, I remember, got short shrift from her. Finally we went into lunch.

When we got to the main course I said, 'Ma'am, I think this roasted beetroot is absolutely excellent. Is there any way I could have the recipe?'

A surprised little silence.

'I don't know. You'll have to ask the chef.'

I did and here it is.

The chef takes a kilo of beetroot, boils it in salted water, peels and cuts it into cubes then he sweats a medium chopped onion in butter with a tablespoon of red wine vinegar. He then adds the chopped beetroot and seasons with salt and black pepper. In the version I have adapted for my own use, I add a tablespoon of tiny capers and very nice it is too.

In my second term I started working for the undergraduate newspaper, *Cherwell*. The offices were in a shed behind the Oxford Union building off Cornmarket. They were irredeemably scruffy and numbingly cold, alleviated by a one-bar electric fire charged by a 10p meter funded by the students rather than the newspaper. *Cherwell* was not assisted financially by the university and was much despised. I recall happening to mention it to my tutor Christopher Tolkien. He looked at me with what I took to be extreme scorn. I suffered for my art. I was doing this voluntarily and sometimes I was forced to ask myself why I was traipsing around junior common rooms, college porters' lodges and the Oxford Union Bar, looking for scraps of stories. I'd hoped that journalism was to be my career but the reality was proving mundane. Being a reporter for an unloved newspaper was like any foot-in-the-door job – excruciating.

I don't have a thick skin and most of the stories seemed hardly stories at all. This was one of mine:

*Girl in Rustication Row*

*Found with a girl in his room early in the morning of the Saturday of Eights Week last term, Mick Watts (Mansfield) was rusticated for a term.*

*'We had crashed Lincoln and Jesus Balls and the chick couldn't go back to Somerville, she didn't have a late key,' said Watts. 'The usual fine is about ten shillings so I think this a bit rough.'*

I was sent to interview the girl in question and she pleaded with me to drop it because her parents would be so upset. I fussed about this and got back to our dingy offices and gave the story to the news editor, Keith Jenkins.

'I really don't think we should use this. The girl's very worried about her parents finding out.'

'Who are her parents?'

'I don't know.'

'Well, go and find out if they're famous. Ring Bill Potter.'

Bill Potter was a local photographer but, more than that, he had been at Oxford and had perfected the art of photographing the offspring of celebrities and sending pictures and gossip through to columns like William Hickey on the *Express*. All he needed was a shred of a story.

He was nice to us on *Cherwell* partly because he realised that some of us would grow into the job and become valuable to him, and indeed a few would end up editing newspapers as was the case with one of our number, Peter Stodhart, who went on to edit *The Times*. There was a story – doubtless apocryphal – that Bill had had a lucrative period before my time with a student who may or may not have actually been an undergraduate called Jeffrey Archer. Indeed the myth has it that they honed the practice to a fine art and that this same Jeffrey Archer once persuaded The Beatles to appear at Brasenose for a fund-raiser and Ringo Starr famously asked Sheridan Morley in the gents who Jeffrey Archer was. Morley replied that everyone was trying to work out who he was, to which Ringo replied, 'He strikes me as a nice enough fella, but he's the kind of bloke who would bottle your piss and sell it.'

I never felt at ease with being a reporter. It wasn't just upsetting people, it was also the dawning understanding that most stories were in reality far less contentious than they ultimately appeared in the paper.

Occasionally I reported on almost serious things. Students occupied the Clarendon Building because it was alleged that the university was holding files with information about the political activities of undergraduates including sit-ins, the digging up of rugby pitches where the Springboks were playing and anything else antisocial. I interviewed a few of the organisers. I remember that Christopher Hitchens was particularly sartorial, wearing jeans and a tight donkey jacket and a fine silk scarf in a nice shade of purple very much in vogue at the time. He was charismatic, and there certainly seemed to be more than his fair share of protesting female undergraduates around him. During the sit-in, one of my colleagues at *Cherwell* asked me to drive past the Clarendon Building and to stop a second. He got out, took a brick out of a bag and hurled it at one of the windows, smashing the eighteenth-century glass. I was outraged. Later that night I went round to my brother John's in Winchester Road in North Oxford and grumped about what a storm in a teacup it all was. John's wife, Fanny, who was going through a left-wing phase at the time, told me to get out of the house.

Keith Jenkins took the job seriously. He introduced me to the Velvet Underground and the prose style of the *Daily Mirror*. He was a fan of Hugh Cudlipp who was the *Mirror*'s editorial director. The *Mirror*, Cudlipp said, provided its public with 'Vivid and dramatic presentation of events so as to give them a forceful impact on the mind of the reader. It means big headlines, vigorous writing, simplification into familiar everyday language, and the wide use of illustration by cartoon and photographs.' Tabloid journalism could actually be a joy to read. Sparely written with a minimum of adjectives, it really worked when describing something totally dramatic such as the assassination of Martin Luther King. The style was, unfortunately, less effective when writing about college gossip.

The main reason I got to be *Cherwell's* editor was most likely because I had a car, a Land Rover, and could drive over to Swindon where *Cherwell* was printed at Wiltshire Newspapers. We would spend half a day putting the paper to bed. It was still lovely old-fashioned letterpress printing – the letters were formed from hot lead. The sight of your own hard work rattling down a chute in the form of blocks of hot type, which would be made up into the solid form of a whole page, was very satisfying. It also meant that headline writing was a precise combination of space and shape requiring verbal dexterity and a lot of convulsive laughter. Here are a few.

**Poor Penetration**
**In Oxford Attack**
(A rugby game)

**Nose Belches**
**Fire and Flame**
(Referring to a fire at Brasenose)

**Police hot**
**up arrests**
**of student**
**heads**
(Drug arrests)

I enjoyed being editor. I attempted to make the paper look like the *Daily Mirror*. I changed the typeface and put a red top to the left of the front page and increased the size of headlines, just like the real thing. The hardest part was trying to make it pay, trying to persuade advertisers that a student rag was worth it. The best part was the people I met. One of the other hacks, Martin Leeburn, is still one of my best friends. I was awed by his aggressive style of writing. He always seemed to be fuming about some fool or shyster, which made for great copy. If he wrote about goings-on in a senior common room, it would be mingled with images of crusty old bores passing the port. He also had the knack of getting interviews with people of some stature, including Rupert Murdoch. He used Bill Potter the photographer a lot. On one occasion he went off with Bill to interview the designer of the hovercraft, Sir Christopher Cockerell, and reported that the famous inventor had been dismayed to be asked to hold an Airfix model Martin had made for the photograph.

Scott Donovan was another friend. We all thought he was going to be prime minister, he was so on the ball politically. We used to joke about his name-dropping but it was just a game to him, flexing muscles, understanding how it all worked. In the end he became a barrister with a social conscience in his native Liverpool. He was also very good at gaining interviews with famous people, he had a lot of audacity. When he and I interviewed W. H. Auden in Christ Church, Scott certainly did the lion's share of the chat. I found it hard to think of questions to ask a hero, and was mesmerised by the lines of the poet's face, the most lived-in skin I've ever seen.

Scott lived on Headington Hill in Oxford in a house owned by Richard Bulmer whose family made cider. Richard was reclining in a cricket catching cradle outside the New College pavilion when I first met him. I was about to hold a party nearby. I'd written the invitation in the style I remembered from my time in Sydney:

**Rick Stein Invites You to a Crash Hot Turn**

I'd invited my friends John Thompson, Francis Bowerbank and Graham Walker down from London, as well as virtually every girl I passed in the street, and there we were on the New College cricket pitch which stretched down to weeping willows and the Cherwell river, with Bulmer dressed in white trousers, a pink flower-patterned Carnaby Street shirt and desert boots. Lying in the cradle, his arms behind his head, Bulmer looked at my friends as if they were a complete intrusion on his serenity. They, for their part, were intrigued by such cool. He and I became friends from then on, and enjoyed an almost hostile banter. He always claimed I had lots of money, which I didn't, and he had none, which he did. We discovered at one stage he had 250,000 Bulmer shares which seemed quite a lot. Sadly, he died in Hereford about ten years ago. We all miss him.

My party was distinguished by the fact that we polished off 27 gallons of Morrells bitter.

Meanwhile I had started a mobile disco. With a sort of nod to LSD – which I was too nervous to take – I had christened it 'The Purple Tiger'. This party was to be its first outing. I had built a simple plinth designed to house two record decks, which in the early days were of unequal shape, one coming from an old portable player and the other my mother's deck from her stereogram in Cornwall, which since she didn't need to listen to The Seekers any more, as I was back from Australia, I reasoned she wouldn't really need. The amplifier I had bought from a hi-fi trip to Tottenham Court Road, the speakers were the ones I made in Shaun's basement, but the new star was a sound-to-light machine. My brother John had commandeered one of the technicians at the physiology lab, John Mittlele, to make one of those sound-sensitive, three-channel flashers from bits and bobs out of the labs. An early example of technology, its output was 110 volts rather than 240, and this was DC rather than AC. I made the light boxes, but the only bulbs I could get for them were from builders' merchants and they weren't coloured so I bought lots of coloured plastic folders from WH Smith and sellotaped them to the front. The DC current was a problem, too, as it was, even at 110 volts direct, potentially a heart-stopper. Tame Boffin (as Francis dubbed John Mittlele) was not completely tame: he had a wild-eyed look about him when describing the special qualities of thyristors, the hurried, slightly demonic chat of someone talking the secret language of electronics. I have to confess I was hard on him. I needed the magic light box to be flashing in fierce spasms to Free's 'All Right Now' in time for the party and would hold no truck with his protestations that he had more important lab work to do. He finished the box in a panic and was testing it when he touched the DC current which laid him out on the floor with a commensurate bang.

He survived but he spent some time sitting cross-legged in the corner, holding his head and moaning.

And I got my sound and light machine. We had our beer. The girls all came, everyone came. It was a thoroughly wonderful party. Unbeknown to me at that time it was another landmark in my journey to opening crash-hot restaurants and I'm afraid a certain ruthlessness with poor Tame Boffin was part of it.

Soon after the party, I went home for the summer vacation and another long holiday in Cornwall. Jill Newstead, who had dumped me two years before, had come back to Cornwall and was extremely keen to carry on where we had left off. I was still suffering the aftermath of my rejection by Fanny Pick, so was wary of being caught on the rebound. But I no longer minded that Jill had favoured someone else previously. She was so attractive that before long we were getting on extremely well and the thought of spending the summer with her was compelling. My mother initially was hostile towards her, but later described how she'd found her curled up naked in the hall in the middle of the night (we'd probably been out and drunk enormously and I think she'd got up to go to the loo and passed out). My mother said she looked so young and innocent with her long hair that she took to her then and adored her for the rest of her life. I was at that time a typical male. I loved having Jill with me in Cornwall, and around my Cornish and London friends, but I didn't want to let her in on the secret society that was Oxford University.

I had met an exotic gay man through *Cherwell*. James Ruscoe was an occasional contributor to the fashion section and the source of stories about celebrities at the university whom I'd never heard of. Although I'd had one or two slightly dodgy experiences when I was doing my round-the-world trip, I have always liked gay men. In the early seventies at Oxford they were very popular indeed. I suspect many a now-happily-married man had had a little fling, and, even if you hadn't, it was fashionable to say that you had. Personally, my leaning in that direction stopped at very flowery shirts and beads but it was nice to come off being a macho man and feel a bit almost pretty. The great attraction about James and his friends was that they were always surrounded by adoring girls. There were far more men than women then at Oxford so any seam of females was a mighty magnet. In the same way, the various tutorial colleges around the city, especially St Clare's and the Oxford and County secretarial college – known as the Ox and Cow – were happy hunting grounds.

Martin Leeburn and I were fans of the cartoonist Robert Crumb, and in his strip cartoon *Fritz the Cat* there is an episode where Fritz, the randy cat, is sitting in the bedsit of a very pneumatic cat called Charlene who is singing folk songs rather badly. He's trying to concentrate and saying things like, 'Interesting, interesting,' which it isn't, but he's really trying to find a way into her knickers. Well, that was me and Martin and many others.

Whenever I made it into a girl's bedroom, usually an attic with murals and collages on the walls, Oz Clark had been there before me. Unlike Fritz, I rarely enjoyed any success, but then neither did Oz. I didn't know him then – I was just his trail – but we are now friends who enjoy reminiscing about the futility of it all.

James Ruscoe wore colourful suits: his shirts were yellow, powder blue, white, flowery and furled. He had the sort of high black boots that girls normally bought from Biba, the trendiest thick black-framed glasses and lots of black curly hair. He also must have had an account directly with Estée Lauder for the quantity of Aramis he wore. Aramis, the ad said at the time, 'is an attitude'. And indeed it was. James and I shared the job of writing 'John Evelyn', the gossip column in *Cherwell*. He supplied the social stuff and I was the guy using the column to pick up chicks. My writing was a bit cringeworthy, James's stuff less so. One of his pieces was about the recently formed Gay Liberation Front and how they would soon be taking over Oxford, 'mincing down The High hurling Aramis gas canisters'.

It was a golden period, the summer of 1970. Parties on college lawns, parties in rooms in Christ Church and Brasenose, and almost every lunchtime spent in the Kings Arms in Holywell Street where the sort of people I didn't know but would love to have done congregated, people like Martin Amis, Ian Fleming's son Casper, Tina Brown and others, all of whom seemed immensely interesting and above me. This also used to irritate me: in my John Evelyn column I listed the most boring people in Oxford, one of whom I said was Rachel Toynbee, because she was so 'nice, so friendly, so entertaining'. It seems very babyish now, to have vented my resentment at not being part of the inner sanctum in the KA. I described Mark Blackett-Ord as, 'An appallingly pretentious youth who invited Maurice Bowra to dine with him last week in his college room.'

I had it in for Mark Blackett-Ord. One lunchtime he had a drinks party in New College and I invited myself, along with my friends John Thompson and Francis Bowerbank. Mark may have mentioned to me that he was having a party but certainly I wasn't at liberty to invite my friends. He was leaning back, with both arms draped across the mantelpiece in his large rooms overlooking the garden quad, dressed in a three-piece suit made of some fine Northumberland tweed, complete with a gold watch and chain. He was not at all pleased to see us and said, 'Rick, would you take your nightmare Cornish friends and get out of my rooms immediately?'

At another party – this time in an old mansion in Wiltshire – one of Mark's friends, I thought, patronised me about my choice of music, so I told him if he didn't fuck off I'd take him outside and punch him. He was disconcerted; those types don't like violence. In those days I was lively and energetic but also insecure. I felt I was quite dim and shouldn't really be at the university in the company of all these bright people, so I tended to hide behind a cover of being a bit of a heavy. Nowadays, I understand that it's a common problem with being at Oxford. There's a perception that everyone else is cleverer and more handsome than you are. Even Evelyn Waugh and John Betjeman suffered from it; you can see the fear in their writings. In some ways being at Oxford is as stressful and competitive as trying to make your way in Hollywood.

As the time drew closer to Finals, I became uneasy. It is difficult to write honestly about myself as I was then but I wasn't particularly nice, and one of the ways I was not particularly nice was in my treatment of Jill. She was there in Cornwall and there I wanted her to stay. But she had other ideas. She wanted to be with me and let me know she had taken a job in a country pub at Sandford in Oxfordshire. She didn't mention that it was four miles from Oxford. When I found out, I was angry. I felt trapped, my swaggering style was being compromised. I was spending time with a girl called Lois Ainslie who was lodging with James Ruscoe in the Cowley Road.

At one stage Jill left a note on my desk in my rooms, typed on my prized red Valentine typewriter, which said, 'I just thought I would tell you that I love you in case you were interested. Get the picture sweetie. I think you are intolerable sometimes, far too cruel for words, but I suppose you are OK.'

But I was still somehow armoured against life outside Oxford. I felt curiously immune in my lovely rooms in New College looking over the Chapel with my King Crimson, Emerson, Lake and Palmer and Jimi Hendrix LPs and my collection of green bottles filled with water with a light behind them to suggest 'green thoughts in a green shade'.

What did it finally was Richard Bulmer, who plonked himself down on my sofa one morning and said if I wasn't interested in Jill he certainly was and he was going to take her out. And then things started to unravel. I must have started talking to Jill because Lois left a note on my desk which said,

*When the girl in your head is the girl in your bed*
*The girl in your heart has a head start.*

I realised that in Jill I had an ally; someone who was not going to make me feel inadequate, who didn't make me feel dim. Jill was among the party of friends who went to Greece in the summer holidays, travelling overland in my very noisy diesel Land Rover.

I came back to Oxford in early October with exams threatening and both my hedonistic lifestyle and my confidence draining away.

～

Jill moved to London at the end of the summer and lodged in Archway in a run-down flat with Francis Bowerbank and his girlfriend Pauline Huddleston. Two weeks after the beginning of term, she came to Oxford for the weekend. She arrived on the Friday evening, but I had gone to a dinner organised by one of those slightly arcane dining clubs for undergraduates called The Boojums. These clubs allow over-privileged young men to drink and eat excessively. That night I was very tanked up when I got to the pub, the Bear, where Jill waited with my brother John and John Thompson.

Unbeknown to me, John Thompson had told Jill that The Boojums was a bit like the Hellfire Club near High Wycombe, famous for orgies. Jill had become extremely agitated and flew at me when I arrived. I reacted angrily but also very lustfully. The combination of all that and the drink was perilous. I snatched her and dragged her to my car, which was a Mini 1275 GT, and drove very fast round the Oxford bypass towards North Oxford and straight into some road works. I hit a 44-gallon drum which had an oil lamp on top. This smashed through the front windscreen and hit Jill on the head and then broke through the rear window.

The first thing I noticed after I came to a shuddering halt was she had blood running down her hairline and she was crying weakly and saying she wanted to go home. Fortunately, even drunk, I was frightened by the blood and took her to the Radcliffe Hospital. Then I drove the short distance home. I carried her little overnight case into the bedroom. It was covered in blood, as it had been on her lap. I opened it and saw all her clothes neatly folded for a happy weekend.

Later that night the police came to the house. They took me to the cells in St Aldgate's, where I was told she was dying.

Next day, Martin and I went to see her. We were both crying. Soon her family arrived. They were so non-judgemental of me, it made me feel even more distraught.

Jill had a fairly large piece of her skull removed and gradually recovered.

All that, and drinking too much, and fear of Finals, precipitated a kind of nervous breakdown -- not helped by some of the stuff I was reading, which seemed to be all about the meaninglessness of life. *Moby Dick* stood for me as an example of the arbitrariness of the world. Edgar Allan Poe completely freaked me out with his tales of entombment and his raven calling 'Nevermore, Nevermore'. I panicked at the idea of being trapped in a white room forever which I took to mean being trapped inside my own skull. At one point I explained the horror of this to my tutor John Bayley who pointed out that Poe was probably suffering from Vitamin B deficiency. It's one of the symptoms of alcoholism: the skin becomes extremely sensitive and you start to hallucinate about the limits of your body. It was my *Waste Land* period. I could see nothing but death everywhere. Even hitherto uplifting music like Paul Simon singing 'Paranoia Blues' and 'Mother and Child Reunion' convinced me that everything was about the shortness of life. I couldn't listen to the Doors' 'The End', just couldn't listen to it. Lost in a wilderness of pain, I couldn't listen to it.

I started depersonalising. It felt like being in a film. I went on a brief trip to Paris and had a panic attack in the middle of the Boulevard St Germain. I was rooted to the spot thinking my death was imminent. Francis asked if I could possibly find somewhere else to collapse, it was bloody inconvenient in the middle of a main road. I became very irate. 'You bastard,' I said. 'This is really serious.' But even in my extreme anxiety I must have seen that my absolute certainty of a heart attack about to happen couldn't co-exist with my anger at my friend's lack of sympathy.

At Beauvais airport, waiting to fly back in a Hawker Siddeley 748, I was petrified in spite of the red wine I was drinking to quell my fears. The plane was going to crash. I became agitated that we were going to miss it. I asked a uniformed man with a handlebar moustache if the plane had already gone.

'Don't worry, I'm Captain Anderson, we won't leave without you.'

I was oddly comforted by that. Maybe people *could* help me, wouldn't let me down like my dad had.

On the way home we stopped off at a pub in Kent and I said to John Thompson, 'I don't know how you manage to get through life without worrying about dying.'

'Look, sweetness,' he said. 'You're going to live forever.'

# IX

I had moved out of college and into the house that belonged to my brother John. It was a tall, thin, limestone Queen Anne house on Winchester Road. John had lived there for about four years, with his wife Fanny who was the daughter of the Master of Balliol, the historian Christopher Hill. John and Fanny were sociable, intelligent and good looking. Their elder child, William, was the most beautiful boy. I remember the excitement when he made it to the cover of a knitting magazine modelling a chunky jersey for tiny kids. His sister Polly had just been born, blonde and blue-eyed.

John was a new junior medical don at Magdalen College. The house was, to me, the last word in style, pale blue Laura Ashley wallpaper in the basement kitchen, crimson and white walls in the living room upstairs which they had converted from an original front room and kitchen into a long main room with windows at the front looking out over St Philip and St James Church and at the back over their very pretty garden with a gate straight into the Gardeners Arms. John had installed a stereo in the sitting room with tweeters and built-in 12-inch speakers. Every time I listen to the Stones' *Let it Bleed*, with the outrageous channel separation of early stereo recordings, I'm back there in number 14 Winchester Road.

John and Fanny were very hospitable. I don't think I ever went into the kitchen without finding someone seated at the big stripped-pine table talking about politics, music or hash. They took in lodgers, and people were always dropping by, most notably Howard Marks who read history at Balliol. He was precociously bright with a slightly sardonic Welsh accent. He always seemed to be carrying a cotton bag containing about a pound of hash from which he'd regularly cut off enough for joints all round. Neither John nor Fanny was much into dope. At the time John was enthusiastic about home-made wine so there were demijohns bubbling all over the kitchen. None of it was any good but wine was expensive in those days. They were always short of money, hence the lodgers. They had a friend called Peter who did all their DIY jobs for them and seemed to be there all the time; the children called him Hay Bags. He never seemed to be without a ratchet screwdriver. He made cupboards everywhere out of hardboard. Not great feats of carpentry but the Laura Ashley wallpaper made it all look great.

Fanny was one of those women who cannot help but attract the young. She had an instinctive understanding of how to make people feel at home. When she talked to me, I felt like she knew everything about me in a humorous, slightly bossy, older-sister way. She was very attractive – blonde with unforgettable green eyes. I had known her since I was very young: she used to come to the farm and trounce Henrietta and me at jacks. She was also very intelligent and a brilliant cook. Fanny and my sister Janey were significant influences in my later career. In both their houses there would inevitably be Elizabeth David's *A Book of Mediterranean Food* and *French Provincial Cooking*, chopping boards, glass storage jars with wooden tops and striped aprons from Habitat. If Janey's dinner parties were organised and relaxed, Fanny's were loud, drunken and stuffed full of cigarette smoke. But both gave me a deep sense that eating was about having fun.

I'm reminded of a poem by Thomas Hardy called 'During Wind and Rain':

*They are blithely breakfasting all –*
*Men and maidens – yea,*
*Under the summer tree,*
*With a glimpse of the bay,*
*While pet fowl come to the knee…*
*Ah, no; the years O!*
*And the rotten rose is ript from the wall.*

⁓

Both are dead now. Janey died of cancer in 1984. Fanny drowned in Spain in 1986. Janey's death was shattering for all of us. After my dad died, she became the central strength of my family. She was very supportive of us all. The last time I saw her in a cancer ward in the Middlesex Hospital, I felt bad afterwards because I talked about buying an old Range Rover simply because I knew she would think it a ridiculous thing and we could talk about something not connected with her imminent death. She never said she knew she was dying, she just told my mother minutes before she died that she did feel very ill. She was like that in life – absolutely protective of her children, her brothers and sister and her mother, but completely private about herself. We all coped with her death badly. Shaun was devastated. She was such a strong person in his life. It took him years to come to terms with it but in the end he married a head teacher called Maggie McLean, and moved to Yorkshire where he has lived very happily for over 20 years.

When my mother died of heart failure, all within the space of a morning at the John Radcliffe Hospital in Oxford, it was a sad occasion but she did it so easily and at 89, it was to be expected and the rest of us were capable of organising everything quite sensibly. When Janey died it was as though our lives had been ripped apart.

There are photographs of my mum with Henrietta and me as children in Cornwall. In one of them my mother is looking at me with protective affection and, looking at the photo, I can see that I was with the person I then loved most on earth. I must have been about eight. Henrietta looks blissfully happy too. My mother adored Henrietta but treated her as a friend. It was almost as if she expected her daughter to be less vulnerable than her son. Certainly she guided me and guarded me. Henrietta could get a bit wry about my 'special relationship' with our mother.

Both Henrietta and I were there at the John Radcliffe when my mother died in 2000. And, in the final moments before she slipped into unconsciousness, it was to Henrietta she turned.

John and Fanny's marriage didn't last very long. It seems always to be something in childhood which spins people off course. Fanny had been neglected as a child – her father was too busy making his name in academia and her mother Inez was really quite selfish. Inez was very attractive. What made everything a little tense in my family was that Inez had had an affair with my father. My mother found a receipt for the Russell Hotel in London's Russell Square in my father's jacket pocket. Since, in those days, wives usually emptied their husband's pockets and hung their suits up, she concluded that he probably had left it there on purpose. I can well understand that he might have subliminally wanted to be found out and stopped, because Inez would have driven him wild. She wasn't malevolent like du Maurier's Rebecca, just slightly psychopathic. I have to say, I enjoyed her company. She was bright and very funny. In her latter years, she was a successful garden designer for people such as Diana Quick and Albert Finney and Jeremy Irons, who all adored her. I don't think her mother, Madeleine, was much of a mother to Inez either. Philip Larkin says it all. They fuck you up, your mum and dad. They may not mean to, but they do. Fanny was damaged, certainly. When she first started going out with John, my father was vociferous in his opposition to her but of course that just made John dig his toes in. She became pregnant with William and they married in their early twenties. By the time I arrived in Oxford the marriage was on the way to disaster. Fanny was having an affair with a close friend which everyone except John knew about. When he finally found out, she moved out of Winchester Road with the children to a house in Leckford Road, North Oxford. John, after living on his own for a short while, moved into Magdalen College and I moved into Winchester Road with two friends, Martin Leeburn and Al White.

Ironically the split-up with Fanny was the beginning of a much closer relationship between John and me. In a large family like ours, the six-year age gap had meant that we split into two groups – John, Janey and Jeremy, and then Henrietta and me – so I didn't really know him before. He was desolated by what was happening to him. I persuaded him to come along to all the parties that I was going to and to meet all the people I was frenetically trying to get to know. I hate to admit it but I was rather using his position as a junior don to give me a bit of cred. He now says it helped him to get over Fanny. It makes me feel guilty about wanting him to be an asset to me rather than the liability I thought he was. He was no liability really. He's always been more sociable and confident than me and, as he came out of his depression, he took to dressing flamboyantly in blue velvet suits and flowing scarves and enjoying himself as much as anyone with a mind like my brother's can ever enjoy himself. He is far and away the cleverest man I'll ever know. He combines a prodigious memory and power of reasoning with a bleak humour about the impermanence of everything. With a bottle or two of wine you can talk to him almost on a telepathic level down into the deep valleys of thought.

Behind our house in Winchester Road was the Gardeners Arms. Martin, Al and I would go there most lunchtimes. It had a jukebox and, while I still couldn't listen to 'Mother and Child Reunion', 'Me and Julio Down By the Schoolyard' lifted me up a little and Lindisfarne's 'Meet Me on the Corner' started to break the clouds. Music and eating. Even at my lowest ebb, I had consoled myself with food in Paris. We had found a hotel on the left bank called Le Grand Hotel de l'Univers which had a spiral staircase up the middle painted red with the steps sloping inward, and tiny toilets with curved doors on the outside wall. Nearby was a place that sold moules marinière and steak frites with bottles of Beaujolais or Cabernet Franc from Saumur and Chinon. It also had a Gewürztraminer which they sold over the bar in tiny thick glasses with long green stems. Those steaks were a massive cheer-up – so deliciously salty, thin and bloodily rare and the chips thin and crisp and the salads made with a creamy dressing clinging to the bitter leaves. The problem, though, was always that in red wine I found calmness but the huge amount I drank eventually made things worse. I cooked the odd dinner party with Martin and Al at Winchester Road. On one notable occasion we did prawns with aïoli and a *civet de lièvre* from Elizabeth David's *French Provincial Cooking*.

Perhaps more importantly, I began to realise that the covered market in Oxford was really quite special. I had become used to having breakfast at George's Cafe after a heavy night. The pleasure of the full English, George's style, and a giant mug of tea was considerable. There was no question but HP sauce was essential but, for me, the crowning glory of the bacon, sausages, eggs, tomatoes and baked beans was the fried bread. Everything was fried in lard which permeated the whole cafe in a blue haze. I still find the hot pork smell of lard deeply comforting. Yes, for breakfast it had to be George's and, in the afternoon, tea at Brown's and mushrooms on toast. Almost as important to me as the architectural beauty of Oxford was that market. It was handsome too. Over 200 years old, it had very high ceilings with curved steel roof trusses and large lanterns hanging down. The food stalls added to the sense of occasion – from a large fishmonger's near the Market Street entrance with lots of whole fish on display to two or three butchers in the middle aisle. Hedges specialised in game and in the winter there would be whole venison carcasses hanging up as well as hares, rabbits, pheasants and partridges. The greengrocer's, Bonners, was an inspiration to get cooking, while Palm's delicatessen was a source for the sort of things you really could get nowhere else in those days, including saffron, Spanish olive oil, feta cheese, palm hearts and bamboo shoots. I bought mackerel, cod and crab from the fishmonger and took them back to Winchester Road for early forays into fish cookery. For someone with a growing appreciation of food, Oxford was a good place to be. I think that market gave me a real sense of ownership of Oxford. To me there's something very reassuring about being in a place where there's good food.

While supposed to be revising for my Finals, reclining on a chaise longue looking out of the window with a glass of port, maybe thinking about Coleridge, I developed a passion for chorizos which, inexplicably, were sold in a deli next to the Rose and Crown in North Parade just round the corner from Winchester Road. I had had no idea what they were, but Martin, who was reading modern languages at St Peter's Hall and had spent some time in Spain, had put me on to them. The smokiness and deep orange colour, the garlic and chilli spiciness were a glimpse into a world of robust flavours. I used to waste plenty of time wandering round to North Parade, perhaps for a pint in the Gardeners Arms and a chat to Cyril, the landlord, then back to the chaise longue for some more Coleridge, but before that I'd make myself a lunch of sliced chorizo with tomato and onion salad and crusty bread. Food was much more interesting than studying English literature.

My last year at Oxford, though wobbly at the beginning with my mental turmoil, ended quite peacefully. I got a third in English, which was about what I was worth. It didn't make me feel any better about myself, though. Jill always maintained that my breakdown was due to fear of doing badly in the exams but I think it was more to do with a delayed reaction to my father's suicide coupled with the realisation that we all have to come to terms at some stage with the fact that we aren't going to live for ever. These fears, of course, are deep in our subconscious – and I had done a good job of burying them even deeper – but I was terribly afraid not only of sudden death, but also of going crazy like my dad.

So I left Oxford with a definite improvement in my culinary knowledge but no knowledge of what I really wanted to do. I made a couple of desultory attempts to get into journalism. I applied for a BBC general traineeship but was turned down. I thought of having a go at advertising. But, after the accident, I knew I wanted to be with Jill and, after Oxford, what I wanted in the short term was to drive to Greece in The Purple Tiger disco van, with Jill and a gang of friends. It wasn't the endless breakdowns of that old van nor the not-always-friendly relations in a slow vehicle which I remember best, nor the fear of travelling down the main road in Yugoslavia which we got to call the crystal highway on account of the horrific traffic accidents we saw all the time. No, the abiding memory of that trip was the food.

There is a popular view that Greek cooking is cold and greasy. The first time I tasted Greek food was in 1966 in Athens on my way to Australia. I ordered a plate of fried aubergines with Greek oregano and a glass of retsina. I found the aubergines too bland and the oregano and the wine too strong. In 1970, I'd got off the ferry from Brindisi to Igoumenitsa and entered a dirty kitchen to choose lunch. There was a giant, rectangular, shallow bain-marie filled with big dented aluminium pans. The first lid I lifted exposed a number of goats' heads in a watery-looking broth. I had something of a hangover: I had been playing cards with the ship's engineer and drinking Fix beer on the ferry late into the night. I formed the opinion there and then that I would starve to death, because Greek food was going to be all eyeballs and oregano. In point of fact, on my post-Oxford trip it was the glorious shock of the new. I grew to love it. The fish – red mullet, cooked outdoors on a little charcoal grill and served with a Greek salad scattered with dried *rigani* and some sliced potatoes fried in a black pan in olive oil. The ubiquitous green beans in a rich tomato sauce and the same sauce with giant butter beans. The lovely potato, olive oil and pounded garlic *skorthalia*, so good with grilled fish. The locally made ewes' milk yoghurt in shallow earthenware containers, always with a soft crust and always with Greek honey. The memory takes me to Matala on the south coast of Crete and an old Bal-Ami jukebox in The Mermaid Cafe where you had to make your selection by turning a big wheel. Here I first heard a Greek song called 'Gelmenden' sung by a pin-up, Rena Dalia, and Ioannis Papaioannou, who was a famous composer of bouzouki music. I played it every day. I took a copy home with me and played it in my disco, where people didn't get it but I didn't care. The tune sparked memories of great times in Lindos on the island of Rhodes, with the bedroom window wide open and the silvery courtship calls of Scops owls in the warm, pine-scented darkness. Jill and I loved Greece: the light, the 'wine dark' sea, the dry sunny climate, the emphatic people and the robust cooking. For my generation, it was like discovering Thailand is for young people today, our own place, not the Florence, Venice and Rome that my parents went to, but Monemvasia, the central market in Athens, the waterfront at Simi. Studying ferry timetables in Piraeus was our guide to the galaxy. The *Evangelistra*, which did indeed have a worrying list and which eventually sank. The *Mimika*, a converted English cross-Channel ferry plying from Piraeus to Rhodes. These were the old ships in which we traversed the Aegean with the disco van hoisted aboard on ropes.

# PART THREE

## Early Days

# I

Back in London I set to work to make my fortune running a mobile disco. I advertised The Purple Tiger in the pages of a new magazine just arrived on the streets called *Time Out*. I was copying other, more successful, mobile discos which had better equipment and better transport. The Twilight of the Gods was one, The Mushroom another (well, you couldn't call it The Magic Mushroom). I got my driving licence back (it had been taken away – quite rightly – after the accident in which I had nearly killed Jill), so I sold the old Commer and bought a blue Volkswagen van. I asked a friend to paint some purple tigers on it. Cecil was a young man of peaceful demeanour. He had long curly hair, was a bit plump and wore his bell-bottom jeans and a tank top with sartorial elegance. His jacket, too, was of a tight cut and shape which said art school. We used to meet at the King's Head in Crouch End to discuss tigers. Cecil was very keen on real ale and introduced me to the world of CAMRA, the Campaign for Real Ale. The King's Head had Courage Best Bitter and Directors' Ale. I was rather hoping for fierce William Blake sort of tigers, in purple hues to give the impression of some acid vision of terrible creatures with 'burning bright' scary eyes. Cecil painted just one tiger, in his own image.

The tiger on the van was purple, yes, and standing among green jungle leaves, but he looked rather little and had the severity of a dog waiting to go on a walk. Cecil also did a purple tiger for the disco console and the speakers. I still have the speaker covers: two tigers, one with distinctly chubby cheeks and an expression of attempted severity, the other looking slightly frightened.

'Well, it's supposed to be sort of a bit druggy.'

'I don't like drugs.'

'Nor do I actually.'

'I thought they should be nice tigers, maybe the sort who'd like a pint or two of Courage Best.'

'Yeah, OK.'

The Purple Tiger roared in many a venue in London: the staff restaurant of John Lewis, a pub in Hampstead, a police section house off Baker Street. I built the whole disco in Janey and Shaun's cellar – the light boxes, the speakers, the disco console. I made a bubble machine from an old turntable motor and a hairdryer. I bought photo-slide changers and had a box of 35mm transparencies of shots of Trevone Beach at sunset, the old graves in Padstow cemetery surrounded by greenery, some nudes from a copy of *Playboy*, pieces of green, yellow, red and blue gel made to look like a Patrick Heron abstract. I'd project these on to the walls. Jill painted a double sheet with a girl kneeling in front of a forest, all in fluorescent paint which would shine under ultraviolet. I had two strobes which I would go mad with at the end of long pieces like the Allman Brothers' 'Jessica'. At the time, quadraphonic recordings were the latest technology; a four-channel hi-fi system. There weren't many quadraphonic records around but I had two: Santana's *Caravanserai* and Miles Davis's *Bitches Brew*. I bought a special quadraphonic converter and sat in the cellar with a four-way amplifier and couldn't actually tell the difference. The music I played was eclectic to say the least. As DJ I didn't say much, just kept it rolling along. I thought I absolutely knew what would get people going. I cringe now to remember some of the Top 20 hits I put on – 'Chirpy Chirpy Cheep Cheep' by Middle of the Road, any of the Gary Glitter hits, 'In the Summertime' by Mungo Jerry, 'Band of Gold' by Freda Payne (the gays were very keen on that).

But I had standards, though they seem a bit meaningless now. I wouldn't play any of The Osmonds and I couldn't stand Chuck Berry's 'My Ding-a-Ling' though I would play anything else by him. The trick was to build a dancing audience by playing a sequence of songs which would get them up and dancing – more and more of them – then climax with a couple of really-throwing-it-around tracks, then kill it with a couple of quiet ones, then go at it again. Towards the end, given that by then a lot of people were really pissed, I could slip in the stuff I really wanted to play – the sort of thing that I felt would single me out from all the other discos, tracks like 'Stairway to Heaven' or 'L. A. Woman'.

Here's the sort of sequence I would play. Actually, it's the real thing from a disco in a bakery in South Parade in Oxford which I recorded on a cassette tape.

'Jig-A-Jig'
'Sex Machine'
'Brown Sugar'
'Ride A White Swan'
'I Hear You Knocking'
'When I'm Dead And Gone'
'Jessica'
'Just My Imagination'
'Nothing Rhymed'
'Spirit in the Sky'

'Strange Kind of Woman'
'Satisfaction'
'L.A. Woman'

I booked some Cornish village halls for the summer – St Merryn, Port Isaac, Crackington Haven, Padstow, Crantock. I hired rooms in pubs: the room above The Swan in Wadebridge, a similar one in the King's Arms in Lostwithiel. I built a second disco and bought a second van and took on an American student, Chris Darkins, to run it. I kept up the advertising in London.

Jill and I would start at seven, playing stuff for teenagers like 'School's Out' by Alice Cooper and 'Hot Love' by T. Rex. Towards pub closing time at 11 the hall would fill up as the Farmers Arms emptied and by midnight it would be heaving, with condensation running down the windows. We'd take about £250 a night. We sold soft drinks and crisps bought from the cash and carry in St Austell. The hall cost £10 to hire, so we were doing well. None of the other venues were anything like as good earners as St Merryn. I always did the nights there and, if there was nothing else on, Jill would take the money at the door, but if we had a double booking she would go off with Chris to other venues. They complained about the quality of the second unit equipment because I was too mean to buy some proper stuff. Well, maybe not mean. I had a clear idea of profit and loss and always kept little notes of what things cost, but I also suffered from a failure to see the difference between cost and value.

And so I came to buy a nightclub in Padstow.

# II

The summer of 1973 had come to an end, the holiday visitors had left and the revenue from the discos had plummeted. Chris had gone back to college in Portland. When I heard that the White House Club in Padstow was up for sale I thought: here's a home, a den almost, for The Purple Tiger.

The owner, Terry Johnson, had appeared in Padstow a year or two earlier. He had made a lot of money buying and selling meat in London's Smithfield market and had decided to put some of it into doing up a rather sleepy little supper club called The Puffin Club. The property was owned by Brad Trethewy who had previously used it as a furniture store. It had been constructed as a granary by a friend of the man who built the Metropole Hotel on the hill above. Known then as the Great Southern Hotel, this had been designed as a railway hotel for the Southern Railway from Waterloo to Padstow. The part of the track which runs from Padstow through Wadebridge and on to Bodmin is now called the Camel trail. The Puffin Club attracted the sort of people that I found hard to take in those days, the sort of people who like to dance to 'Tie a Yellow Ribbon Round the Old Oak Tree'. But Brad, who with his mutton-chop sideburns looked like a slightly dodgy sea captain and was locally known as Lord Puffin, was a shrewd operator. He knew his audience and he spent very little money on his club.

Terry converted the Puffin Club into what he billed as the most luxurious club outside London's West End and renamed it The White House Club. It had swirly purple carpets and purple faux leather high banquette seating. There was a white baby grand piano and a small dance floor with aluminium chains hanging down from the roof. The bar was deep blue and long and backed with mirrors. It was the sort of place you wouldn't dream of entering without a tight, double-breasted suit with flares and a shirt so stretched across your chest that your nipples stuck out. The White House Club was singularly out of place in the then prosaic fishing port of Padstow, a world of rusty chains and lobster pots and the salt smell of fish bait. I'm fond of saying it was a bit like finding an opera house in the Peruvian rain forest city of Iquitos. It was Terry Johnson's dream, like the dream of *Fitzcarraldo* in Werner Herzog's film. On the top floor, Terry had built a steak bar with an open kitchen and a view over the Camel Estuary. He booked acts from London. On a radio programme recently I met Dave Stewart who reminded me of how he had been booked to appear with Annie Lennox in the White House Club in the early seventies. They'd played for a couple of hours with no one interested and finally had been told to pack up. He said Annie had cried all the way back to London. He assumed that I owned it then, but it was TJ. Terry was an amateur heavyweight boxer, very handsome, dark and Italian-looking. He was tall and broad and very fit. He was charming and funny but there was also a slight air of danger about him, like a sort of Medici prince; everyone was a little scared of him, not least me and my friend Johnny Walter. Johnny and I had decided to buy the club jointly. Our negotiations with Terry for the purchase price were pathetic. We tried to get it a bit cheaper than the £65,000 we eventually paid for it, but we were never in with a chance.

Johnny and I started negotiations in early January and by May we had the keys. Johnny put up two-thirds of the money, £38,000. I put in £19,000, and the final £8,000 we borrowed from Terry Johnson. Much of my share came from a sum I had inherited from great-uncle Otto, who had lived in Dusseldorf. I never met great-uncle Otto and didn't know of his existence until he died and left me about £12,000. I feel forever grateful to him because a bit of capital in life is a great thing. The rest of my share came from Jill's compensation for our accident, henceforth called her head money. The balance was put up by my mother.

I never for one minute tried to consider the reality of what it would be like running a club. All I wanted to do was get it open. I pressurised everyone to make it happen quickly – my solicitors, Johnny's solicitors – and I gave in all too readily to Terry. The fact is I couldn't wait to take it over. The country was going through a low time. The Conservative government under Edward Heath had introduced a three-day working week to conserve dwindling coal stocks during the miners' strike of 1973. In my little world that meant the editor of the *Western Morning News*, who had held out the promise that he would give me work as a sub-editor, wrote and told me the job was no more. It was then a simple decision for me: I wouldn't become a journalist after all. I'd become a nightclub owner.

I still have nightmares about opening the club. The almost crippling sense of claustrophobia when you realise that you're stuck. No more trips to Greece, no more 'What shall I do with my life', no more 'Let's drive off somewhere nice'. You're stuck. You haven't got anything like the staff you need, and the ones you've got are terrible because you've no idea what to look for. You become overtired and as you do you get more demoralised. All these strange people, most of whom you've never met before, checking you out, especially the ones from the old Puffin Club, the members of the chamber of commerce, the Freemasons, the happily-married couples who like to go out on a Saturday night and dance cheek-to-cheek and drink Double Diamond and Babycham, who wear Burton suits with striped polyester shirts and Dorothy Perkins dresses. Even the customers you know have become strangers to you because you're so convinced it's all terrible. And all the time you're asking the question: Why? Why didn't you see this coming? How could you have been so stupid? Why ever did you think it was so like a New York club, though you'd never been to one, and why did you not see the long, green abstract fibreglass fish hung on the wall above the longest run of purple banquettes was not fabulous modern art but just a piece of fibreglass?

When The Purple Tiger was at its height, I'd had the idea of running another type of event which I was going to call The Peace Machine. I would hire a hall or pitch a tent and invite people to enjoy a serene experience. I would play soothing music while projecting calming scenes all around and the sound – naturally – would be quadraphonic. I had thought of the club as being the sort of place where I could do this. It would become a very special venue in the south west, do some great food, put on some great lunches.

The gap between my vision of the way it was going to be and the reality was frightening. Padstow was then a gritty fishing port and, like it or not, many of those fishermen were going to become my customers. They were a long way from the bright young things I wanted. They'd normally arrive when the pubs closed. They were already tanked up and often aggressive. We needed all the business we could take, as we were undercapitalised. Doubtless we were warned about this at the time but we didn't understand why you needed money in the bank just to open. In fact we had no working capital at all and we soon realised that we'd have to let anybody and everybody into the club.

The rules for operating a licensed club are simple. You are required to admit only members – and their guests. The members have to go through a process of application, followed by acceptance or rejection, and this should not happen instantaneously at the club door. We regarded strict membership as not important. At either end of our bar we had poker machines which had a jackpot of a sufficiently large pay-out to make them legally for the use of bona fide club members only. We also skimped on the food. The rules stipulated that we had to supply our members with what was classed as 'a substantial meal' and that any drinking had to be 'ancillary' to the food. Our substantial meal was Batchelors ready meals. These were freeze-dried chicken curry or beef stroganoff mix, sold in the shops as Vesta. Every night one of us would go up to the kitchen on the middle floor and prepare a 24-pint pan of mix by adding water and heating, then a bigger pan of boiled rice, then send both down on a rope-driven dumb waiter to be picked up near the bar. Small portions were then slapped on paper plates and handed out with plastic knives. Most people declined. Some actually ate the stuff, sitting on the steps of the bar.

Plenty of other clubs were very lax about observing the rules. What we didn't take account of was the pubs in Padstow. In those days pubs officially stopped serving at 11 p.m. Most would then close their doors and draw the curtains over their small windows, and invite their favoured customers in for a cosy late evening's drinking. This was called a 'lock-in', an illegal but not usually penalised activity which went on everywhere. Thus, the publicans did not relish a club on their doorstep, let alone a club open till 1 a.m. with music and dancing and pretty girls. Many a lock-in customer came to take a look at us, and business in the London Inn, the Harbour, the Golden Lion and Shipwrights took a downturn.

None of us had any idea that we were causing this sort of trouble. We had plenty of our own to deal with anyway – our policy of letting anyone in was already causing problems. We got over the opening. The Puffin Club lot left, never to return. We started to attract some young people, and renamed the club The Great Western. We had yellow headed paper with a brown, puffing, steam train at the top. I had seen a few hamburger restaurants – Browns in Brighton for example – decorated in brown and cream with potted palms everywhere, so we copied the colour since it approximated the original livery of the Great Western Railway which ran from Paddington to Penzance. We failed to notice that the original railway company that came to Padstow was, in fact, the Great Southern Railway, probably because their livery colours – green and cream – wouldn't have looked so classy.

It wasn't too long before The Great Western Club had been renamed locally The Wild Western Club. The slogan was that you didn't sign in at The Great Western, you weighed in.

The fighting was mostly on a Saturday night. On the door we had a local called Richard Bate who was big and broad. Jill and I usually left him to sort out the fights but occasionally we wondered if he wasn't actually causing more brawls than he was preventing.

There were two bars, and the smaller one was run by two very pretty girls from Manchester. Jill and Teri thought they were a couple of scrubbers who were robbing us blind. Johnny and I would not hear of such a thing. Johnny had married Jill's best friend Teri in 1970.

Our main barman, Tiggy Old, was as fast behind the bar as anyone I'd ever seen. You didn't bother to enter every drink on the till, you added everything in your head. Or you did until you knew everyone was too pissed to remember, then you'd just think of a number and add a bit more on to cover yourself. The speed with which you delivered a round of drinks was staggering by today's standards, but under-ringing was rife. No one drank much more than beer, cider, whisky and dry ginger, gin and tonic, vodka and orange, Bacardi and coke, or Babycham, so rounds were easily assembled. Almost all the men drank Double Diamond, a beer so sweet it would make Coca-Cola taste dry, or Whitbread Tankard, a so-called beer which these days would probably fail to satisfy the Trade Descriptions Act. Johnny and I were very keen on real ale and usually had a barrel of Bass or Devenish Wessex in the cellar behind the bar. We took the business of cellaring the real ale seriously, but it was not chilled and when the club was heaving it became hot and the beers became volatile, so much so that the walls and ceiling were splattered with the hops which would blow through the spill hole on the top of the barrels. Once a senior member of CAMRA, the Campaign for Real Ale, came down to check us out. He was an older man with handlebar moustaches who looked like an ex-RAF officer, rather red-faced. He started shouting at me about how we shouldn't be in their guide running such a rough place and selling good beer in a nightclub. I told him to fuck off but it didn't make me feel any better about the club.

Running the club was an ever-increasing strain, but we didn't help ourselves by staying on far into the night after it shut at 1 a.m. We'd sit and talk for hours with Richard Bate and his wife Maureen and their coterie of locals. Richard would hold court. He was about six foot five inches tall and heavily built, slightly running to fat but immensely powerful. He was also extremely intelligent, but dangerous. Like many locals, he had lived a life that was hard, and he made do as best he could – poached salmon a bit, went to sea occasionally, worked manual labour, had a few extra children here and there, drank copiously and entertained us wonderfully with highly embellished stories of old Padstow. He introduced me to a whole world of energetic local life and a deliciously coarse humour.

Richard was protective of us four – Jill, Johnny and Teri and me. I think he felt sorry for us, that we were so wet behind the ears. He really tried to sort out the increasing fights. It wasn't just the fishermen but the occasional farmer who threw a punch or two, and then of course there were the resentful landlords or resentful friends of the landlords. The landlady of the Harbour Inn got into a fight near the bar one Saturday night. She hit my brother John by mistake; he was only staying for the weekend.

One Saturday in early June I was called to the door. Richard wasn't on, and a mild-mannered school teacher called John Newling was trying to block half a dozen men who were trying to get in. (They were, I learned later, a jousting team who were taking part in a tournament on the Royal Cornwall Showground in Wadebridge.) I became very angry and walked aggressively up to the ringleader and started swearing at him, telling him to get off my terrace. The next thing I remember was being in Johnny's car, asking if he could remind me what my name was. I had been knocked out with one punch. I spent a night in Treliske Hospital with concussion. Next time I met the sister at the A & E, I was concussed again, with a black eye and suspected broken nose. She said she was sure she'd seen me somewhere before.

I was getting regular visits from the local PC, Fred Hardy. He kept warning me that the trouble had to stop. He was friendly, but said there was a lot of notice being taken 'from above'. The end was in sight.

A group of men in their thirties, known collectively as the Watford Boys, had been drinking in the Customs House for most of the day. I couldn't possibly comment on whether some conversation about the badly run club just down the road had taken place between them and the landlord. All I know is that at about 11.30 that night they arrived en masse. Richard Bate refused them entry and one of them hit him with a stool. They swarmed into the club and beat me up. I went back to casualty to be patched up and was kept in overnight.

The next day I got back to learn that revenge had been taken. A lot of the Watford Boys had been staying in a caravan outside Padstow and they had been blasted with both barrels of a shotgun late at night. The assailant had had the grace to shout to tell them to get down on the floor.

I rang Terry Johnson.

'Hi, Terry. I suppose you've heard what happened?'

'Yeah.'

'I think that it might have been Richard Bate.'

'Yeah, of course it was.'

'Well, I'm a bit worried. He could have killed one of them. They'll come after us now.'

'They're nothing. Nothing.'

'I see. Well, thanks. That's reassuring.'

It wasn't reassuring, not at all. All that day I expected the Watford Boys to break in again, but this time with steel bars or knives or guns.

The police came round and took photos of me and I gave a statement. Gradually the fear receded. The police prepared a case and a date was fixed for a couple of Watford Boys to appear at Wadebridge Magistrates Court. The one who assaulted me was sent to prison for a year. For some reason – nod, wink – the local police never found out who had shot up the caravan.

Meanwhile there were more fights and, finally, frightening violence. I found myself with Johnny hosing blood off the terrace at the front of the club the morning after a glassing and a stabbing. The paving slabs were large cheap textured-concrete ones, and the blood was hard to shift because it had sunk in. It was a dark early morning, oppressive with black clouds, a mood of dark grey and red.

I said to Johnny, 'This is like a film, I can't believe it's happening.'

A local from St Issey had attacked a fisherman from St Merryn, first with a broken glass cutting most of his nose away from his face. He had staggered out to the terrace bleeding profusely and his assailant had picked up a piece of angle-iron from a half-finished road sign in the quay car park across the road and run back and stabbed him in the chest. We were now absolutely four-square in the sights of the local police and it was only a matter of weeks before the end came.

A plain-clothes police couple signed in on the door as a member and a guest on two occasions. No one checked their names or consulted a membership list, they were just signed in and given instant access. No one offered them food with their drinks. Each time they came, they purchased alcohol and they played poker on the fruit machines. Every drink and every pull of the handle was an offence.

# III

I put on my best suit for the court case. This was on the advice of my solicitor, Eric Church. His firm, Cole and Cole, was based in Oxford. They were my mother's solicitors, and had done the conveyancing on my original purchase of the club. It might have been a mistake employing them to defend me: a firm of poncy lawyers imported from an ancient university town was perceived locally with suspicion. But, of course, our real mistake lay in our childish disdain for the law, our naive lack of forethought and our ignorance of businesslike management. We were something of a laughing stock.

The police prosecutor had got hold of a leaflet for an Old Time Music Hall show that we had booked. The advertisement was a poster headed 'A Night of Wild Abandon', which he took as an example of the sort of thing that went on in the club. Wild Abandon! The old-time music hall was three very senior actors and an MC called Knox Crighton with handlebar moustaches and a dicky heart. Then there was 'The Nation's Heart-throb' Jeanette 'Bombshell' du Barry who wore a black wig as she was bald after chemotherapy, and a small man in his early sixties who would appear as a black-and-white minstrel and sing 'Mammie' wearing a straw boater. He had a prosthetic hand which he would unstrap and leave on a table upstairs after his performance.

Eric Church had also advised me to seek respectability by making an honest woman of Jill and getting married. But nothing worked.

I was declared not a fit and proper person to hold a licence, and so was Johnny.

In fact I was very happy to get married. The wedding took place in a marquee on the lawn at Redlands. Jill and I paid for it all but it didn't cost much as we made all the food ourselves: poached salmon, rare roast beef and my mum's ham with cloves, mustard and brown sugar. I bought a few barrels of Bass and we got the champagne at trade prices. All my friends came – Francis Bowerbank, John Thompson, Graham Walker, Martin Leeburn, Richard Bulmer and many, many more – and all my large family. My strongest memories are my love for my beautiful young wife, so lovely in her clinging wedding dress, and the perfume she was wearing – Guerlain's Shalimar.

The service was in St Merryn Church opposite the pub. The stag night had been in The Hanging Tree, a rather jerry-built pub in a chalet estate next to the Second World War airfield behind St Merryn. There, the Wadebridge Camels, with whom I played rugby at the time, got me completely pissed on full-strength Navy rum. First, they threw me in the pool, which was filthy. To avoid drowning, I had to swim through water which was literally darkened with cigarette ends. After I finally got home and into bed, they manoeuvred me and the bed through the downstairs window and into the marquee, so that I woke next morning in the tent wondering how on earth I'd got there.

I suffered a lot from being declared not a fit and proper person. I pulled in for some petrol at the garage in St Merryn and the owner John Ball came out with a grin and said, 'Ricky Stein, the man they couldn't hang.' I hated the stigma and felt very low.

The club limped on for another year after we lost our licences in February 1975. We took on an ex-pub landlord, who got a licence till 11 p.m. in his own name, but no one came and he helped himself at the whisky optic to any meagre profits we might have made. We struggled with entertainment on the second floor. We booked a lot of dance trios, including one with Jill's dad Jack and his best friend, but they didn't attract much of an audience. We occasionally put on Big Al Hodge which filled the venue but didn't pay for itself. We often booked the Rod Mason Jazz Band; we had lots of fun drinking with them afterwards but we always lost money on the evenings.

There was only one glimmer of hope. Due, I suspect, to a processing error, though I like to think it was a spark of humanity with the police, a separate table licence for the restaurant on the top floor was never challenged in court.

Many years later I recalled those months after we lost the licences. And remembered that after my dad died I went to see *The Sound of Music* three times because it cheered me up. I remembered the words in 'Climb Every Mountain' which sound a bit like what Dame Edna Everage would say, 'When the Lord closes a door, somewhere he opens a window'. And there it was – the open window. We would plan a fish restaurant.

Not long ago, I received an invitation to tea in St Austell with a retired policeman called Inspector Hooper. He had been in charge of the case against the troublesome little club on the quay in Padstow.

By then my restaurant was very well known, but the invitation was to remember the past.

'We felt sorry for you both,' he said. 'When we turned up that afternoon to check the register, we were amazed you hadn't destroyed it.'

'I know,' I said. 'I couldn't. The doorman kept saying throw away the register, but I couldn't lie.'

'The signatures in it were the evidence we needed.'

'It was the best thing that ever happened to me,' I said. 'You left us with one restaurant licence. Did you do that on purpose?'

'I don't remember,' he said.

I'll never know.

# IV

My friend John Watt, who knew a lot about French food and smoked Gitanes, had a friend called Mark Righton who was running a hole-in-the-wall restaurant in Falmouth called Mark's Seafood Bar. This was in a narrow street, Quay Street, which ran down to the harbour. You went down some steps through a door with a porthole in it into a tiny little bar. As soon as you walked in, there was a smell of garlic butter and grilled shellfish. Downstairs, in two tiny rooms, old pine tables and chairs from household sales were crammed in. The walls were festooned with herring nets and the room was lit by old ship's lamps and candles. In the tiny kitchen he had a six-burner stove and grill. Here Mark would grill lobsters with garlic butter, and serve moules marinière and classic French fish dishes – chowder, Dover sole and whole lemon sole with a prawn and cream sauce. He was attracting well-heeled customers – retired admirals, captains of industry at their holiday houses or off their yachts … After my diet of drunk fishermen and locals complaining about the price of Double Diamond (I think at the time we'd just put it up from 19 to 20p a pint), this was a glimpse of a civilised life.

There was a fish place in Padstow called The Blue Lobster above The Shipwrights, a pub on the other side of the harbour from the club. I had been there a few times with the composer, Malcolm Arnold.

Malcolm and his wife Isobel were friends of my parents who had moved from London in the late sixties to St Merryn. You couldn't fail to get to know Malcolm if you ever went into any pub in Padstow, St Merryn, St Issey or Porthcuthan. Wherever he went, he'd buy everyone in the pub a drink. Not unnaturally, wherever he went the pub would fill up. Malcolm had received an Oscar for his score for *Bridge Over The River Kwai* and was riding high on this and other successful film scores including *Whistle Down the Wind*. He was very generous, and he'd invite Jill and me, Henrietta and Johnny and Teri over for lunch or dinner and give us exotic beers like Budweiser from Czechoslovakia and Russian cigarettes with long cardboard filters and Cohiba cigars. He also took us to The Blue Lobster for lobster Thermidors. It seemed like the height of luxury, and I began to realise that Puligny-Montrachet and lobster had enormous affinity for each other.

The memory of those great nights at The Blue Lobster stayed with me and I thought we could do the same sort of thing, but simpler. I decided not to set up in direct competition with them but to create a Mark's Seafood lookalike. We went to household sales at Button Menhenit and Mutton, and bought tables, chairs and old pictures. We also bought a couple of large dining-room tables and some chapel pews from an army camp which was closing down on Dartmoor, and a second-hand chiller display cabinet to put the white wines in. We transformed what had been a room that looked like a Wimpy Bar into something that looked like a junk shop, so keen were we to model it on Mark's hole-in-the-wall atmosphere. Downstairs was the club, while the top floor was earmarked for the fish restaurant. The middle floor would also be put to use.

I took on a secretary, an elderly lady named Helen Stevens whose job was to do the books and write letters for me and Johnny. I built an office for her on the top floor, bought the materials for stud walls and papered them myself with woodchip paper to avoid the cost of plasterers, and got a carpenter to hang the doors as it was beyond me. As 'the man they couldn't hang', I was trying to build some sort of credibility with ordinary nice people, rather trying to compensate for the den of iniquity that had been going on downstairs. Helen suggested a family restaurant, the sort of place where ordinary nice people would come to eat roasts and sponge puddings, on our middle floor.

I took on a cook – a girl called Tessa who lived with her husband in an old mill house in a remote village down a very narrow leafy lane. They smoked a lot of dope down there and lived the sort of good life which seemed idyllic to me at the time, growing their own vegetables, making home-made wine, their little children growing up knowing about flowers and herbs in a damp but pretty house by a stream. It was Tessa who decided she wanted to work for me. She had made friends with the sort of locals who used to come into the club with Richard Bate. She once described herself to me as witch and temptress. I wasn't attracted to her physically but I found her conversation electrifying. She loved talking of the Padstow fishermen, and had spent plenty of time in some of the rougher Padstow pubs. She said that she would be able to cook the sort of food I wanted – roast lamb and roast beef, Irish stews, carrot soup, apple crumble – so I let her get on with it.

The afternoon we were due to open the family restaurant there was no sign of Tessa. She finally arrived, pissed, from the pub at about 6 p.m., incapable of doing anything. Fortunately, there were no customers.

The next morning Helen told her she'd have to go.

'I can't possibly go,' she said. 'I'm in love with Rick. I have to go on working for him.'

'You've no business loving him,' said Helen, 'he's already married.'

I was a bit flattered and a bit shocked – and agreed with Helen that Tessa should go. I had grown nervous about a family restaurant, anyway. It was definitely not me.

We decided to open a burger bar on the middle floor instead. The first McDonald's had only just opened in the UK, but US hamburgers were becoming increasingly popular. The Hard Rock Cafe near Hyde Park Corner opened in 1971. The waitresses wore white cotton overalls and plimsolls; they looked like Nurse Ratched in *One Flew Over the Cuckoo's Nest*. Long queues formed down Piccadilly. The Hard Rock Cafe was modelled on the look of an American diner and sold drinks such as Dr Pepper and Schlitz beer as well as American Budweiser. There was loud rock music and the large, rare, burgers were served with relishes such as chilli or sweetcorn. I also loved the fact that the owners had named the place after the picture on the back cover of *Morrison Hotel*, an album by The Doors, whose 'Roadhouse Blues' was a favourite in my disco.

I actually found a supplier of American-style burgers in Cornwall. It was in Bude and also did frozen buns and, most importantly, shoestring chips. We tracked down a company in London that did hamburger relish, and another which sold an Australian beer called Fosters Lager which I remembered from my trip. There was a charcoal grill left over in Terry Johnson's steak bar, and we already had a chip fryer in the kitchen there. Thus begun The Great Western Hamburger Express. We produced a poster with stars and stripes all over it and a rather more wild western version of the train that was puffing along the paper of the club downstairs and the fish restaurant upstairs. The posters were printed on flimsy paper and we put them under car windscreens in all the car parks around Padstow and the beaches.

The hamburger restaurant took £4,500 in the only season it was open. Not a great deal of money, even in 1975 – but those who went there loved it. Rather more, I guess, than the two cooks, Richard Gibbs, aka Fuzz, and Dave Stout, aka Sprout. There was no extraction in the kitchen on the middle floor so I bought a plastic 12-inch fan and replaced all the window panes in one of the windows with a big piece of plywood with a 12-inch hole cut out of it. I put the chargrill under the window. Unfortunately there was no way of controlling the flare-up from the fat oozing out of the burgers on to the hot charcoal below, so that after a week the fan blades had melted. From then on Fuzz and Sprout had to cook with the window open. Whenever you went in there on a busy night, the two of them would appear out of the smoke wearing swimming goggles with wet tea towels tied round their faces. Heroes.

We closed in early September and realised, even then, that it wasn't going to reopen next season.

The fish restaurant fared little better. We had taken on a girl who had previously worked at The Blue Lobster. Sally Prosser brought most of their menu with her but the problem was getting people to walk up two flights of stairs to the top floor. It is a general rule in restaurants that people don't like going upstairs. If the restaurant is on the ground floor you can peer through the windows to see if you like the look of the place and, almost more important, if there's anyone else in there. Interestingly, basement restaurants are less off-putting, perhaps because once you're upstairs it's an embarrassment to turn round and go back down.

It was in 1976 that I decided I would have to do the cooking myself. We couldn't afford to pay anyone else to do it but, almost more importantly for me personally, I felt I had to pin myself down to something. It's a source of some embarrassment to me to have to admit that I came into cooking by default, but it's true. I had a pressing need to do something worthwhile after so much, as the Australians say, 'stuffing around'. I started cooking the same dishes that Sally had cooked the summer before. A good cook, organised and methodical, she made me keen to have a go. We used to make a fish velouté together by gently cooking flour with melted butter, then adding fish stock. This would be made in a large 24-pint aluminium pan, just as at the Great Western Hotel in my youth, and stored in a gallon ice-cream tub in the fridge. For the service we would take a couple of handfuls of finely chopped shallots and cook them down with white wine, cream and fish stock. When the original volume had reduced by about three-quarters, we would stir some English mustard into the velouté which we had by then warmed up. When a Thermidor was ordered, we grilled a little lobster meat, prawns, scallops and some white fish, added some white crab meat, then poured on the warmed sauce, sprinkled it with grated mature Cheddar, paprika, cayenne pepper and dried breadcrumbs, and browned it under the grill. The white fish was normally monkfish which nobody knew at that time, so there was no point naming it.

In those early days we couldn't afford the sort of gratin dish I really liked – an oval dish with 'ears' at either end. Instead we bought round shallow baking dishes from the cash and carry in St Austell but, as these were normally end-of-line runs, we ended up with a collection of different-shaped dishes and, being much cheaper than the French versions, they broke frequently. I had about five of the fine French porcelain dishes. If there was a large order, the seafood Thermidor would come out in lots of different dishes. I guess it's testimony to how little the restaurant was regarded that on one occasion the host of a large party from across the water in Rock appeared the next morning and complained vehemently about how I had short-changed them by serving big and small portions at the same price. Unusually for me, and not to be repeated henceforth, I didn't tell him to eff off but patiently poured water from one bowl to the next to show that indeed the volume was the same. He had written a note on the bill the night before: 'A bill's a bill but the cook's a crook.'

Our menu was short and very simple – baked crab with cheese, which was just a scallop shell filled with lots of white crab meat and a little brown meat heated up under the grill with some melted butter and black pepper, sprinkled with Cheddar and gratinated. There weren't many other starters. We didn't even do mussels or oysters, we couldn't get them. Occasionally, I would find time to gather some mussels myself off the beach at Booby's Bay or on the lifeboat pillars below Polventon, our old holiday house on Trevose Head, but you couldn't buy them. There were no fresh scallops and only frozen prawns. We simply grilled whatever fresh fish was available – lemon sole, sea bass, sea trout. We bought in frozen Dover soles from Young's Seafoods.

There wasn't much to be said about the first version of The Seafood Restaurant, except that it had a pleasing homely quality, if you respected that sort of thing. If you ordered sea bass or sea trout, the fish was served with local new potatoes, sometimes from my own garden at Redlands. Your salmon came from the Camel Estuary, poached like my mother used to do and served with mayonnaise which I made with olive oil. You could also order a whole cold crab with the same mayonnaise, or a good fish pie. Fresh, local and simple. Many of the customers liked what I was doing.

A couple who owned Marine Villas, a slate-hung house next to the restaurant with interesting curved windows, were regulars that year. Herman Friedhoff was quite a lot older than his wife Polly. He was Dutch and had been a resistance fighter during the war. He was quite happy to talk about it, which I found fascinating. He was always well dressed with lovely manners and a genuine interest in what Johnny and I were doing. Polly was very pretty. They were important to me because they were the sort of customers I craved, and the very fact that they liked the plain grilled sea trout and bass was a terrific confidence booster. Indeed, I would go so far as to say that people like the Friedhoffs kept me going. Johnny and I were certainly not making much money. Jill had taken up running the travelling disco again and had turned Redlands into a guest house. I paid a couple of teenagers, whose parents ran the Tregloss Hotel, to do the discos at St Merryn parish hall. We had very little money.

We kept the restaurant open through the winter of 1976/1977. Most nights nobody came. It was more or less a waste of time but we thought that a little money coming in was better than none. We also ran a disco on the now-unlicensed middle floor for teenagers. I hated the sort of music they liked – 'Living Next Door to Alice', lots of Bay City Rollers, The Sweet, Racey and Showaddywaddy. The fact that they also liked Abba helped a bit but mainly I felt I was in purgatory. Most nights we earned about £10. These days I sometimes meet those kids, now in their late forties, who remember those days with enormous affection and I feel mean about it.

The favourite song of Peter Billings, the boy who worked for me upstairs in the restaurant, was 'Seasons In The Sun' by Terry Jacks. Billings, as I used to refer to him, worked hard but had the most annoying line in teasing.

'Rick, you see those lumps in the plaster over there?'

'Yes, I can see it's a textured plaster designed to give a rustic finish. I don't really like it but we're stuck with it for the time being.'

'No, it's not plaster, it's Thermidor sauce and people have got so bored with it that they've thrown it on the walls and it's dried.'

He was like a young puppy dog, friendly and massively energetic. Whenever he heard 'Seasons In The Sun' he went all dewy-eyed.

'Can't you see what a pathetic spastic song it is, Billings? It's got as much sincerity as a crab stick.'

Well, I couldn't have said that because crab sticks hadn't been invented then.

I became frustrated with turning up to cook for no one. I realised the only way the restaurant was going to work was if it was on the ground floor, so I suggested to Johnny that we split up – he take over the top two floors and turn them into flats and I take over the now-closed club and try and turn it into a restaurant. We organised a sale of all the club equipment and most of the catering equipment. We got very little for most of it. The purple faux leather club seats did quite well and the abstract fish got 30 quid. Jill's old employer at the Brentwood Hotel in Treyarnon where she had worked as a girl bought the chargrill from the Great Western Hamburger express for £60. He came back and gave me abuse because two of the elements had burnt out. It was the only time in my life I ever said 'tough' to anyone. I still feel bad about it, but just couldn't give him back his money – there was so little of it.

I moved all the rest of the equipment downstairs – the old blue six-burner cooker, a grill, a fryer, and a fridge and a dishwasher. I took down one of the plasterboard walls at the back of the club and dragged it to the middle and stuck woodchip wallpaper over it to create a division between what I wanted to be a small restaurant and the weird-looking kitchen which was just the old club bar. I didn't bother with any extraction; just put a big electric fan at the bottom of the dumb waiter shaft which I hoped would blow most of the smoke up and away. We made more trips to household sales for more tables, old pictures, lamps and general bric-a-brac for the walls. I bought a catering sink from a second-hand sale held at Wadebridge Cattle Market every spring. I plumbed it in myself, as well as all the gas equipment. We opened just before Easter 1977.

We had spent some time trying to come up with a new name as we felt that The Great Western Fish Restaurant was pretty meaningless now that the club had gone, and 'fish restaurant' suggested fish and chips. We wanted ours to be more upmarket. The Blue Lobster was, alas, as good a name as you could get for a seafood restaurant … and my friend Martin suggested The Gay Lobster. The Pickled Prawn. Rick and Jill's. Whatever we came up with seemed too familiar or ran the risk of becoming outdated too quickly. In the end we chose The Seafood Restaurant out of frustration. At least, I argued, it implied it was THE Seafood Restaurant.

Opening up for a new season is always a time of excitement. Every winter you work out the new things you are going to do – an expansion, a change to the kitchen, a renewal of tables and chairs, new windows, new floors, bigger cookers – there was always something. I can't these days smell freshly drying oil paint without a sense of spring in Padstow, lighter evenings, a chill wind blowing up the Camel Estuary but a hint of summer days to come. That first opening on the ground floor was no exception. New tables, red-and-white gingham check tablecloths, candles in Verdicchio bottles and the promise of better business downstairs. The summer of 1977 our turnover went up from £9,000 to £20,000. These were still tiny sums but the 120 per cent increase in turnover was enough to tell us that we were on the way. Johnny, meanwhile, had started turning the top two floors into four holiday flats. It was Johnny's family money which saved us from bankruptcy – not only did he put in twice as much money when we bought the property, he also had sufficient cash left to develop the flats which gave Jill and me the freedom to build up the restaurant. Each year we were able to plough most of our profits into improving it. We never borrowed money to do this, except for arranging an initial overdraft which we could pay back in the summer months. Each season we would open just before Easter and close at the end of September. I would then spend much of the winter working with a local builder, Roger Bennett, on the latest improvement. Within a few years we had a proper kitchen and a restaurant with white cement-rendered walls, white tablecloths and a parquet floor. Jill had found some large old mirrors and we began to put posters on the walls, mostly framed prints – originally things like David Hockney's 'Bigger Splash' – and art exhibition advertisements.

The menu had started to change too. Seafood Thermidor was still the rage but I now had two Garland stoves back-to-back in the centre of what was still a small kitchen and had installed some lobster tanks near the back door. I had also bought a cold room which went in the gap behind the new restaurant wall and the old wall of the building.

I was beginning to get hold of a lot more local fish and shellfish than previously. Mostly, it had to be said, because many of the fishermen who used often to be a problem in the club were supplying me. I got lovely salmon and salmon peel (sea trout from Jim Chown, who had on many occasions been incoherently drunk at the club; never any trouble, but very difficult to understand). He turned out to be a salmon netter of extraordinary skill. Often he would come in with an 18-pound salmon wrapped in a damp towel, complaining about the 'bastard seal' that had stalked his every move and slipped into his net as soon as it saw a fish in there. Seals in the Camel Estuary were clever enough to retrieve a salmon and then get out of the net. What really used to irritate him was that if they weren't hungry they'd kill the salmon just for the hell of it. He often threatened to borrow a gun and shoot the seal, but never did. He was soft-hearted.

The fish were firm, silvery and sleek. I soon developed ways of cooking them, other than just poaching them and serving them with mayonnaise. One method, which I still do, was to cut the fish into steaks, season the steaks with salt and pepper, and fry them gently in butter, turning them over after four minutes, then again after another three. I added half a glass of Muscadet, let it reduce gently, added roughly chopped parsley, and served the fish still quite pink in the middle with a bunch of watercress and some potatoes as recently dug out of the ground as possible. The fishermen sometimes brought in large crayfish which I would split in half and grill. Some of them were really large – six or seven pounds – and I used to reckon on a pound per person. I relied very little on the markets for any fish. Most was off the boats. Everything is regulated these days, but back then you could buy a couple of boxes of mixed fish – cod, monkfish, pollack, all sizes of Dover sole, hake and haddock – off a trawler and pay cash. Generally it was legitimate. Once it wasn't: a fisherman had stolen a box of fish from the skipper and sold it to me. Next thing I found the skipper mouthing off at me at the back door. I got quite shirty with him saying, 'It's not my business to check who's stealing your fish!'

We'd also get large bags of scallops off the trawlers. In those days it was difficult to find scallops that hadn't been soaked in water. They were soaked so that they swelled up and then they were frozen, but when you defrosted them the soaking water would leach out and you'd be left with a small scallop minus a lot of the flavour. Because of this we'd have to clean them ourselves, and this was hard work. Serving scallops in the shell, therefore, seemed like a sensible thing to do, so I would just grill them with a lump of parsley butter or garlic butter in each.

We were blessed with lots of very cheap mackerel. A man called Billy would come round every morning with a home-made cart with mackerel he'd got off the daily fishing trip boats. He'd charge 5p each for them. Fred Murt, who had lost a leg in a motorcycle accident when he was a teenager, sold mackerel, too, for the same money. I grilled the mackerel and served it with thin chips and a tomato, onion and thyme salad dressed with wine vinegar and olive oil.

Billings and I parted company when we moved downstairs. I had help from a local farmer's daughter called Frances Partridge, and a boy from Padstow called Patrick Bate. Patrick – distantly related to Richard Bate – is of course a grown man now. I see him from time to time. I remember him as a tall, very thin boy with a rather startled expression in his blue eyes because he's standing by me when a man, yelling at me, rushes in the door and punches me three times in the face. So hard, in fact, that I fall backwards and slide along the line of Seafood Thermidors we are preparing at the bar, which is now our worktop, scattering half a dozen all over the floor. I'm overwhelmed by the force of it. He's shouting, 'Don't you shout like that at my kid, you bastard.' I'm seriously thinking he's going to kill me but in my confusion decide I've got to keep him here so I can hand him over to the police. 'Shut the door,' I shout at Patrick. Which he does. By then the assailant has, I realised afterwards, done what he came for and is trying to leave in a hurry, but I grab him and now I'm really angry and he's getting frightened. There's a big tussle, with him trying to get away and me holding on to him. We burst through the double doors and my chef's jacket has pulled off and his shirt rips away as he's struggling to get free. I chase him over the car park yelling I'm going to kill him and catch up with him near the harbour's edge. We are lined up facing each other. I have my hands in fists like a Victorian prize fighter, he's right on the edge of the quay and I'm seriously threatening to knock him into the mud below. Fortunately by then lots of people have pulled us apart and there we are both covered in my blood. Someone leads me sobbing for breath back to the restaurant. I'm filled with a red feeling of outrage but also complete shock at my uncontrollable anger – and a sense of the ridiculousness of two men stripped to the waist about to fight in the middle of a car park.

It turned out that the night before he had been in the restaurant, leaving a very young child in the car with the window open. The child had been screaming out of the window. In the kitchen with the back doors open and a really tough service, the screaming had become intolerable, so I had run out of the back door and shouted to who, I knew not, to calm that child down. Just as I was doing this, the mother had walked out of the restaurant to do just that, and was so upset by my yelling that she persuaded her husband to go into the kitchen and sort me out the next day.

The couple persuaded the police to charge me with intent to commit grievous bodily harm. I was very upset by this because I felt his attack on me was far more severe than my yelling at his child. I spent six months terrified that this, coupled with my not being 'a fit and proper person', would close the restaurant. In the event, the charges were dropped the morning we all arrived at the magistrates' court in Bodmin. I have been more than happy to be a non-violent person ever since.

It was 1978, the year after the summer of the big fight, that we took on two of the girls who had worked in The Blue Lobster, Marie Hill and Penny Rabey. Marie went on to work for us for 27 years, Penny for about five.

Penny worked with me in the kitchen and, from the moment she started, life changed. I had enjoyed cooking with Frances; she was intelligent with a great sense of humour but she didn't really like working in a kitchen. Penny, on the other hand, had worked in kitchens most of her life. I wouldn't exactly say she liked it but she put up with it. Some nights, when it was particularly hot, she'd gaze wistfully out of the double doors across to the other side of the estuary and say, 'It's nice over at Rock.'

It always looked magical over at Rock when I was stuck in the hot kitchen. I sort of liked cooking and sort of didn't. I liked it well enough when we were really busy, but on quiet nights it was a bugger. Some nights in those early days we'd get no one in, just hang round disconsolately, hoping at first we'd get some customers, then hoping we wouldn't because if we'd got no bookings by half-past eight I'd say that we were going to the pub and we'd be out of there as quick, as they say in Padstow, as a rat up a drain. If someone came while we were packing up we'd have to serve them, then we'd be on till 11 or later.

Penny was originally from London and had a strong cockney accent. She loved the gossip in the town and had very strong views about many of the locals who used to come into the club. She had been married into one of the main Padstow families, the ubiquitous Bates, and knew them all only too well. She didn't have much time for her ex-husband Joey, but admitted that they had got married far too young. Later, after she had stopped working for us, Joey himself did the washing-up. I was initially a little wary of him because of her stories, but he worked hard and filled us with laughter about the goings-on in Padstow. Penny was always tidy and quick. She brought in a friend to wash the dishes. She was called Dianne Lobb and didn't have a lot of time for her husband either. I look back with fondness on those early days when the kitchen was run by working mums. Later, when I employed chefs, working relationships became more complicated and often frustrating. These girls just got on with it, never complained, just gossiped all the time while they did an absolutely competent job. Padstow was a bit like *Coronation Street*. Were I a sociologist I'd say that it was a port in transition from a male-dominated society, where fishing was the only livelihood, to a place far more diverse. In the early days of the restaurant, the men were still the men and if they didn't treat their women too well, so be it. Boys were brought up to think of themselves as the breadwinners, and the power in the family. I've had quite enough Padstow wives working for me over the years to realise this situation. But young men – fighting, binge-drinking, womanising – have changed. Those old macho fishing days have gone. Many of the characters I now meet on the quayside are keen gardeners, not averse to going to the theatre or even travelling to see married sons or daughters in Australia. The days when two young fishermen stood outside The Shipwrights and attacked each other with anchor chains are no more. Male aggressiveness is tamed, but maybe that's why May Day is still so powerful a celebration of fertility where the vigorous reality of male and female sexuality is acknowledged.

Penny was the cornerstone of the kitchen and Marie provided the same stability in the restaurant. Jill and Marie worked well together. Jill was on the surface smiling, slightly innocent-seeming, but underneath much tougher than she appeared. Marie was on the surface Liverpudlian, blunt and to the point, but underneath much softer than she appeared. They needed each other for support, dealing with sometimes very difficult customers and in the height of the season large numbers with not quite enough tables to go round. They evolved a form of service which was efficient but refreshingly informal. This is the best type of service for a restaurant in rural Britain. They made me behave better, too. Like most young chefs, I wasn't averse to throwing my weight around. They were far more concerned to get the food to their customers.

With those two in charge out in the restaurant, I grew to love my little domain, the kitchen. It's a busy Saturday night, with Penny moaning about too many orders, and me pushing a couple of lemon soles under the grill. Sliding the door down on the leaky microwave into which I'd just put a sea trout with cream, chives and fish stock sauce, while reducing some more fish stock – white wine and velouté – to go with some chopped tomato and broadleaf parsley for a piece of brill with Dugléré sauce. I always worked in the centre of a pile of debris – parsley stalks, onion skins, splashed velouté. Penny used to say it was like Casey's bleeding court wherever I was.

I evolved a strategy for dealing with panic. Some nights were so busy that the orders stuck on nails driven through an old narrow floorboard would be lapping themselves, i.e. all nails would have one paper order and would be starting to pick up a second. I just used to say to myself, 'Don't scream, because if you can stand the next ten minutes it will get better.' And it did. Once, though, I felt like giving it all up. It was August Bank Holiday Saturday; we were full to bursting. Jill's family were in for dinner: Jack and Mary, her parents, and Veronica (Roni), her sister, and Roni's husband Chris. Roni was working in a smart restaurant in Manchester called the Beaujolais and Chris owned a trendy hair salon in the city centre called Christopher James. I wanted to impress them – they were used to really good restaurants. Jill's younger sister Mary was down as well, with her boyfriend Nick. She worked in Waddington's art gallery in Cork Street in London.

Much later we learnt to space out the tables better, but that night the orders kept coming in for two terrible hours from about 8.45. So bad was it that, I confess, I moved the family order back three nails hoping they wouldn't mind. The time between the orders coming in and the main courses going out increased so much that I refused to notice it, one hour, one and a half hours, and worsening. Finally, I sent their mains out: grilled sea bass mostly.

Within minutes Roni came into the kitchen and said, 'Rick, love. The bass is raw in the middle.'

She said it with such sympathy and kindness that it cut straight to my heart. I wanted the nightmare to end and to wake up as a journalist. I must remember to remind her about it. She's now the sommelier in The Seafood Restaurant.

Sometimes on a really busy night I'd go into the cold room and stand there cooling down and eating raw green beans. It was quiet in there, just the whir of the fans. Outside, it was crazy. I used to hum the Peter Gabriel song, 'A Normal Life'. It didn't quite fit the words but the sentiment did.

That Peter Gabriel song actually came out in 1980. Soon after that Paul Sellars started working with me. He had been coming to the restaurant at lunchtimes. I always got to know the regulars, and appreciated people who liked my food. Sometimes they asked me to have a drink with them, other times they passed a message into the kitchen and I went out after the service to talk to them. Paul came round the back door one morning and said he'd like a job.

'Where have you worked before?'

'Well, I was in the House of Commons for five years, but now I'm working at the Lantern in Surrey.'

'OK. Do you fancy a pint at the Customs?'

At the Customs House pub, just down the quay from The Seafood Restaurant, he told me that he was tired of cooking French food and wanted to move down to Cornwall to surf and cook seafood. His wife Sue was with him – very Geordie, a coalminer's daughter, very direct. I liked them both and thought, I'm about to take on a real chef.

Paul was deft and neat and tidy. I was in awe of him but felt threatened by him, too, because I knew very little and guessed he knew everything. He caught me boiling new potatoes at much too rapid a boil and suggested I turned them down to a simmer. I got cross and said what difference did it make, boiling was boiling. But it did. His knife skills were a joy to watch, the way the filleting knife neatly parted the two top fillets of a lemon sole and flew across the backbone, leaving it clean and the fillet whole with no nicks in it, or the way he could take a side of salmon off the bone with no tearing of the flesh and remove the pin bones just using his thumb and a potato peeler. His peeled, deseeded and chopped tomatoes were a perfect dice and his brunoise of shallots were like Demerara sugar. I didn't always warm to some of his ways of presenting food. He liked to do a Sole Mousseline where he freed the top two fillets of skinned Dover sole and piped fish mousse under them, then braised the whole fish with a little white wine, chopped shallots and fish stock, where he then reduced the cream and finished with some egg yolk and gratinated under a salamander. I pointed out that the finished dish, with two curves of fillet on the top and an extrusion of soft mousseline looked slightly pornographic. I didn't like the way he cut lemon wedges, either, with a little tail of peel which he'd curl up decoratively. These, however, were the sum total of my reservations.

With Paul in the kitchen the menu grew significantly in size and scope. It was now about 1982 and nouvelle cuisine, which arrived in the UK in the mid-Seventies, had finally got to Padstow. Nouvelle cuisine was a reaction, by a number of young and highly regarded chefs in France, to classic French cookery and the almost-hallowed recipes of Escoffier. Paul Bocuse, Alain Chapel, the Troisgros brothers, Michel Guérard and Roger Vergé had pioneered ideas about flavouring sauces with fresh herbs and fragrant stocks which were thickened not with flour but with cream and a little butter whisked in at the last minute. The emphasis was on the freshest possible produce, and the presentation of exquisite, tiny portions on the plate was very important. I bought all their books, some in

French, the others translated. It was an exciting time to be cooking but much as I longed to be able to create dishes like those French stars, the reality of a small kitchen, limited equipment and, most importantly, limited chef's skills put an unnecessary strain on the kitchen. Delicate colour presentation is very demanding and requires time and effort at the last minute.

I certainly came up with some difficult ideas. I wanted to get the best possible value out of our glorious Cornish lobsters. This would have been fine with a kitchen full of trained chefs, but in those days we had one commis chef on the larder, who portioned all the fish for cooking; me and Paul on hot starters and main courses; one chef on the veg and another on the sweets. Just five of us on nights when we might be doing 80 or 90 covers.

I went and put on this two-course lobster dish. First course, a fresh bisque made from the shells. Main course, a nouvelle cuisine version of *homard à l'américaine*. I would take a live lobster, briefly boil it in salted water so that the colour changed from blue to red, cut it in half, remove as carefully as possible all the meat from the body and the claws. Then I'd make a stock from all the shells except a small triangle of red shell to which the long red feelers were attached. I'd then make a fresh bisque out of the stock with chopped onions, shallots, carrots, tomato, white wine and tarragon. I'd put all this in a food processor, pass it through a fine chinoise, add a little cream and send half of the bisque out with tarragon leaves, diced tomato and a few very thin slices of lobster meat. While the customers were eating their lobster soup, I'd be reassembling the lobster meat to look like a lobster, without the shell, garnishing the plate with two red feelers and making a sauce out of the rest of the bisque which I'd reduce down with a stamen or two of saffron. I'd add cream, whisk in a couple of pieces of chilled butter, and finally pour the sauce decoratively around the plate, which by then was a 12-inch Wedgwood Insignia white plate with, as the brochure said, a thin band around the edge and 'a little nosegay of flowers'.

Usually we'd get an order of three of these on a table at the same time as we were dealing with the main courses for tables of ten, six and four. In the ensuing chaos, I couldn't help noticing that a lobster laid out on an oval plate without its shell looked a bit like my Jack Russell terrier, Chalky, when he jumped in the sea and came out shrunk.

This idiocy was not the end of my ambitions. I devised three fillets of three different fish – say John Dory, monkfish and brill – cooked in three different ways: the John Dory sautéed in butter, the monkfish grilled over charcoal, the brill steamed. They were served with three different sauces: the John Dory with sautéed cucumber, the monkfish with a roasted red pepper dressing and the brill with a cream and sorrel sauce. All on the same plate.

When people ask me for a tip about seafood cookery and I say, 'Keep it simple,' it's in the light of bitter experience.

Gradually Jill and I found time to visit other restaurants to get ideas from them. Just across the Tamar in Devon at Gulworthy, near Tavistock, was The Horn of Plenty. It was our favourite. The owners were Patrick and Sonia Stevenson. Sonia, an ex-violinist, was the chef and Patrick, an opera singer, ran the restaurant wearing tails every night. The menu seemed to us to be a wonder of sophistication, and we loved the ambience of the large manor house overlooking the Tamar. I don't quite know why but the smell of the deep, dark-green gloss paint in the toilet, and the way the Stevensons provided real fabric hand towels that you dropped into a bin when you'd used them, are a lasting memory of comfort. In the restaurant was a log fire that ran right through the wall in the main dining room into the conservatory outside in which Patrick often had a barrel of Bass which he'd drink out of a pewter mug. Sonia put on regional French dinners with wines from parts of France we'd never even heard of. For the 'Poitou' evening they devised a large folded card with a scene from the Poitou countryside around Poitiers, near the Loire, and a menu handwritten by Patrick made up of special dishes from around that area. It was enough to set me off with a determination to do the same sort of thing in Padstow. Within a year, I'd found a supplier of the two wines on that menu, Sauvignon du Haut Poitou and a red Gamay. The Sauvignon was our house wine for 30 years. I was influenced by Patrick's sense of place to the extent of copying a drawing from Elizabeth David's *A Book of Mediterranean Food*, for use on our own menu. It was a harbour scene with a girl, holding a basket of grapes, talking to a young *matelot*. In the foreground is a cloth spread on the ground with scallops, whelks, a red mullet and what looks like a turbot. It was by John Minton, who illustrated her first two books, and it worked for me because the fish were the right ones and the sailor looked like one of the local Padstow fishermen, Bernard Murt, in May Day whites. It was our little logo for about ten years and it set the tone. It wasn't the Mediterranean, it was Cornwall. It felt different from the rest of England and the delightful Minton drawing seemed to sum up the romance of Cornwall.

# V

Before 1978, there was no chance of a baby, our future was too uncertain. Then it took a long time to happen. I began to blame the ancient kitchen microwave for making me sterile. I thought it might be the electrons, and I started to stand well back and to press the button with a stick. This did the trick! Jill got pregnant.

She went into labour on a cold morning in January. There was a deep frost and driving her to hospital in Truro I saw a hare standing motionless in a silver field. I will remember this forever and ever, because it seemed the perfect way to introduce my first son to the world. It was prophetic. Edward has always had a unique love of nature. The minute I saw him born, I felt he'd been here before. Edward is one of those Old Souls.

Two years later I was at the birth of Jack. When the baby arrived and proved to be another boy, I blurted, 'Oh no! My tools!' My father used to tell me that I could borrow his tools but I always had to put them back. When I took Edward in to see his new baby brother, a look of shock passed over his face, followed by consternation. He, too, knew that in future he'd be sharing his tools.

I missed the birth of Charles in 1985, and have regretted it ever since. Looking back, it seems symbolic. Already – only four years after Jack's arrival – the restaurant had become all consuming, to the point where business was more important than family life.

One of my brightest chefs, Peter Richardson, once said to me, 'Catering's not a vocation, it's a disease.'

It's a *sine qua non* that anyone seriously involved in the catering industry doesn't have a family life. The sheer exhaustion of working 16 hours day after day, the frustration of having to deal with complaining customers, the indignity of having to clean out blocked urinals at midnight. The mistakes you make when you're tired, how your judgement is increasingly impaired. How you once dropped four treacle tarts when your builder, Roger Bennett, yelled 'Afternoon' as he came into the kitchen and you looked up just as you were lining up the tray to put it in the oven. Then you had an hour to make four more tarts before service. Or the time when, exhausted and angry with someone who sent back your lovely grilled Dover sole because it was tough, you snapped and went out to the large round table just by the reception desk filled with a party of regulars from Rock and shouted, 'The trouble with you upper-middle-classes is you're so supercilious.' Afterwards you realised they were right: the sole was like rubber.

Actually, Jill and I were lucky for the first 15 years of running The Seafood Restaurant: we took the winters off. In 1990, however, we decided to stay open all the year round because it was almost impossible to find enough good staff on a seasonal basis, i.e. pay them off in October and re-employ them in March. But for a long while, when our boys were little, we had plenty of time for them in the winter. We had a pleasant home life which I'm pleased to say they still remember, partly because of the stories I used to tell them most nights before they went to bed.

The stories sort of progressed out of *Treasure Island*. In the 1960s, a small tanker, the *Helmsley*, had run aground in thick fog at Fox Cove, near Treyarnon Bay. She was close enough to the coast for her crew to get off on to the rocks and up the cliff. People scrambled down the cliff to remove bells and other small pieces of booty from the ship, which was wedged firmly on the rocks and was later cut up and winched to the cliff top and taken away in trucks. I told my sons about the *Helmsley* and suddenly started imagining what it would be like if three boys of their age had come across the boat shortly after it had been wrecked and decided to patch it up and set out in it. Near Stepper Point at the mouth of the estuary had been a jetty for ships to load the stone from a quarry there, and I had heard that there was a diesel tank dug into the ground, so I had the boys refloat the *Helmsley* and sail it round to Stepper to refuel. The jetty became the base from which they sailed away on adventures all over the world, finding smugglers' islands, wreckers' islands, vampires' islands, getting becalmed in the Sargasso Sea and surrounded by giant turtles in the Galapagos. Some nights I found it so hard to think up new stories that I repeated the old ones, to howls of 'Dad we've been here before'. None of them has forgotten the voyages of the *Helmsley*.

When I returned to Cornwall after Oxford, I moved into Redlands, the family home. My mother was still living there, but I cohabited happily with her, and eventually Jill moved in too. I lived in Redlands from the age of 18 until I was in my mid-forties. It was bliss. I adored Jill, our business was expanding, and our three children were born there. I had plenty of time to spend with my boys. Even when working flat out, I made a point of taking every Sunday off so that we could go out. These were days of simple country pleasures, the sort of things boys love – traction engine rallies, festivals, exhibitions, dog shows. I restored the ancient black Mercedes I'd acquired from a local farmer who had a shed full of cars. My sons shared my delight in the eccentricity of rural Cornwall. I seem to remember that once we found a ghost train at a farm show. When I dream of home, it is always Redlands.

In 1974 my mother moved out. She missed her Oxfordshire friends, and decided to live in Burford. Jill and I made Redlands our own. It had nearly an acre of land, and I had visions of growing most of the vegetables for the restaurant. I read a book about wine-making in England and planted about 50 vines which blew out of the ground in the winter gales. But the veg thrived in the quick-to-warm sandy soil. I was always happy pottering in my garden, albeit always under pressure to return to the restaurant to cook. An early enthusiast for recycling, I made a wall out of the wine bottles from the restaurant. It's still there, a bit higgedly-piggedly because I used only sand as infill. Remembering my father's meticulous constructions from the lovely Cotswold stone at the farm back in Oxfordshire, I wish I'd done a better job. But my empty-bottle wall is, nevertheless, now a local landmark.

~

In 1978, the year that Jill was pregnant with Edward, I rather ungallantly decided to bunk off on holiday with John Thompson. I bought a book called *Visiting French Vineyards* and off we went to explore Burgundy, the Jura and Provence. We drove to Paris where a neurophysiology graduate, Susan Greenfield, who my brother John had taught at Oxford, was doing research. Springy, as we know her, now Baroness Greenfield, was and still is one of those people who enjoy every moment of life, hence her name – she does everything with a spring in her step. Well that's how I think she got her nickname. Because Susan Greenfield = spring greens. Her enthusiasm meant she was more Parisienne than the locals. She mastered the language in a couple of blinks and knew every cafe and bistro. She took us to what is still my favourite brasserie anywhere, La Coupole, where I ordered a *plateau de fruits de mer*. It was the best I've ever had, and the ideal for all the thousands of *fruits de mer* that I've produced in Padstow since. Was it the quality of the mayonnaise, made not with olive oil but rapeseed oil with lots of mustard in it? I couldn't afford the lobster version but the langoustines, prawns and shrimps with their wispy feelers still intact were the star attraction. There were two crabs, half a brown crab and a whole *etrille*, a velvet swimming crab. *Bigorneaux* (winkles) were salty and sweet *bulots* (whelks) small and therefore not as intimidating as the ones that come to us from lobster pots. All the bivalves – oysters, mussels, *praires* and *palourdes* clams had been opened whilst still alive, so the mussels had that bitter but exquisite mineral taste alleviated only by a sprinkle of shallot vinegar. The platter came on a deep round aluminium tray. There was a chrome wire stand and seaweed on a pile of crushed ice. You chucked oyster and mussel shells into a bowl beneath.

And it wasn't just the dishes: the service at that restaurant was of a sophistication which we in Padstow, with the local girls and the lack of waiters' stations and the cramped hot kitchen, could only see as unattainable. For a start all the waiters had the most chic uniforms: white shirt, black trousers, white apron and black waistcoat built for the job with pockets for pens, pads and corkscrews. The amount of last-minute preparation that they did at their waiters' stations was fascinating to watch. They filleted Dover soles and napped the fillets with the nutty butter from the serving pan; they sliced *côtes de boeuf* with speedy accuracy; they served up steak tartare and spooned out navarin of lamb from a copper pan. I've been back to La Coupole many times since then, and it's still fabulous. The entrance in the Boulevard Montparnasse looks like a first night at the Odeon, Leicester Square. The interior is art deco, the pillars painted to look like green marble.

Visitors today are spoon-fed information. I prefer to experiment and find out for myself. That's why I don't like entries in Trip Advisor which moan about the brusqueness of the service at La Coupole. I find the service refreshing. It's what you get from Chinese restaurants in Hong Kong. The waiters (usually middle-aged) are similar, and they do a perfectly efficient job of getting your food to you as quickly and professionally as possible. Not that I would allow brusqueness in my own restaurants, where customers expect to be treated as something close to royalty. But what's wrong with bloody good service without any exchange of sweetness?

After Paris we drove to Beaune and visited a number of vineyards in Burgundy. At the Hospices de Beaune, possibly because of too much indulgence in wine, I felt chastened by the Rogier Van de Leyden painting 'The Last Judgement'. Such a frightening scene with all the little beds with their red blankets in that very hospice where the poor of the area went to die. We tried a few Macons on the way to Provence, and just outside Orange I saw a promising vineyard near the town of D'Eath and, momentarily forgetting which side of the road I was on, I turned directly into the path of a Citroën. The young driver of the oncoming car, though shocked, was also humorous: subsequently I paid a large sum of money to compensate him for his very old, very mechanically imperfect car. I was shattered by my stupidity but no one was hurt and the police didn't materialise. My bright yellow Golf was drivable, with smoke emanating from the front tyre where the bumper was pressing into it. I vibrated into a garage where a very tall, old garage mechanic with a bad back manoeuvred himself into a position to jack the bumper away from the tyre. What was so touching was he could, without language, feel my shock and guilt and told me in French to calm down.

We limped down to the coast and stayed in Le Lavandou where my spirits revived at a restaurant in St Tropez on the Quai Jean

Jacques with a lunch of *Aïoli Provençal* and *Bourride*. These two dishes and the *fruits de mer* in Paris were instrumental in moving my culinary horizon a long way. The aïoli was the deep yellow garlic mayonnaise that they call the butter of Provence, served with a magnificent platter of vegetables – artichokes, green beans, carrots and warm potatoes with some quartered boiled eggs with bright orange yokes very slightly runny. The *bourride* – a sort of soup with whole fish – was made with red mullet, rascasse, John Dory and monkfish. It came as the rich garlicky stock into which piles of the aïoli had been stirred. The fish, which had been cooked in the stock, were filleted at our table. Naturally we drank a lot of rosé and wandered around St Tropez afterwards feeling as full as it's possible to be. I formed an opinion then, which I haven't altered, that both dishes, but particularly the aïoli, are best eaten at lunch; they're just too rich for the evening.

Jill was never totally at home in Redlands, which after all had been my parents' place. In the summer, the nearby lanes were jammed with caravans. Eventually, she found a large family house in the village of Trevone and we moved in 1988.

My three sons went to a village school in St Eval. It wasn't quite our local school, but I selected it because it was the choice of RAF families whose married accommodation was nearby and it had good facilities. I admired the headmaster, Paul Bordeaux, for his forward-looking teaching ideas. Edward didn't do particularly well at school, and I was impressed when Paul said that gaining and retaining knowledge isn't necessarily the most important thing in education. Too much emphasis is put on exams, and he looked to identify the latent talent in every child, and develop that, whatever it was. He saw that Edward was artistic and good with his hands. I think that it is due to him that Edward is a sculptor today.

⁓

I had been cooking for five years by the time Edward was born. I was aware that my palate was good and that my liking for simplicity and my ability to produce dishes which tasted special were somehow instinctive, second nature. But my learned skills were crap. I didn't know how to make puff pastry, or a soufflé, or croquette potatoes, or how to prepare a rack of lamb. I wanted to master the technical and business side of restaurant management, including portion control, budgeting and finding the best prices. I therefore enrolled at Camborne Tech in Poole as a catering student because I felt I wanted to learn the basics of French classic cooking. The other students on the course were all working in the industry, two from the RAF base at St Mawgan, a couple from the hotels in Newquay.

My tutor, Tom Chivers, was a chef who had worked in some legendary restaurants in the fifties and sixties – Quaglino's, Le Coq d'Or, The Caprice, as well as the Dorchester Hotel. He filled me with lots of the detail I had so crassly missed during my all-too-brief experience at the Great Western Hotel in Paddington. This time I was thirsty for knowledge. We made fricassees and blanquettes, mousselines and farces. He taught me inventive vegetable dishes: a potato gratin from Le Coq d'Or, now Langan's, which we still use in Padstow to this day, the correct way to produce Carrots Vichy which should be made with genuine salty Vichy Water and *petits pois à la Française*. We mastered *champignons à la Grecque* and presented salsify in a reduced blanc of flour, water, lemon juice and butter. We made proper fish stocks and beef stocks and discussed the origins of Lobster Thermidor and *Lobster à l'Américaine* (I bought lobsters down from Padstow and we made both).

Tom called me Colin. 'Chef, I'd just like to say my name's actually Rick,' I said one Wednesday, college day.

'Yes, yes, all right, Colin.'

He claimed I looked like a Colin.

He used to tell hair-raising anecdotes of his past life in the Dorchester kitchen and other busy basements with lesser pedigrees. One of these – a favourite – was about a Russian chef de parti called Victor and a commis chef on the roast section. Of course, when I was the audience for this shaggy dog story, the young wet-behind-the-ears commis was always called Colin. Thus Colin had been pushing his luck with Victor by maintaining that all Russians were baby-eaters, after the terrible siege of Leningrad. Victor had picked up a cooks' knife and threatened Colin with it. Tom, the hero of the story, who was a sous chef at the time, had grabbed a copper sauteuse hanging from the extraction canopy, and had whacked the Russian over the head and dropped him. Tom told it well, with glinting eyes recalling the drama and his starched toque on the table beside him. Of course the subtext was an instructive little lecture about good manners in the kitchen.

If you've ever seen a play called *The Kitchen* by Arnold Wesker, you'll know how these rows in kitchens evolve, especially where the heat is immense and where the numbers are, too. Wesker's play is about a very large kitchen with about 30 chefs and kitchen porters. The action takes place over a busy lunch service, during the lull in the afternoon and then the dinner service. I first went to see it with my sister Janey in the sixties. It's the sort of play which would make you never want to set foot in a commercial kitchen and yet there is a catharsis about the sometimes violent interaction between the characters, English, German, Irish and others, very like the kitchen I worked in London but much busier. Anthony Bourdain's *Kitchen Confidential* also gives a vivid picture, as does Rose Tremain's novel, *The Road Home*.

The part of the course that I really didn't care for was chaud-froid, the process invented by Carême where hot food was left to go cold then coated in a mixture of aspic and velouté, béchamel, mayonnaise, cream or reduced stock. Cooked whole chickens, chicken breasts, poached eggs or trout would be coated in a sauce. You'd chill it to let it set, then add decorations. We were taken to Hotel Olympia to look at examples of chaud-froid as well as chocolate moulding and sugar paste creations in pale pinks, greens, yellows and blues. Snow White and the seven dwarfs and nativity scenes were the most common. Most bizarre of all, though, was fat carving: the Venus de Milo, Michelangelo's David or an eagle on a crag, in white fat. I found it all at odds with what I wanted to do in cooking, yet held a sardonic admiration for the effort put in. Back at Camborne Tech, chaud-froid decorations for a chicken were a black-and-white chequerboard or a harlequin pattern. The black, which in Marie-Antoine Carême's day would have been thin slices of truffle, was a black cylinder of what was called truffle paste, which tasted as though it was made from charcoal, flour and gelatine. This would be sliced and cut into little squares, diamonds, lines and circles. I just didn't get it and was hopeless at it, except that I did once do a couple of poached eggs with flowers on them using chives for the stalks, tarragon leaves for the leaves, and egg white and yoke for the flowers. The teacher, Gerry Boriosi, said it looked 'very natural'. 'Natural' was what I saw in the *fruits de mer*, the *bourride* and the *aïoli Provençal*. That's how I wanted my food to look.

It was Paul Sellars who helped me turn out *fruits de mer* and *bourride*. The problem at that time was the availability of seafood. Crabs we had in abundance, and lobsters, but that was about it. I was still going out and picking my own mussels. Oysters by then we could get from the Duchy Oyster Company at Port Navas near Falmouth, but no one would deliver them so we had to have them sent by train to Bodmin Road station and then persuade a Western National driver to pick them up for the Padstow bus. Some of them refused to do this because the cardboard boxes always leaked oyster water. We finally managed to get langoustines for the *fruits de mer* on the overnight train from Glasgow, which caused similar problems – in fact, leaked prawn water is a lot smellier. Initially the clams were from the Camel Estuary, a very soft-shell variety which the locals called Hens. We got cockles in the same way. I found someone who would pick mussels from the estuary, too, by the bagful; but I realised these mussels would have to be purified before I could sell them. So back at the house on Trevose Head, I set up an ultraviolet purification system in the coach house, scene of many a party in years gone by. Here, on my day off, I would collect water from the slipway at high tide in big plastic tanks in the back of my VW Caddy pick-up, and take it back to purify the mussels. These mussels were really good quality. The main mussel that grows in the Camel Estuary is from the Mediterranean and has an almost black shell which is rounder than the local beach mussel. It may be fantasy but I am transported to some beach-side restaurant on the Costa Brava whenever I taste them. We began to put on moules marinière and stuffed mussels. But getting all the ingredients for a *fruits de mer* had been a labour of love.

Not any more, though. I was in The Seafood kitchen last night and ruminated that now it's just a matter of picking up the phone and shrimps, prawns, langoustines, razor clams, palourdes all arrive next day in perfect condition.

These days, I just go in and stand on the pass and watch what everyone is doing. It's a scene of quiet concentration. Nobody raises their voices. I love it in there, always have, for all the hard work, sweating, stressing, yelling. Nowadays, it's almost like a temple. It's a friendly world where stocks and soups are simmering and fish and shellfish are grilling. The chefs are pleased to see me. I don't say much, just notice that the horseradish and beetroot salad with smoked salmon is a little chunky. Mental note to ask them to cut the beetroot finer. I taste it. Needs more horseradish and a little more sugar. The sauce for the new season's garlic with the monkfish is a little on the dry side. Will mention that. Grilled lobster looks perfect, as does the bass with the vanilla dressing which is hard to get right. Too much vanilla and it tastes weird; just a trace and it's exciting, seems to make the chargrilled bitterness of the skin taste memorable.

In 1996 we bought the house behind the restaurant and dug out its garden, then knocked through to form a massively bigger space. We put the garden back on top of the roof. To me it's like the Home Underground where Peter Pan and The Lost Boys lived in Neverland. It's complete with its chimney, the extract duct now tiled with local Delabole slate to conceal it. The new kitchen is big, divided into four sections. The main part has a central island Rorgue range. There are two solid-top stoves, a deep-fat fryer, a plancha (the stainless steel griddle beloved by the Spanish) and a chargrill on one side for the main courses and vegetables, and on the other side – for the hot starters and what we call bar snacks, little *amuse-gueules* – another plancha, a solid-top stove, a four-burner stove, a deep-fat fryer and a fierce wok burner. The wok cooker is also used for the large number of Singapore chilli crabs we do, where we split whole brown crabs and stir-fry them with ginger, garlic, chilli and soya sauce. There are also two salamanders at the end of the range nearest the pass for grillling whole fish like dover sole or bass, and browning fish pies. There are worktops on the back wall and side walls interspersed with two Rational cookers and another salamander.

The fourth side of the main kitchen is the pass where the food is passed from chefs to waiters. On the pass is a chef whose job is to check the food as it goes out and assist with adding last-minute sauces and garnishes. We made our new pass as long as possible, half heated and half cold, so that we could occasionally do a banquet service which needs lots of plates being assembled with, say, roast *trançons* (steaks) of turbot, a nap of fish stock flavoured with fish sauce, butter and *fines herbes* and, finally, a thick yellow slick of hollandaise sauce.

Next to the main kitchen is the pastry kitchen which has two ovens, a grill and an ice-cream maker called a Pacojet.

Next to that is the fish prep area or larder, as we call it, where all the fish and shellfish is portioned and delivered to the main kitchen, and the platters of seafood, prawns or oysters and the cold crabs and lobsters are put together. The initial fish prep – gutting, scaling and filleting – is done in a chilled kitchen upstairs. Next to the fish prep area is the pot wash, and just in front of that is the still area for slicing bread and preparing teas and coffee, and in front of that the wine room.

In addition to having a good extraction system, the kitchen today is air conditioned. I've only cooked in this kitchen on an occasional service or when filming some cookery sequences. The kitchen that I worked in was about one-fifth of the size of the current one. The area where it was is now a small part of the restaurant. It had a terrible extract system and a low roof, so that we were always very hot, particularly as I insisted on having a real charcoal grill in there. Near the back door were the lobster tanks; I put them there as it was the coolest part of the kitchen. It was also where all the fish came in, most of it, in the early days, literally across the quay. We always kept that double door wide open so that in the summer it was the most comfortable place to work. In winter you wore an overcoat. I heard much later that at least one enterprising Padstonian used to nip in the back door when no one was looking and help himself to two or three lobsters from the tanks, then come in later to sell them to us.

There were six of us in the old kitchen. We used to get hot, very hot, while coping with large numbers of customers, up to a hundred a night in the height of the summer. I had difficulty in recruiting staff. I used to ask any chef coming for a job if he surfed. If he did, the chances were that he'd stay, because the beaches either side of Padstow – Summerleaze, Widmouth, Crackington Haven, Polzeath, Trevone, Harlyn, Treyarnon, Porthcothan, Watergate – are great for surf. We were also lucky in that Padstow is close to Newquay, where there's plenty of night life. It was a typical scenario: not enough resources to ensure that the kitchen is correctly equipped and not enough reputation to ensure that a regular supply of talented young chefs will come through. My aspirations were always well ahead of what was possible. I also have a tendency to get over-excited about a new dish and put it on at the last minute without ascertaining if it will work with the existing menu. The only way to get through a busy lunch or dinner is to be completely prepared for each dish with what we call our *mise en place*, which is where all the parts of a dish – chopped herbs and onions, peeled, deseeded and chopped tomatoes, reduced stocks, sauces in the bain-marie – are laid out ready to cook.

So not unnaturally, for reasons beyond my control and others which were of my own doing, service in the old days was often extremely fraught and my temper was not always level. I've realised now after many years that I'm not naturally a bad-tempered person, nor are most chefs. It's just that the conditions, the *coup de feu* as the French call it, can be of such immense stress that the only way is to erupt. The only thing I can say is that I never hit anyone and, after I'd finished letting off steam, I always apologised.

But it was tough. Recently I asked Claire Cross what it used to be like. Claire, who still works for me as a waitress and has done so off and on for over 20 years, wrote,

*Every night was like being on a stage or in a performance and you were never sure what would happen next. The further into the season we were the harder it got as everyone had been working six days a week and all the hours God sent and tempers got frayed. Towards the end of the summer, I remembered asking you to pass the large catering jar of English mustard as a customer wanted some for their steak. You told me to take that out to them as it was. When I said I thought it might be better in a ramekin, you blew your stack and said no, just effing take it out to them like that. I put it in a pot anyway where you couldn't see! Every season's end I went to Australia for the winter. Once I mentioned to you that I'd be leaving in a couple of weeks. You were mortified because you'd just lost it again and thought it had caused me to hand in my notice. You kept apologising saying sorry you'd lost it and were so sweet. It was no use answering you back when you were shouting as you'd just get worse! But you always, always apologised. No matter how cross you were. I knew it was because you had such a passion for your food, and you were always salting and tasting*

205

*your food and if the chefs didn't do this you'd get upset! Pressure in
the kitchen is so different to front of house, if you mess up a dish
you have to start from scratch but if front of house makes a mistake
there's always a way round it.*

*We had an agreed golden rule with all the front of house staff
if there was something wrong with a dish and it would have to go
back to the kitchen we weren't to tell Rick directly, it always had
to go through Jill because you would go ballistic but she knew how
to handle it and soften you up!*

*Nowadays everything is so different, there's training, every-
thing is tidy and organised now. I had no training but it was such
good fun. I used to love seeing how the customers were dressed, very
odd yellow trousers with tartan jacket, all colours, every one dressed
in the same odd way, I used to say they all came from one egg! Some
of the customers were really eccentric and some very rude. One chap
was being really awkward and was very big. Usually Jill dealt
with them and was very calm when they were pissed and kicked off
but he was so rude and intimidating to her, as she was only small
and he so big, that she just yelled at him. 'Don't you talk to me like
that you bully', then turned to me and said: 'Get Rick, get Rick.'
You marched out and said, 'Why don't you fuck off,' he yelled back
to you and said 'Don't you tell me to fuck off, you told my brother
to fuck off last week!' But he left and I remember he was yelling at
you outside through the kitchen door.*

The staff were our refuge from difficult customers. We knew each
other very well, since we spent so much of our time working together.
We didn't get much opportunity to socialise outside work, so we
socialised within it. It's a cliché but it's true to say that you only get
out of life what you put into it. A lot of the work was really tough,

but when we were off we took delight in letting our hair down. We liked each other and we had lots to talk about, simply because we worked under such pressure and there was so much to remember with pleasure and happiness after a few glasses of wine. We had some great parties. In the early days, we'd throw an annual party just before Christmas at the Bedruthan Steps Hotel which had a Sicilian chef. Later, we started having barbecues on the beach where we played volleyball, had a clam bake and ended up completely plastered with lots of surfers and my boys and their babysitter Liz dancing uncontrollably to Lynyrd Skynyrd's 'Free Bird'.

These were innocent times: our children growing up and the restaurant increasingly successful but still small.

# VI

When I started living in Cornwall full time in 1974 I also started playing rugby again. I joined the local team, The Wadebridge Camels: Camels because Wadebridge, like Padstow, is on the River Camel which if course meant that the emblem on our brown and yellow rugby shirts was just that. The team was made up largely of local farmers. Up to then, most of the Cornish people I knew were fishermen. Cornish fishermen are apt to be men of few words, not unfriendly, but rugged characters filled with the harshness of their job, putting up with the all-too-real danger of gale-force winds and mountainous seas. They tend to moan about government intervention and the high price of diesel and the low price of fish, but that's inevitable because their lives are so precarious. They are the last hunter-gatherers and as such represent a past world where men went out to bring back the food for the family. Sometimes, out with my friend Johnnie Murt, I found it impossible to see why a life on a small, pitching, tossing, wooden boat could be anything but miserable. It's relentless work, cold, wet and hard, the lifting up of pots over the side of the boat, the rapid removal of lobsters and crabs, the speedy replacement of the old half-eaten bait with a new smelly salted scad. Then, when all the pots are stacked at the back of the boat, the ropes snake across the deck as the string of pots is tossed overboard again with the engine running all the time. This process is repeated maybe 20 times in a day. Then there's the clean-up –

hosing the weed, the crushed whelks, the starfish, out through the scuppers. Maybe a mackerel spinner or two over the stern on the way home, the flurry of gulls above and behind if you were gutting fish. At sea, though, you somehow feel the serenity of it. It's men without women and, as Hemingway would have said, it's doing what men have always done.

Farming is tough too, but the difference is you own some land – maybe just as a tenant – but your peace comes from land. I imagined myself leaning on a gate, looking down a field newly green with spring rain in the late afternoon when there was still a brightness in the sky and a chill wind coming down the estuary from the north-east with some pink blossom scattering the ground from a crab apple tree in the hedge. That's how it felt, for me, with the farmers who formed the Wadebridge Camels. John Warwick, Richard and Robert Hicks, John May, Dave Polkinghorne, Anthony Wills, Ted Wills, John Treglowen, Doug Yelland, Terry Gardener, Al Rowe and Geoff Rowe, who we called Jethro, who was just beginning to make a bit of a name for himself as a very Cornish comedian.

The Camels broadened my understanding of Cornwall. Previously, in my local world, it had been the romantic Cornwall of men of the sea, a sort of amalgam of Daphne du Maurier's *Jamaica Inn* with a bit of *Treasure Island* and the rugged fishermen who I met in the pubs of Padstow. Rugby introduced me to a mellower Cornwall. Some of the farmers would actually consider coming to our restaurant and even liked my cooking. For example, the restaurant was always full for the Royal Cornwall Show in June. The same people would come back year after year. Tony Hackett, who had a small caravan at the show selling bull's sperm, and his friend Michael Rosenberg, who kept a flock of Ash sheep in Devon and was a leading light in The Rare Breeds Survival Trust. The journalists from the *Farmers Weekly* came too. The show is a very important week in the life of rural Cornwall. It's still a rare time in the year when the older farmers put on a smart suit, always a nice shade of green and brown tweed, but still with the calloused hands of hard work on the farm.

Michael Rosenberg, who was very well off, had lobster almost every night. He and his friends ordered Dover soles and turbot, and drank our best white Burgundy. They still hold the record for the highest number of *plateaux de fruits de mer* sold to one table – 17. They spent with abandon and after the Cornwall Show each year we were left with a warm feeling of having done some good business with some really lovely customers who were also our friends.

We also started getting regular visits from a group of holidaying young married people from around Oxford who would appear in late June and virtually take the restaurant for two weeks. The leading lights were Philip Minty and his wife Margaret Anne who, like the show people, took my cooking seriously. Philip, whose family made Minty furniture, worked in the catering industry and knew everyone – Roy Ackerman, Anton Mosimann, Raymond Blanc. He'd been joint owner of The Bear in Woodstock. Mingling with him and his friends made me feel we'd finally arrived.

My brother John had married again. His second wife, Clare, had been a catering student at the Bay Tree in Burford. The owner, Silvia Gray, was a good friend of my parents and part of the pleasure of going there, for me and John, was being served by well-mannered girls learning the industry. Clare, who had big brown eyes and an almost Eastern poise, now worked for Corney & Barrow, one of the smartest City wine merchants around. Their managing director was John Armit who had a legendary palate and who had pioneered the practice of buying wines straight from the growers, most notably those of Château Petrus. He was personal friends with the Leoville Barton family and knew the famous white Burgundy-maker Leflaive, as well as Angelo Gaja, the most admired Barbera-maker in Piedmont.

Clare introduced me to her boss, Richard Peat, whose father had started a modest accountancy business, now one of the world's biggest – KPMG. When Richard first visited Padstow it was like nobility arriving. Dressed in a suit of some sort of fine country cloth, he drew up in an old Bristol and produced a couple of boxes of wines from its voluminous boot. The taste of these wines had the effect on me of John Donne's poem 'The Good-Morrow':

> *I wonder by my troth, what thou, and I*
> *Did, till we lov'd? Were we not wean'd till then?*
> *But suck'd on country pleasures, childishly?*

Richard was the perfect gentleman. Lean, handsome, impeccable Old Etonian manners, house in Norfolk, fly fisherman. How could I not buy wine and lots of it from such a paragon? He went on buying trips to Europe every year and of course was an astute businessman underneath all the charm. He gave me good advice about how to run things more efficiently but never in a patronising way. He'd produce bottles of Brouilly or Moulin à Vent and Fleurie and discuss the differences between them. Having got used to the fact that, yes, a smart wine merchant was indeed interested in taking on my business, I became slightly more blasé about his fine wines.

All wine merchants greet you with effusiveness. I soon realised that a couple of boxes of samples and a drunken meal paid for by the wine merchant inevitably ended in orders. There is indeed no such thing as a free lunch. When charming experts came to call bearing gifts, I found I couldn't refuse. The problem is that having a lot of different wine suppliers means lots of accounts and paperwork and lots of lunches.

Two men, one short and a bit plump and the other tall and very plump, started to come frequently to the restaurant. It was clear they liked my cooking, so when I eventually went out from the kitchen to talk to them I was well disposed, and when they told me they were in the wine business I sat down with them. It was like a new chapter in my restaurant life was opening. They were called Charles Reid and Bill Baker. Bill was the leading light of their company, Reid Wines in Bath. He sold wine to Simon Hopkinson, Shaun Hill, Joyce Molyneux at the Carved Angel in Devon and George Perry-Smith at the Riverside in Helford – all chefs whom I was beginning to admire. He made regular trips to Scotland and supplied Grete Hobbs at Inverlochy Castle, David Wilson at Peat Inn in Fife, David and Hilary Brown at La Potinière at Gullane just outside Edinburgh and in Stirling a precocious young chef called Nick Nairn who would go on to be the youngest-ever Michelin star winner in Scotland. Bill ate with them all and remembered everything he ate. Not only that, he had been to every one of the Michelin three-starred restaurants in France – Alain Chapel, the Troisgros Brothers, Bocuse; indeed he had eaten Bocuse's famous *volaille de Bresse truffée en vessie 'Mère Fillioux'*. His wines were sensational; he had an exceptional palate. It turned out that he had been born in Harlyn and retained a love of Cornwall. Whenever Bill came to the restaurant, there was a warm feeling of fun. After cooking, I would sit down with him and share a great wine. Those occasions – with Jill and Bill's wife Kate – are among the happiest in my life.

Of course, Bill's discerning taste buds enjoyed fine food as well as fine wines. With us, he'd eat a large lobster, sometimes two, and start with at least half a dozen oysters. He was very overweight but he carried it well. Every morning he walked his Labradors, however late he'd been to bed. He was a character from another age. His good humour, intelligence and forthrightness were endearing; I never heard a bad word said of him by anyone, even his competitors. Richard Peat spoke of him with commendable warmth. The truth was that Bill didn't reciprocate, he always frowned on my continuing allegiance to Corney & Barrow and, under all the delightful charm, was ruthless in his business dealings. He wanted my whole wine list. In the end I let him write a lot of it, because his comments about wine were always such fun. Not for him the 'hints of peppermint and cedar'.

I've escaped from the kitchen and gone to the table where Bill always stands out, with his vigorously striped shirts and thick green tweed jackets. He wears Church's brogues with thick soles and steel caps so you can hear him coming miles away. His table is a litter of oyster and lobster shells. He has with him a basket with 12 compartments, different red and white wines. The whites are chilled. Some bottles are opened – he has had a taste already. Others are destined for me.

'Ricardo! Sit down. Delicious dinner. Try this, it's a Zind Humbrecht Pinot Blanc. It was fabulous with your scallops. I've kept you some.'

'I've never tasted a Pinot Blanc like it.'

'I was there with Olivier Humbrecht last week. Great dinner at L'Auberge de l'Ill. I had *truffe-sous-la-cendre*, a whole truffle wrapped in foie gras, then pastry, then baked in ashes. Fabulous. But I want you to try this. I've just had it with your lobster.' He then produces a Beaune Clos des Mouches, a white burgundy about which I know nothing. Then follows Montrachet, and he's saying, 'I know you buy all your Burgundy from Richard Peat. You are *so* sweet. But, you know, Raymond Leflaive's handed it all to his nephew Olivier, and I don't think he's any longer making the great wine. Try this.'

'God Bill, that's fantastic. What on earth is it?'

'Ampeau, straight Puligny.'

'Just ordinary Montrachet? I can't believe it.'

'Well, that's Ampeau for you.'

Needless to say Bill had hit it off with Robert Ampeau and seemed to be able to magic old vintages out of his cellar like no one else.

I have come straight from my kitchen and haven't eaten anything. By the time we've tried a couple of reds, maybe a Guigal Côte Rôtie and a sip or two of Sassicaia, and then a sweet wine like a Muscat from the island of Pantelleria off Sicily, I'd be raving with euphoria, at which point Bill says,

'Couple of cases, then?'

'No. Four. And the Clos des Mouches – oh, a couple at least.'

'And the Rôtie?' he adds. 'You know Guigal will only sell me his prize wines if I take plenty of his Côtes du Rhone.'

'Well, two of the Rôtie and 15 of the Côtes du Rhone.'

Next morning, back in the kitchen, I can't quite remember what I'd ordered but by the following day the invoice is in the office.

# VII

These days newspapers and magazines often ask me to do what they call Q & As. Sometimes the questions have me groaning, things like 'What would your last meal on earth be?' If I'm feeling charitable I'll say langoustines and mayonnaise followed by turbot and hollandaise. If not, I'll say, 'Well, I'll probably be feeding through a tube so does it matter?' But sometimes the questions fit in with the way I'm feeling. Such was the case when I was asked who I'd most like to have dinner with.

This happened to be soon after Bill died. He'd suffered a heart attack in 2008 while en route to a wine tasting with me at The Seafood Restaurant. I missed his funeral at Wells Cathedral because I was filming in Cambodia. I still regret not having been there. Missing him terribly, I imagined my ideal dinner party: Bill and his wife Kate, Bill's friend Johnny Apple and his wife Betsey. Len Evans and his wife Trish. Peter Herbert and his wife Sue. Peter had been very helpful to Jill and me when we were building up the restaurant. There was only one problem about this imaginary dinner and, I would guess, most fantasy dinners containing successful people: none of the men apart from Bill and me really got on with each other; they were all a bit alpha male. By then, though, there would be one other at my dinner who would have made everyone get on, who would have read all the undercurrents and simply steered the party into clear air, a lively Australian, a book publicist used to dealing with talented but often difficult authors, Sarah Burns, or Sas to her friends. She had met them all and liked them, particularly Johnny.

I first met Johnny Apple, who wrote as chief political correspondent for the *New York Times* as R. W. Apple, in the early nineties when he and Betsey came to The Seafood with Bill. I knew from Bill that Johnny, as a political correspondent, had been everywhere, even spent time under fire in the Vietnam war. He had run the paper's bureau in London, lived in Washington, had a farm in Connecticut and a cottage in Lechlade in the Cotswolds. Betsey (née Pinckney) was from Charleston, South Carolina and came from a very distinguished southern family. They loved my restaurant and loved my food. He was very keen on the soft-shell crabs from the Camel Estuary, and wrote a piece for the *NYT* in which he described Padstow as 'plug ugly'. I was a bit pissed off. Years later I reminded him what he'd written. 'Well it's not plug ugly now,' he said. Padstow had come up in the world. While travelling everywhere for the *New York Times* Johnny wrote about food, and was far more informative than any food guide. He knew the inside of every Michelin three-star restaurant, of course, but he also loved prosaic food if it was good. He would enthuse equally about the lobster rolls in Maine and the secret spices with the fried fish at Cha Ca La Vong in Hanoi. There was nothing he didn't know about Southern barbecue – the subtle differences between North and South Carolina, Kansas, Memphis and Texas. Like Bill, he seemed to come from another age, maybe pre-revolutionary France; he might have been a guest at one of Brillat-Savarin's lunches. Johnny's ancestors were German immigrants to Akron, Ohio. He used to say that with their can-do attitude, Americans were like Germans – just by a quirk of history they ended up speaking English.

The last time I saw him was at a dinner in Washington at a very good fish restaurant called Pesce. I had been over for a long

Edward, me, Jack and Jill in a publicity shot for a feature in *Woman's Realm* in 1984, at Tregirls Beach, Padstow.

More publicity in the late 1980s.
I quite like these tricksy shots these
days, but you can see from my face
that I disapproved then.

Most of The Seafood Restaurant staff outside in the early nineties. Me, Jill, Heather Bettridge, my nephew Sam O'Riordan, Maxine Avery, Roger Rees, David Wong, Fiona Cock, Gareth Eddy, Paul Hearn, David Pope and Dave Miney.

With Johnny Walter, my best friend and former business partner, flogging me a few lobsters in the early 1990s.

Jill and me in the early nineties looking proud as our restaurant really begins to flourish.

Filming in Padstow with Keith Floyd for the first time. Lunch on a trawler and a glass of Alsace Riesling before sailing out of the harbour to a life in TV.

My brother Jeremy in his garden in Westbourne, West Sussex.

Chalky, me and Mr Copas's Bronze turkeys near Cookham, Berkshire, filming *Christmas Food Heroes* in 2005.

The Denhams TV crew's audience with the Dalai Lama. He described us as the oldest TV crew he'd met, nearly as old as him. Some of our younger members didn't find it as amusing as those of us who had to admit he had a point. Arezoo Farahzad, Chris Topliss, Pete Underwood, David, me, the Dalai Lama, Bernard Hall, Chris Denham.

David Pritchard and me having a theatrical argument about vindaloo in Himachal Pradesh, India. Cameraman Chris Topliss and sound recordist Pete Underwood look on.

Charles, Edward, Jack and me visiting a grappa maker on a truffle hunting trip to Piedmont, Italy, in November 2011.

Sas and me at The Bathers' Pavilion, Balmoral Beach, Sydney, April 2013.

Olivia, Zach, me and Sas at Pipeline Beach, Hawaii, April 2013. Could even have gone for a wave myself that day.

weekend with my brother, John, selling the idea of omega-3 fish oils to the great and the good at a couple of dinners at the Willard Hotel. Johnny was absolutely in his element – politicians and journalists dropping by to say hello, included Seymour Hersh who broke the story of the My Lai massacre in the Vietnam war. Johnny had caught up with my TV programmes and recognised that they were indeed about more than just cookery. He understood that it gave us our reason – our platform – for filming somewhere like Cambodia, but that cookery was just the starting point from which we could go on to say whatever we needed to about poverty and the Khmer Rouge, the atmosphere, the architecture, even the civil war.

I had lunch with Johnny and Betsey in Sydney, once at Tetsuya's and once at Est, both great restaurants, and each time he knew the chef and knew the dishes. Both times I went with Sarah Burns. At Est, a favourite of mine where Peter Doyle is head chef, Sarah's little son Zach was building a shopping centre out of a white shoe box at the end of the table and Johnny stopped talking about food and spent 20 minutes discussing the construction with Zach. He took delight in many different things. He died in 2008, the same year as Bill.

Len Evans was like a second father to me. I had first met him in the 1980s when I was once more staying in Australia with the Ifoulds. Ed Ifould's mother, Mary, suggested that my friend Johnny Walter and I should go and see Len. I protested he would be far too busy but she insisted I give him a ring, that he wouldn't mind. Later, he liked to tell people he had arranged to see some Cornish boys at 11 a.m. and expected to be through by 11.30. 'I was,' he said. 'Through by 11.30 that evening.'

Even then, Len was famous as a wine maker and it proved to be quite a day. When we arrived, he was firing a batch of tiles he'd made in a small kiln he had installed in one of the corrugated iron and hardwood outhouses on his farm which he called, with typical humour, Loggerheads. The largely figurative designs had an almost medieval simplicity about them and when fired the tiles were vividly coloured, bright yellows and blues. He'd already started plastering them into the walls of the arched entrance to the rambling single-storey house. He had only just come out of hospital from heart surgery but that wasn't going to stop him opening bottles of Evans family wine, a choice malolactic Chardonnay from his company, Rothbury Estate, and later that night a 30-year-old Château Margaux. There were bottles from wine-making friends like Murray Tyrrell, Brian Croser and James Halliday, and a couple from further afield, including a Bâtard-Montrachet.

After lunch Johnny and I retired to our motel for a snooze but after what seemed no more than a couple of minutes, Len was on the phone demanding we meet him in the pub in Pokolbin. We had a quick look round the winery at Rothbury, then he took us on a drive through his property in his four-wheel drive Mitsubishi Pajero with kangaroos hopping away to left and right as we drove through the gum trees past a dam he'd recently put in and a sculpture he'd created out of antique wooden gears. We went back to Loggerheads where he and Trish cooked us a three-course supper starting with scallops in the shell with a wine and cream sauce, then simple lamb chops, then Trish's trifle, made without fruit which is the way I always make it now. I can't remember the very old vintages of Bordeaux which we had with all this – after the first bottle of Margaux one became a bit blasé.

I saw Len and Trish many times in the following 20 years, both in the Hunter Valley and in Padstow. Though very Australian, he was born in Suffolk of Welsh parents and always had an affection for his country of birth. He loved fish and chips. He suggested that a simple white-tiled restaurant with slate floors and wooden tables and a rigorously pure menu celebrating traditional fish and chips would work in Padstow. He was right: we opened Stein's Fish and Chips and it has proved very successful.

Len had persuaded Jill and me to invest in his new wine-making company. He called it Tower Estate, and we've had its wines on the list at Padstow for 15 years. Len's infectious optimism seemed to be the answer to everything. It was his sense of humour which I most remember.

The last words on Len go to Jancis Robinson, one of his close friends:

> 'We were served more than two dozen great Australian wines blind, plus a magnum of Le Montrachet as "quaffing white" and almost a dozen other treasures including an 1890 Chambers Rutherglen Muscat. Afterwards, we reeled out into the night counting the blessings of this 30-year friendship as we blinked up at the Southern Cross. The next day, we learnt via a newsflash in Sydney airport that he had been found dead in his car that morning while picking up his wife Trish from hospital. The heart that had struggled for 75 years against all the odds to keep up with the appetites and passions of this pugnacious hedonist finally gave up.'

Johnny Apple, Bill Baker, Len Evans – probably all of them would have lived longer if they hadn't enjoyed the pleasures of the table so much. It was almost as if their enthusiasm for eating and drinking was an act of defiance. They had a sense of the heroic about them which I admire. I don't think any of their wives admired it too much, though. All left families who miss them very much.

I like rather loud men. In spite of the fact I was a little afraid of my father, I look back with fondness on my childhood with a loud man who] was larger-than-life and pushy and naturally always the centre of attention. I think that, however uncomfortable it was at times, it was reassuring that my dad was the lion. Johnny was just such a man, often irascible, often cross with Betsey, but he was always in charge – as was Bill, as was Len, as is Peter. Lions, all of them.

PART FOUR

# Giddy Times

# I

In 1984 *The Sunday Times* ran a national restaurant competition in conjunction with the RAC: they invited members of the public to nominate their favourite restaurant. Tony Hackett who spent every night of the week of the Royal Cornwall Show in The Seafood Restaurant, put us forward – and we were voted best restaurant in England.

At the time I had started writing monthly fish recipes for *Woman's Realm* magazine. I got the job simply because I knew the editor, Richard Barber. I found writing these articles really hard. I had no idea what the average reader of *Woman's Realm* wanted and I didn't get a lot of feedback, but Richard seemed happy with my recipes and the cookery editor, Christine France, was so keen on them that she arranged a photo feature. We worked on that one picture for about five hours. I still have it. I'm holding a copper pot of fish stew and I look horribly nervous.

Getting a regular cookery column in a magazine gave me an insight into how publicity worked, so when we won the Best Restaurant Award I typed a single sheet of paper with information about the prize and, on Richard's advice, sent it to all the local TV and radio stations and local newspapers. It had an immediate effect. Television South West sent a journalist who took one look at the menu which, of course, featured lobster grilled and lobster cold, and proceeded to conduct an interview with me of the I-can't-believe-you're-still-in-business-charging-these-prices sort of thing. I was too naive to stand up for myself and point out that, yes lobster was £10, but everything else was under £5. I didn't have the nous to argue that here was a restaurant staffed by young people who were trying to do something excellent in the West Country. The journalist from BBC South West, Sue King, couldn't have been more different. She liked what we were doing and sampled a meal in the restaurant. Not only did she do a very nice piece on the local news about us but, more importantly – much more importantly – she mentioned my restaurant to a friend of hers who was working for the BBC in Bristol. He was called David Pritchard.

David was a habitué of Keith Floyd's restaurant in Clifton, Bristol, and had featured Keith on a Friday night TV programme called *RPM*, distinguished, as he hilariously pointed out in his book *Shooting The Cook*, by an enormous number of appearances by The Stranglers because he liked them so much. David also employed Keith to do some cookery slots and together, in Keith's restaurant, they hatched a plan to produce a series for the West Country called *Floyd on Fish*. They were looking for places in the south west where the fish cooking was of note. They chose The Horn of Plenty and – thanks to the good word that Sue King had put in for us – The Seafood Restaurant.

I decided to do a new bass dish for the occasion. I took a julienne of carrot, leek and celery and simmered it gently in butter, then added some white wine and stuffed the cavity of the bass with the mixture. I roasted the fish in the oven and served it with a sorrel sauce which was a food-processor version of a hollandaise with lots of sorrel thrown in at the last minute so that the greenness of the leaf came out in the sauce. (You don't want the sauce to turn brown as soon as the sorrel is cooked.) I'm still proud of this dish.

I'd already met Keith a couple of times because he visited Padstow with his second wife, Julie, and their daughter Poppy. Keith knew North

Cornwall well because his first wife, Jesmond, had come from Port Isaac. He had been complimentary about the restaurant and had given me some good advice about the Provençal fish dishes I was cooking at the time, notably the *bourride* which I had worked out from my memories of eating the dish in St Tropez and what I'd gathered from recipes in Alan Davidson's *Mediterranean Seafood*, as well as recipes by Elizabeth David and Jane Grigson. Keith gave me an idea for serving it with a slice of baguette fried in olive oil and rubbed with garlic, then spread with harissa, the North African paste of pounded chillies, red peppers, cumin and coriander. He had a confidence about him. He had cooked classic all-French dishes such as *bourride* and *bouillabaisse* for French people in their own foodie heartland of Provence – and had passed the test. He used to claim that local French restaurants were so regional that a perfect *boeuf Bourguignon* was available only in Burgundy, while only in Alsace could you eat a perfect *coq au Riesling*. I was in awe of him. He spoke with public-school swagger, drank whisky with American dry ginger ale and smoked many Marlboro reds which gave his voice an attractive gravelly edge.

I was excited when the crew arrived. David Pritchard – with a mischievous sparkle in his eye – gave the impression of only being interested in what was for lunch. His PA, Frances Wallis, was attractive, Scottish and constantly exasperated by David's ever-changing plans. The tall, slightly patrician cameraman was called Clive North. Keith treated Clive as if he was rather stupid and never in the right place at the right time with his camera – a clever ploy because it made the viewers feel they were sharing directly in Keith's culinary secrets and that the filming, though necessary, was an intrusion. Then there was Timmy West, the sound recordist, who was all over the place with dynamic youthful enthusiasm. The net effect on me was of a world much more attractive and much more dynamic than my own.

Keith and I cooked together. He said, 'Now, Nick, what exactly are we cooking this morning?'

'Roasted sea bass. Actually, old boy, it's Rick, not Nick.'

'Nick, Rick, you new young chefs are two a penny.'

I wasn't fazed by this one bit, and I loved cooking with Keith. After we'd cooked the bass, they all ate my lunch. I had spent some time worrying about this. Even then, I sensed that showing off would not go down well. I cooked small sirloin steaks, thin crisp chips and a salad of tomato, red onion and fresh thyme with the dressing I've always used – four parts olive oil and one part red wine vinegar with a pinch of salt and a pinch of sugar. I served a bottle or two of Beaujolais with the steaks and instead of pudding I produced some cheese so we could finish off the wine. No big deal. But it was exactly right; the sort of food both Keith and David absolutely loved.

After lunch we got down to filming. It was a lovely sunny afternoon. David decided to shoot the bass not in the restaurant but on the quayside. A table was prepared on the edge right next to a trawler which was almost level with the quay as it was high tide by then. It was to be just Keith and me with a bottle of Trimbach Riesling.

David suddenly said, 'Let's put the whole thing on the boat.'

So it was that Keith and I found ourselves sitting at a table with a white cloth, eating sea bass and toasting each other with Alsace Riesling as we sailed down the Camel Estuary in the golden light of late afternoon – and I felt I was sailing off to a new and exciting life with all these fabulous new people.

*Floyd on Fish* was a great success. It was originally intended to be a local programme but even I could see it was going to become a lot more than that. Keith was a real bloke, slightly arrogant, drinking while he cooked. He also had a mission: to make the British enjoy the great seafood in our waters all around the British Isles, and to show an enthusiasm equal to that of the French and Spanish. The fact that Keith didn't cook in a studio was radically new. Keith reminded me of Graham Kerr, the Galloping Gourmet who I'd worked with in Sydney so many years before – but Keith was much more dangerous. Cocky on-screen, he lived life at full speed. He really was like a rock and roll star, rather like what The Byrds wrote in their song 'So You Want to Be a Rock 'n' Roll Star'. When he and I filmed again in Padstow, I cooked porbeagle shark. Keith's son Patrick later came to work with us for a few years, a lovely boy. Then each time I saw Keith he seemed a little less fun, a little more into being a star. He took to wearing very expensive suits and Burberry coats. He was always sartorial but the new Keith was in a different league. He bought a white Bentley and had the first mobile phone I'd ever seen; he used to phone our house to say he was outside in his car.

In 1991 I was invited to appear on Keith's *This is Your Life*. When the time came for me to be revealed he was very un-pleased to see me. This was unsettling, to say the least. I put it down to Keith's resentment of my growing friendship with David Pritchard. Meanwhile, Keith's drinking was creating problems for David and the crew on their next project *Floyd on Oz*.

He had become a little insane, I would go so far as to surmise, but fortunately he employed a Kiwi girl called Maggie McClaren to act as the tour manager who also drove them, and who was not afraid to stand up to him and he in turn liked her for it. I have a great affection for Australians and Kiwis, and from my formative years there often think of myself as half Australian. I admire their straightforwardness and fearless approach to people. Maggie was a shining example. She would have told Keith exactly what she thought about his less-than-perfect behaviour while filming. But it was Maggie's mistake, perhaps, to fall in love with David Pritchard, which Keith wasn't happy about. After the series Maggie came to England to be with David, and when David and Keith finally parted company after *Far Flung Floyd* in 1994 it was Maggie who helped steer David in my direction for TV.

David had been instrumental in getting me a slot in a local TV programme called *Village Green*, on which I was the judge of the best cooking. I wore a purple striped blazer and mostly the food was appalling – I mean utterly appalling. It's hard to recall how terrible cooking in Britain could be in those far-off days before everyone watched food programmes and reality TV. Of course there were exceptions and standards – and the wondrous Women's Institute – but *Village Green* had me filming in a pub where the landlady was cooking in her dark kitchen at the back. It was tiny and there was no extraction. The filming lights and the landlady's stew made the smell of two aged Labradors in unspeakable dog baskets almost unbearable. I did it, though, because my brief appearances with Keith had given me the TV bug. I started appearing on local TV whenever I was asked, doing little slots on barbecues or what to do with summer mackerel.

Speaking directly to a camera, however, is much harder to do than passing judgement on a fish pie with no seasoning or filleting a mackerel. It's a bit like bursting into song or dancing a foxtrot on your own, you just have to let yourself go – but if you're shy as I am, it's very hard. I tried some tests but my TV delivery was terrible – limp and stilted. David said, 'Think of the camera as your little friend, someone who you're confiding in. And don't be you, *play* being you.'

I tried again, and David said, 'Can't you talk on camera like you talk in the restaurant? After we've had dinner? And three bottles of wine between us?'

I went to Plymouth to do what I knew would be the final camera test – last-chance saloon. I stood on the quay feeling hungover after an indulgent evening but with that sense of euphoria you get after talking late into the night. I just didn't care. That did the trick. I got the job.

It's always been the same ever since. The thought of doing a piece to camera is nerve-wracking, but doing it, getting over my natural reserve and getting on with it, gives me a wonderful sense of achievement.

Before filming started a few months later for our first cookery series, *Taste of the Sea*, I got glandular fever. This was really hard as I was cooking all the time in the restaurant. I had to give up for a couple of months and leave Paul Ripley, our excellent sous chef, to take over. When we began to film the series I felt really ill. I struggled to cook, sweating all the time and feeling weak. David was all for abandoning the project but Maggie, bless her, said, 'We will persevere.' Years later, I asked her about it.

*You were shocking and David was convinced he had made a great error of judgement. I remember the scrunch, scrunch of his shoes pacing on the gravel of your drive,' she wrote. ' "What am I going to do? He is terrible. He just ain't got it. How am I going to tell him? I've made a big mistake. I'm fucked." He was very distressed, if he had any hair he would have been tearing at it. He'd put all his future hopes in you being fabulous.*

*But we were really partners in those days, Rick, and he used to listen to my opinions and of course he did this time.*

*'You are wrong. He is really sick and it was his first time with that kind of pressure in front of the camera. It is totally unrealistic to expect anyone to be brilliant first time confronted with a camera and you don't help him. He is a sensitive soul, not*

*brash and full of bravado like Floyd. This is better. You have to*
*give him another chance. And let me tell you the most important*
*thing, he has that illusive quality, that men will relate to him*
*and women will love him ... he is like a teddy bear, you want*
*to hug him.'*

Looking at that first series now I can see how weak I was from the
fever but it doesn't really show to others, even the sequence which
got the family dog Chalky a part. We had been filming in our kitchen
at Trevone. I think it was salmon with sorrel sauce, and David was
trying to get me to voice my thoughts about what it's like working
in a restaurant. We moved into the living room and I sat on the sofa
and, almost as a prop, David lifted Chalky and sat him next to me. I
started talking to camera and Chalky started growling. I asked David
if he wanted me to carry on and he nodded. So again I started but
by then Chalky was growling so loudly, that I said, 'Chalky are you
all right, old boy?' and then Chalky gave a great snuffle and the next
minute he had leapt up and bitten the fluffy cover on the microphone
above my head. I keeled over laughing. It was particularly funny
because I had been gallantly trying to keep the show going, as ever.
David, of course, saw it as a perfect bloopers-type sequence, and so it
turned out to be: Chalky's performance on that day got him a part in
every series till he died in 2004.

Richard Barber did me another favour. He mentioned to a friend
at Penguin Books that they might want to publish a book by me. I
was amazed. I did not realise at the time that publishers are always
on the lookout for new young writers, that that's how it works. I
was contacted by a non-fiction editor, Eleo Gordon, but I was not
hopeful when I went to meet her. I suppose I thought that it would

be a bit like going to see a tutor at university. I was, at that stage, very much a chef and, though I still read all the time, I felt remote from the world of literature. She was a bit academic but also jolly, funny and relaxed. She had already seen some of my pieces and seemed to have no doubt that I could manage to write a whole full-length book. I was rather overawed by her position because Penguin published the cookery writers I loved: Jane Grigson, Richard Olnay, my mother's best friend at Cambridge Elizabeth Ayrton, who had written a book on English food which I very much admired. Penguin had them all, including the star in my firmament, Elizabeth David. 'Elizabeth David could be the most disagreable woman,' Eleo said. 'She once threw a cookery book at me.'

Eleo gave me a copy of Josceline Dimbleby's *Favourite Food*. She told me to read it to get some ideas. I worried over it for days. It painted a picture of joyful family life, with Josceline stopping every now and then to jot down another favourite recipe, and it rather drove home the fact that I didn't really have much family life. True, I cooked every Sunday evening for Jill and my two sons Edward and Jack (Charles had just been born) but my life was the restaurant day after day, night after night. Any books by me would have to be a book of recipes from the restaurant. I decided to call it *English Seafood Cookery*.

My mother lent me a book called *Good Things in England* by Florence White. Out of some 360 pages of recipes, only ten were for fish and the recipes seemed to show a heavy-handed approach to cooking such dishes as eel pie, breaded smelts dropped into a pan of boiling lard, stewed oyster and fish roll. The recipe for Cornish Stargazey pie had pilchards in a pie dish with lots of butter and double cream; the heads stuck through a rich shortcrust so that as they cooked the fish oil ran down into the cream. I wrote in my introduction, to 'fill a book with recipes with an English flavour one has to look elsewhere than in traditional English cookery and this is where the recipes from my restaurant come in'. I continued by describing English seafood cookery as 'the cookery by English chefs of fish from English coastal waters in an English port for English people. I may borrow from France, Italy and even China, India and Japan but everything is finely filtered by the place where I work and the people I cook for'. Would that I had substituted the word 'British' a few times to appease the Welsh, Scottish and Irish!

It took a long time to write that first book, mostly because I was cooking in the restaurant every night but also because I had to test all the recipes without any help. These days I work with a home economist. The recipes in *English Seafood Cookery* are a mixture of French and English dishes such as moules marinière, Provençal fish soup, bouillabaisse, skate with black butter and poached halibut steaks with hollandaise. Alongside this classic food are dishes that I made up. I'm proud of these, and many of them are still on the menu at The Seafood Restaurant, even, occasionally, poêlé of conger eel. Tom Chivers at Camborne Tech had taught me how to poêlé. Usually it's done in a casserole with slightly tough pieces of beef like silverside or a shoulder of lamb, which need slow cooking, and you use lots of root vegetables including carrots, onions, garlic, leeks and celery, sweated in the casserole dish with the lid on. In this case, I larded a loin of conger eel with slivers of garlic and wrapped it in pig's caul fat to enrich it before slow casseroling it. I served it sliced and suggested a chilled Beaujolais alongside. The red casserole dish used for cooking this is on the original cover of the book.

The book was illustrated by an artist called Katinka Kew who's sadly died since the book was published in 1988. I love the illustrations. We can't go back, people like photographs of food these days but this book was made by her drawings. She came down for two or three weeks and sketched me in the kitchen and in my vegetable garden at home. She went down to the quay and politely asked many a tourist to bugger off when they came up to question what she was doing while she drew a platter of fish. She drew a couple of the staff, Wendy Tarby and Linda Dakin, sitting on the sunny terrace above the restaurant, another of my friends David Evans offloading fish from his trawler and Jill, Johnny and Terri eating in The Seafood Restaurant. *English Seafood Cookery* is a lovely-looking book. I used to be rather embarrassed by one recipe – Anchovy Ice Cream – but these days, thanks to Heston Blumenthal, I'm not.

I finished the book in a flurry of activity in early December 1986 just days before my fortieth birthday and departure for Singapore and Australia for a six-week holiday with Jill and my three boys and Johnny and Terri. I was looking forward to going back to Australia. It felt like a reunion with a long-lost love. It lived up to expectation and we went there again in 1988. Good Australian restaurants had begun to appear everywhere. Neil Perry was cooking at Barrenjoey House at Palm Beach and then he opened the Blue Water Grill at North Bondi. There was simply nothing like it in the UK; it was always crammed and the cooking was right up my street, chargrilled seafood. Very simple decor but you didn't need much with that view over the sea. I remember feeling very envious of the name too: the Blue Water Grill, very California but very Sydney too. I was also influenced by a restaurant in Clareville in an old clapperboard house with wooden floors called The Kiosk; I can still remember a pan-fried whiting with a brown butter sauce and capers. And a couple of very smart young Australians – tanned, languid and long. He had on some beige linen trousers, she in a blue cotton dress. He had a pair of memorable shoes, pointed thin-soled brogues but with wide slits in the leather so you could see his bare brown feet. These little details – the simple lovely fish, Pittwater outside, the trendy young Aussies, the homespun nature of The Kiosk – were a powerful pointer to where I wanted to go.

In Singapore we stayed at Raffles. Nasi Lemak and congee for breakfast and for lunch, fish head curry in the Apollo in Little India which was rugged: a spice grinder with whirring pulleys in the kitchen and everything eaten off banana leaves. We ate chicken satays in hawkers' markets and Hainanese chicken rice in a restaurant with lizards running down the walls.

One evening Johnny and I hailed a taxi outside Raffles.

'You want girls?' asked the cabby.

'No, we want chilli crab.'

He jammed on his brakes and, somewhat shamefaced, we got out on Purvis Street yards away from the hotel. I've made many a chilli crab since then. Indeed, we do a version in The Seafood Restaurant recently praised by a Singaporean for the quality of the brown crabs we use. Nothing, however, will ever live up to the delight of that first one. I remember my surprise at the amount of white meat in the local swimming crabs (Thalamita spinimana) and the ease with which I could extract the thick white meat from the thin flexible shells, so much easier than the thick, sometimes sharp, shells of ours. The fragrant chilli sauce had a deep redness and a sweet heat. It was also perhaps the first time I truly realised the pleasure of eating spicy food with copious amounts of boiled rice and also the recognition of the exquisiteness of combining all this with large bottles of ice-cold Tiger beer. Johnny and I smoked roll-up fags and talked a lot with delightful euphoria. Later I went out back for a pee and narrowly missed tripping over a rat in the kitchen.

That first trip was marked by parental neglect. The boys got sunburned by the pool in Raffles, and Ed and Jack – playing that irritating game of running up the down the escalators, commonly indulged in at airports after 24-hour flights – disappeared into countless upstairs storeys in a large department store. I feared they'd end up in the street somewhere in a strange oriental city, and knew with paranoid fatherly certainty that they'd be sold into slavery. These days I realise that it's more likely to happen in London than Singapore. Jack and Charles have inherited my wanderlust – and perhaps they got a taste for it on trips when they were children.

At the Ronil Beach Resort in Goa I found the owner, Rui Madre Deus, happy to share his recipes. I would stand in the kitchen on hot evenings watching him turning out pomfret recheado and shark vindaloo made with hammerheads. I got to know his chefs and realised that there was no difference: the delights and the frustrations of cooking in Goa were the same as Padstow. After my wonder about the spice grinder in the Banana Leaf Apollo in Singapore, I became intrigued by the two grinders that Rui had in the basement. I realised that the secret of Indian cuisine was that the spices and masalas were all freshly ground. In a shop in Panjim I found a little grinder about the size of a Honda generator. I bought it and took it home on the Monarch flight. It had stone wheels and worked like a mortar and pestle, though driven by an electric motor. I made Goan masala paste with it for sale in the deli that I opened in 1982. I featured it in the first series *Taste of the Sea* where, almost on cue, the plastic retaining nuts on the stone wheels split and the whole thing came hilariously apart, never to be reassembled, though Rui did send some spare nuts over from Goa. During the filming of *Taste of the Sea* I managed quite a few mini-disasters. I suppose my cuts and abrasions have become a bit of a trademark of my TV persona. Perhaps it's appealing to the viewers that I so graphically illustrate that I'm as capable of making a mess of things as the next man, and of giving the cheerful impression of not minding. I do mind, in fact. But I realise that upsets and a good laugh make excellent television.

Rui used to pack a kilo or so of vindaloo paste into a coffee jar, then wrapped that in foil. I secreted it in my suitcase and it always ran into my clothes. But I was grateful because it gave me a chance to try to copy the flavour, armed, too, with Rui's recipe for the vindaloo. Even so, the vindaloo I make in Padstow doesn't taste quite the same. I'm never quite sure why. Maybe the cloves are different, perhaps it's not having any toddy vinegar – or maybe I'm not eating the hammerhead shark vinadaloo out in the warm wet evening air of west India, with the smell of burning rubbish, joss sticks and cheap perfume and the sound of dogs barking in the fields.

# II

In 1982 The Seafood Restaurant was open seven nights, but not lunchtimes. I started to feel I wasn't getting enough value out of the chefs, so hit on the idea of making food for a shop. There was a wool shop for sale for £32,000 in a street behind the cinema. Middle Street was not a great location but it was cheap. I discovered that the house behind was also for sale for £35,000. I was beginning to see the sense of having some staff accommodation, so we bought them both. In the premises of the wool shop, we opened a deli. I equipped it with a second-hand chiller cabinet and we started selling things that we made in the restaurant kitchen, including fish soup and fish cakes. We boiled gammons and roasted them with mustard, cloves and brown sugar, a recipe that my mother always made for Boxing Day. I did rare roast beef and the potato salads and coleslaws that I remembered from childhood. We poached salmon and made hummus and taramasalata from the products of a Greek company who sold us the Kalamata olives for the restaurant. In Elizabeth David's *English Bread and Yeast Cookery* I discovered an easy-to-make wholewheat bread called the Grant loaf to which I added walnuts. I invented a bubble and squeak cake, which I made with balls of the left-over spring cabbage and new potatoes we'd served the night before, passed them through beaten egg and breadcrumbs made from left-over bread then fried in beef dripping. School food, but delicious.

I made pâtés and terrines, I made gravlax with the abundant salmon from the Camel Estuary and gravad mackerel with the same cure. Sunny Saturday mornings with no lunch service were a hallowed time for me at my worktop, the back door open to the quay, Radio 4 on, Jim McOwen dropping in a salmon caught at dawn that morning. My worktop was only about five foot long and two wide but it was my special place. One of my chefs told me years later he'd had sex with one of our waitresses across my worktop, almost just because it was my prized worktop.

You can't earn much money out of a deli because the time and cost of making small quantities of lots of different things is never justified by what you can charge for them. Eventually, I realised I'd have to turn the upstairs of the shop into some sort of cafe to make the deli pay. By then I'd turned the basement of the house behind into a bakery where we also made Cornish pasties. I don't think we made much money in the bakery either, but my figures weren't good enough to confirm this. Or perhaps I didn't want to know. I loved our pasties; still do. They've been criticised for not using the correct pastry, but I make them as I like them, using beef skirt, swede, potato and onion, lots of salt and pepper, and rough-puff pastry made with butter only. Our pasties were on the menu, of course, in the cafe, as well as quiches, sandwiches and espresso coffee.

In 1990, we expanded the cafe into the building next door. It has a more ambitious menu including salt and pepper prawns, Vietnamese pho, huevos rancheros and steak frites. It's still there in Middle Street but I had the sense to change its name from the original Middle Street Cafe to Rick Stein's Cafe, after I realised that being on TV had serious commercial advantages.

I had an additional reason for opening the deli and the cafe: I wanted to attract more people to The Seafood Restaurant and I realised I should also try to attract more people to Padstow. The Seafood Restaurant had flourished to the extent that Jill and I were able to buy Johnny's holiday flats above for a sum which reflected our indebtedness to him. We converted them into eight bedrooms. We bought all the beds second-hand from a large warehouse in Cambridgeshire (they had been taken out of a Hilton) and the carpet came from a roll in the same place. We made sure that every bedroom had its own bathroom. We had to install a noisy macerator pump, a bit like a waste disposal unit, which whizzed everything into a mush and sent it down a 22mm pipe. Many was the time when I had to dismantle this pump after someone had put a baby's disposable nappy down the loo. My job entailed picking tiny bits of crappy plastic out of the impeller inside the unit.

Every year we ploughed most of our profit into improving the rooms and we installed proper sewage pipes just before an Easter opening for yet another season. We then quickly discovered water dripping through the new recessed low-voltage lights in the restaurant ceiling on to the starched white tablecloths below. I panicked. I thought it was our new wide-bore sewage pipes. I knocked on the doors of all the rooms above and discovered the source of the leak in bedroom 5. The guests had gone out for a walk. The bath was empty but the bathroom floor was still damp, and soaking wet towels everywhere. We assumed they had left the taps running and then done an inadequate mopping-up operation. Meeting them again some years later, they admitted they'd over-filled the bath, then become far too excited with each other in it and, though they knew water was slopping all over the floor, they hadn't been able to stop.

Ah, the life of an innkeeper! The stuff that some people take – towels of course, and sheets sometimes, and pillows – but also the things they leave behind ... Letting out rooms, however, is much more profitable than restaurants. Once the building, decoration and fittings are paid for, the main expenses are loo paper, soap, breakfast, bed-making, cleaning and service. For about 15 years we were able to buy cheap properties to convert into rooms.

St Petroc's had been built in the sixteenth century by a friend of Sir Walter Raleigh. It had been added to over the centuries and, by the time I came to look at it in the early eighties, it was a substantial house, with about seven bedrooms, but it had been a semi-derelict doss house for a long time. I looked over it with the owner George Mott, and was fascinated by its history and faded splendour. It had a ballroom on the first floor with a vaulted ceiling and a fireplace with arabesque vine scrolls in the Adams style. But I was overwhelmed by the atmosphere of decay that prevailed. Mushrooms, moss and ferns everywhere, the depressing smell of damp, an acrid odour of coal fires and bodies, and pathetic attempts here and there by the residents to bring a little humanity around their sleeping bags or stained mattresses with a splash of paint or a photo torn out of a magazine. George offered it to me for £25,000, but even my willingness to have a go was daunted by the size of the job. I said no. Some years later a man called John Shaw, who had made some money working on oil rigs, did it up. It was 1988, the country was in recession and he wanted £230,000 for it. Our accountant and bank manager tried to persuade me not to buy it, but all I could see by then was a growing demand for our rooms.

It's pure nostalgia to remember that bank managers were once local people with offices in small towns like Wadebridge and green leather-topped desks with matching blotting paper holders, blotters and pen holders in pale blue. Ours was called Mr Sharp. He looked a bit like Martin Sheen and he is my hero. He enabled us to buy

St Petroc's out of our turnover at the height of that season and he extended our winter overdraft.

St Petroc's has been the conservative heart of our business ever since. The Seafood Restaurant, though now really smart, was always just a rather ugly converted granary. St Petroc's was a lovely Elizabethan house and, as we improved it, it became our own comfortable hotel in the heart of Padstow. Even though we had two restaurants by then, The Seafood and the cafe, I couldn't resist re-opening the hotel restaurant. We served breakfasts there anyway, but I decided to establish a little bistro serving simple French food like gigot of lamb and steak frites. I reasoned that if I could give the hotel restaurant a meat inclination it wouldn't compete with The Seafood menu. The first summer we opened it, 1989, I cooked there two or three times a week, leaving the new sous chef who I'd just taken on at The Seafood, Paul Ripley, to hold the fort down the road. I remember walking down St Edmunds Lane from St Petroc's to The Seafood one summer evening and feeling rather entrepreneurial at having two restaurants within walking distance of each other and thinking that one day I might own all one side of the lane because I'd just bought the old garage on the same side for car parking for the hotel. It almost turned out like that. Puffin House, just behind the restaurant, became more rooms. Then in 2001 we bought St Edmund's House, the only other large house in the lane, and turned that into four large rooms. By then we owned all the lane except for the last house on the corner across from St Petroc's which I turned down recently because property prices have become too steep to justify buying large houses to turn into rooms. Indeed by the time we bought a little house further up the hill out of Padstow called Bryn Cottage, in 2008, it was becoming impossible to do any more. I think the expression is 'hoisted by my own petard'. Not that we hadn't done well with our accommodation. Earlier, we had turned the rooms above the cafe into what we called bed and breakfast rooms, still with their own bathrooms but smaller and therefore cheaper. We'd bought the house next door to St Petroc's, St Decamon's, which had been part of the original Elizabethan house, and converted it into four rooms looking out over either the estuary or the prettiest part of Padstow.

By then, 2008, I had made seven TV series and written nine books, and had generated more than enough publicity for Padstow. So much so, that a journalist had dubbed it 'Padstein', a name which stuck. I was embarrassed by it but slightly chuffed too. Many of the locals, that is the Padstonians who have lived there for generations, regard the effect of our business on the town as a good thing because we bring employment – but not all. No, by no means all. We were met by a barrage of complaints when we put in planning permission for Prospect House in 2005. There was lots of opposition from residents nearby. It was a difficult location off a narrow street bordered almost exclusively by holiday accommodation. The owner of one such holiday home had set his heart on buying Prospect House and when we outbid him we'd made an enemy. What irritated me was that none of the owners of these houses was local: most had recently bought properties to let out, cashing in, I reckoned, on the prosperity brought to Padstow by our popularity, so we were being opposed by people whose reason for being there was us. But this was a dangerous attitude to take, as I learned to my cost.

Prospect House was behind St Petroc's. Eventually we demolished it and built a brand-new house in its place. The complaints mounted: mud on the road from the demolition, road closures while the drains were laid. We received letters demanding compensation for lost business in March and April. I felt indignant. 'If we hadn't been there,' I argued to our general manager Rupert Wilson, 'they wouldn't be attracting *any* business in March.' He agreed but advised a diplomatic response.

Like a fool, I wrote an email to one of the outraged holiday home owners saying, in effect, give us a break, it's only a modest house. I concluded by pointing out that we were all benefitting from the 'rosy glow of publicity' which me being on television had brought to Padstow.

He promptly sent my email to the local paper, the *Cornish Guardian*, which published it the following day. The next thing, I was the villain of the piece. National newspapers picked up the story but worse was to come. I had apparently alienated the 'Cornish Liberation Army' which at the time was keen to get all non-Cornish entrepreneurs out of the county, notably me and Jamie Oliver who has a restaurant at Watergate Bay near Newquay. I received a letter informing me that the 'rosy glow' they'd seen in my email in the paper would shortly be my restaurant burning down.

Someone smashed every window in the front of the restaurant in the middle of the night. We had the glass replaced by 8.30 a.m. and, miraculously, avoided the rosy glow of publicity.

All this led me to rue the day I ever got cross with those holiday home owners. It's part of the price you have to pay for being well known. But also, I admit, the price of hubris.

～

When I was first a success on TV and people started recognising me in the street it made me feel claustrophobic. It's a shock, losing your anonymity. But I wouldn't say it's all negative. We all like to be noticed, it's one way we cope with our essential isolation. But realising that you have to respond in some sort of official way to people greeting you is unnerving.

I was tipping kitchen waste into the large wheelie bin outside the kitchen door.

'You're Rick Stein, aren't you?'

'Look, I'm emptying the rubbish,' I said, straining to get a bag full of fish guts over the edge.

'I'm so sorry,' the man said. 'I love your programme.'

'Yeah, OK, but can't you see I'm busy?'

'Sorry,' he said again. His body language was crestfallen as he walked away and I felt awful.

I made a resolution to be good-humoured with anyone who spoke to me. I saw it as self-protection. If I didn't react nicely I would come off worse then or later, because I would feel bad about it. Why should I care? Some people don't. It's something that slightly irritates me about myself: I still like to be liked. I can't bear people thinking ill of me. There is a practical advantage though; a smile and a 'nice to meet you' keeps the conversation short. Neither you nor the person who has greeted you really wants to prolong the exchange. It's not what recognising celebrities is about. What is it about? I think it's a wish in people, myself included, to make contact with someone we perceive to be somehow not subject to the normal human frailties, doubts and uncertainties. We like to invest our royalty, prime ministers, film stars and even cooks with an aura of stardust.

I was looking for videos in a Woolworths in Lymington, Hampshire. A woman came to me and said, 'It's you. Isn't it Rick Stein?'

'Yes, it is,' I said, smiling.

'I can't believe you come shopping in Woolworths like ordinary people.'

I'm human. I like to be praised; it's pleasing when someone says they like my work. And when viewers say they don't like me, I try to avoid getting angry or at least showing I'm angry.

# III

My first TV series *Taste of the Sea* (1995) was about my life as a cook in Padstow. It's nostalgic watching it now, particularly the scene on Bodmin Moor when I'm salmon fishing. My very young son Charles is with us and he's so bored, saying, 'How much longer, Dad?' to which I reply, 'Two hours,' and he says, 'Two *hours*! That's 120 *minutes*!' He preferred Harlyn Beach. Framed on the wall in my house I've still got a postcard he wrote in a wobbly childish hand saying '*Dad I always want to go to Harlyn*'.

David Pritchard and I followed *Taste of the Sea* with *Fruits of the Sea* (1997) which was essentially the same thing with some travel thrown in. Next we made *The Seafood Lover's Guide to Britain and Ireland*. At the time, David and I were becoming increasingly worried about overfishing. We'd both read *Cod: A Biography of the Fish that Changed the World* by Mark Kurlansky which told the story of the collapse of the cod fishery off Newfoundland. We had the apparently difficult task of drawing people's attention to declining fish stocks while at the same time rhapsodising about the great seafood off our coasts. I saw no dilemma in this because as I said in the introduction:

*The more we love seafood and the more we know about it the greater will be our diligence in preserving it and the more we will prefer to eat it ourselves rather than see it trucked overland to the fish markets of Spain and France. There is no reason why fish*

*conservation shouldn't work, I just have this nagging doubt that*
*it won't if we don't care enough.*

I've made all my cookery programmes for the BBC. The production
company has always been Denham Productions, owned by Chris
Denham, and the director has always been my friend, David
Pritchard, who also writes a lot of the voice-overs. The creativity
of the programmes comes only partly from me. Most of it comes
from David and the cameraman, Chris Topliss, who can get a
better picture out of a mobile phone than most of us could manage
with the best camera in the world. The rest too, Pete Underwood,
the sound recordist, and Arezoo Farahzad, who keeps everything
going when we're filming and who's known as Our Mum, create a
specially optimistic and convivial working atmosphere. None of the
shows would have the impact they do without Malcolm Ironton,
who composes the slightly yearning music, or indeed the film editor,
Chris Waring.

The ideas are worked out by David and me, either in a pub or in
a restaurant. The London Inn in Padstow, The Seafood Restaurant
in Padstow, The Miners Arms in Hemerdon just outside Plymouth –
that was a good one, it was David's local. We'd go there and meet Chris
Denham and Billy Edwards who lived at the back of the car park and
installed sound systems, and Anthony who was a local auctioneer,
and David and Linda Honey, the landlord and landlady, would be
behind the bar pouring the Bass. We'd talk about, well nothing to do
with making TV programmes. Chris might be praising the quality of
the draught Bass, and we'd possibly exchange a few thoughts about
the very pretty wife of the local used-car dealer standing at the other
end of the bar. Someone might be trying to interest me in flooring
for one of my restaurants. Billy would be telling me about a song he'd

written about Chalky, my dog, and David would say he had bought a smart motor cruiser.

'You once said the best part of owning a boat was the day you bought it and the day you sold it.'

'Yes, but this one is different. It's got a lovely cabin and the deck's really shiny.'

'So where've you been in it?'

'Well, I've been out to the Plymouth Sound breakwater and back, and last Sunday I tried following the Roscoff ferry out to sea but I couldn't keep up. But I did go all the way to Salcombe.'

'I love Salcombe. Stayed there once at the St Elmo Hotel with a friend from school and knocked a girl over in the laundry by mistake. Saw her knickers. Early sexual awakening.'

'I've been reading this little book about a yachtsman who brings his boat back from Majorca to England across France by canals. He starts at Marseille, and did you know you could get all the way to Bordeaux?'

'No, I didn't. That's quite interesting.'

'Well, I was thinking. If we did a journey going the other way, I could use my boat and get the BBC to pay some expenses. We could pretend you were on it on your own going to vineyards and fois gras farms.'

'With Chalky?'

'With Chalky, of course. One man and his dog on the Canal du Midi.'

'That sounds OK. Another pint?'

That was the sum of discussing *Rick Stein's French Odyssey*. We didn't need to say any more. Once we've got an idea it grows.

In those days we went to Bristol to see the commissioning editor, Tom Archer, and sat down to lunch with him at a restaurant called the Quartier Vert. In line with its French bistro appeal, it had thick white paper tablecloths and, long ago, we could smoke and we did. I was going through a last love affair with Gauloises. Tom then went back to the office and David drew a map of France on the tablecloth and started sketching pictures of vineyards, prune farms, cheese-makers and cherry orchards with some enthusiastic additions from me. By the end of lunch, complete with a couple of cigarette burns and a Beaujolais stain or two, we had the series sketched out. We got hold of a large envelope, folded up the entire tablecloth, slipped it in, addressed it to Tom Archer and dropped it off.

Within a couple of days we got his answer: he'd talked to the powers that be and it was agreed but could we just do a page of A4 for formality's sake.

These days we have to plan everything and write what they call 'the treatment'. Then David has to plot a detailed account of each programme which can run to about 30 pages.

What we really liked to do was to follow our noses, because it gave the programmes a true spontaneity and, I think, engaged the viewers in feeling the same excitement as we did when we found ourselves, say, in Galicia facing a large platter with half a steaming pig's head with glistening teeth, a curly tail and a backbone, all long simmered, plus a big bowl of *grelos*, turnip greens cooked even longer than the cabbage I remembered from my prep school. Filming, for me, has been like going on holidays with Denham's tours. I guess it's mostly because David and I have a good creative relationship.

It's a world of its own. Sarah Burns calls it Filmingland. Filmingland is the sort of place, I suspect, where lots of people would like to be, where life is simple, or so they like to imagine. All we have to do is go out and find a nice programme and bring it to screens in people's houses. We don't have to worry about our real families or real businesses back home. We just have to get up, have breakfast, go out filming all day, come back tired to the hotel, have a few beers, eat dinner, then go to bed and fall into a trouble-free sleep, get up and do it all over again. The reality is, of course, tougher and greyer, and I find it hard work but it's never boring. Mostly I suspect because David is so thoroughly entertaining, whether he's enjoying himself or not, whether we're laughing at his unpredictable take on things or outraged by his appalling behaviour – demanding too much and stomping off if he doesn't get his own way. We're a Filmingland family.

For me, it's like when I was a child before my father was ill. We would be driving to Cornwall in our Jag when my dad insisted we stopped to see Wells. On other occasions we were forced to go round Exeter Cathedral or unwillingly to climb up Glastonbury Tor. I even remember, too, a diversion to buy baskets on Sedgemoor in Somerset. Sometimes – a habit which I've copied – we'd stop in the car while we waited for my dad to have a ten-minute nap. My mother would be complaining about the time it was taking to get to Cornwall. Henrietta and I and John, and Rupert the dachshund, would be scrunched up in the back of the car, feeling sick and longing to see the sea. Filmingland is like that to me. It's frustrating, there are diversions and halts; but it's a safe place to be and there's always something wonderful to look forward to.

I have to do my bit and make sensible comments about the places we're in, but that's not difficult because, almost without exception, I like where we are. I get irritated with David because he often wants me to bang on about things that I find tedious, but that's because he needs what I'm saying to be part of a narrative. He sees filming in terms of the finished programme. Often we argue; sometimes we film the arguments because they say quite a lot. Once in Sydney we went to the restaurant of the famous chef Tetsuya, and filmed his elaborate Japanese take on Western food. Afterwards in the crew van, we filmed David talking to me about the lunch we'd just had. I thought it all wonderful.

He said: 'Well, if you like a tiny chunk of salmon with some tea oil and minute pieces of carrot and pink peppercorns on top, that's your business. Give me lamb chops and green beans any time.'

'You just don't get it, do you?' I said. 'You really like Bisto gravy with your roast beef and Yorkshire pudding.'

We were in Australia making *Fruits of the Sea*. This series, which started in Padstow, established, on TV, the essence of what I was doing in Cornwall, trying to broaden the scope of my menu and to increase my knowledge by adding to my understanding of exotic and different ways of cooking. I've always had an uneasy feeling that many people don't really like fish. If, like me, you desperately want to specialise in fish, you need to fight hard to attract punters.

When I was playing rugby for the Wadebridge Camels, I once asked Jethro why he didn't come to The Seafood Restaurant.

'I don't eat fish,' he said.

'Yes, but we do steak too.'

'In Padstow even the steak'll taste of fish.'

Humorous, but revealing too. I had already realised that if I wanted to make the restaurant even busier, which I did, and if I wanted to convert the no-fish-for-me brigade, I would have to bring in tempting and original fish dishes from all over the world. The family holidays in Australia, South East Asia and India had filled me with excitement for travelling and now I visited and revisited many far-away locations in *Fruits of the Sea* and *Seafood Odyssey*. I wrote:

*Travel changes you. The way I cook now, the recipes I write, the way I look at food can never be the same again, as a result of my travels and my quest for seafood dishes. I suppose a certain purity, innocence and simplicity in the way I used to cook have been lost because of what I have learnt on the way. But I can't go back. I keep thinking that it would be nice to retire into some sort of Cornish cuisine but it's just not enough anymore. I need to keep travelling to find those perfect simple dishes from all over the world.*

I revisited places I had been to before. In India the team and I went to Goa and filmed at the hotel where Jill and I and my boys, Edward, Jack and Charles, and our friends Johnny and Terri, had enjoyed so many holidays. In Thailand, we went to the Station Hotel in Hua Hin where I had stayed with them all 12 years before. In Australia, the autobiographical element was to do with my journey to Queensland when I was 20. This came from a conversation in the London Inn in Padstow during which I had rather over-optimistically told David, when planning the *Seafood Odyssey*, that Noosa was just north of Brisbane. I hadn't actually looked at my diary since the 1960s but so keen was I to go back to Australia that a little thing like checking the facts or looking at the map never came into it. Indeed only when reading the diary recently did I realise that what I thought of as Noosa was in fact Tweed Heads. It was about 200 miles away from where I thought it was.

By the time we got to Noosa and the pub didn't look anything like I remembered, I said to David: 'I'm not sure I have been here after all.'

'Well, you *have* been here before. *If* you catch my drift.'

I did a piece to camera in which I stood in Hastings Street saying that in the sixties it had been a mere strip by the sea but that the whole town had changed out of all recognition since then. Not that much of a white lie, really. I'm sure it *had* changed radically, certainly from a gastronomic point of view. We ate in a different restaurant every night, and they were all good.

*Seafood Odyssey* included trips to Italy, the USA and Galicia in Northern Spain as well as Goa, Thailand and Australia, but what I still think is one of the most magical sequences we ever did was actually filmed at the mouth of the Thames. I was trying to liken my travels all over the world to the way the empire builders voyaged all over the world appropriating stuff to bring back to Britain.

We managed to get a near-perfect sunset over the Thames and I quoted a passage from the beginning of Conrad's *Heart of Darkness*.

> *The old river in its broad reach rested unruffled at the decline of day after ages of good service done to the race that peopled its banks spread out in the tranquil dignity of a waterway leading to the utmost ends of the earth. We looked at the venerable stream not in the vivid flush of a short day that comes and departs forever, but in the august light of abiding memories. And indeed nothing is easier for a man who has, as the phrase goes, 'followed the sea' with reverence and affection than to evoke the great spirit of the past upon the lower reaches of the Thames. The current runs to and fro in its unceasing service crowded with memories of ships and men it had borne to the rest of home or to the battles of the sea.*

This was weighty for a cookery show, and I wasn't unaware that this passage is setting a scene which is on the dark side of exploration and exploitation.

I didn't want our programmes to funk the dark side or to trivialise cooking. On the surface it's only food, but there's an underlying seriousness about what I wanted to get across. I was trying to put world food into its context in life.

In *Seafood Odyssey*, we filmed in Porto do Son in Galicia. We were there for fishing boats returning with their catch in the early evening. If it's sunny, the hour before dusk is the best time to film because the light has a rich quality which bathes everything in lustrous warmth. It's called the golden hour. Earlier that day, we had found a little bar on the harbour with about 15 friendly locals sitting at it drinking Estrella Galicia beer and small glasses of wine. The bar also had a few tables and a short menu, all of local seafood. Things like *necoras* (velvet swimming crabs), *gambas* (Mediterranean prawns), several hake dishes and *centolla* (spider crab). I wandered off and walked along the harbour and found a grassy area where schoolchildren were playing. One of them, a boy aged about ten, was particularly animated, scampering about with a sense of joy on his sweet face on that sunny morning.

I returned to the crew and we sat down to lunch and started with some grilled sardines as sweet and fresh as young hazelnuts. We shared a couple of the spider crabs. We drank Alborino, the local white wine, which is grown on stone trestles to keep the grapes off the damp ground, and then a local fragrant red called Mencia. After the fish we had rare steaks: very fresh meat cooked on charcoal, a little tough but juicy and full of sweetness. The whole meal, the bar, the locals, the spontaneity of it … I was overwhelmed with joy, starting with the boy on the green. David filmed me coming out of the bar and saying that I'd just had a lunch of such delight that it felt to me like being in love.

And indeed, I was in love. I'd fallen for Sas – Sarah Burns – and, for better or worse, being in love makes you much more aware of the world around you, in all its variety and colour.

David and I went back to Porto do Son last year when we were filming my Spanish series. We had lunch in one bar, walked into another, but could not find our original. I'm sort of glad we didn't, the memory is so precious to me.

# IV

Around the time I was filming *Seafood Odyssey*, a radical change was happening on the quay of Padstow. The old fish market and fish sheds dating back to the beginning of the twentieth century, which had been gently falling apart for years, now began to cause alarm because it appeared they were also falling into the harbour. They stood quite close to the new quay built to land the considerable tonnage of cod and haddock that was coming in on the new steam trawlers. The fish market had closed in the fifties to be replaced by a series of small fishermen's stores and a fish shop with lobster tanks. But by 1998 our end of the harbour was collapsing and the town council decided to demolish the sheds, and relocate them further away from the quayside, and repair the quay. The result was a very attractive wood-clad industrial building, designed by an architect from Plymouth called Ian Potts who won a prize for its innovation. It soon became clear that the new building, much larger than the old, could take some new tenants and I decided to move our deli next to our cafe to a quayside location.

Everyone renting space in the new building had to abide by the terms which were that your business had to be marine-related; so I decided to call our deli a seafood deli and sell only fresh and preserved fish with a few things which could loosely be termed as accompaniments to fish dishes such as sun-dried tomatoes, olives, olive oil, lemons, garlic, onions, parsley and fresh basil. I thought a few of our own home-made jams and chutneys could be loosely interpreted as going with fish and, while I was about it, I applied for a wine and beer licence to sell the sort of drinks that might go with fish for dinner too. Then I thought: why just sell fish? Why not cook it too, and sell fish dishes to take away?

I put in a little kitchen and wrote a menu.

Fish Tacos
Po' Boys
Fried Squid
Goujons of Lemon Sole
Fish Soup with Rouille and Parmesan

We were swamped from the day it opened. But in spite of that we couldn't make it pay. We were charging £3 to £5 for each dish but to cook that sort of food well we needed two good chefs in there; quite often, I was one of them. We weren't taking enough money to cover the costs. All the time our customers were asking for fish and chips but we didn't have the equipment to cook what they wanted. Gradually I realised that I had to buy a large fryer. We could then charge double the money and halve the cooks. So Stein's Seafood Deli lasted just one year. But by the start of the next season, we'd opened a fish and chip shop next door.

At the same time, we took over the space on the first floor for our offices. I consulted the architect, Ian Potts, because I realised that the unit next door upstairs had enormous windows over the estuary and could be something more than just an office. It was Jill who came up with the idea of making it a cookery school open to the public. To start with, I thought it should be the sort of place where we taught the rigorous secrets of fish cookery, maybe offering some sort of diploma in fish filleting, but having visited Raymond Blanc's school at the Manoir aux Quatre Saisons in Oxfordshire I realised that we would be much better off teaching simple skills to people who just wanted to do a day or two to hone-up their cooking at home. Right from the start, we decided to make it seemingly unstructured so that a day's teaching was about preparing things for lunch, but the menu for lunch would contain as many techniques, cooking methods and types of seafood as we could cram in. We realised that after lunch and a relaxing glass of wine or two, it would be better to get the students to watch demonstrations rather than prepare and cook things themselves. Our scheme has worked well. I'm sure the main reason has been because all the fish we use is of the best quality. I love simple reasons for success – and ours is very fresh-looking, very fresh-tasting and very fresh-smelling fish. Most people simply don't get a chance to handle stuff as good as this. When they realise what fresh fish is like, their previous difficulties vanish. It is as simple as that. We opened the school with Paul Sellars as head teacher. Teaching cookery is something which chefs do rather well if they have any communication ability.

I love demonstrating. I began doing demos in earnest about 25 years ago when the man who started the BBC Good Food Show at the National Exhibition Centre in Birmingham, Tim Etchells, pioneered the idea. He invited chefs such as my chum Brian Turner, Robert Carrier, Ken Hom, Gary Rhodes, Raymond Blanc, Keith Floyd and Antony Worrall Thompson to cook on stage. No one had had any training in teaching cookery. Previously, some chefs had conducted their demos pissed, and some people had demanded their money back. After an inauspicious beginning, Tim asked us all to go and receive tuition in cooking demos from a TV producer called Peter Bazalgette, now chairman of the Arts Council, the same man who went on to create *Ready Steady Cook*, *Changing Rooms* and *Big Brother*. We each spent an hour or so running through things in his house in Holland Park. Most demos last for only 30 minutes and it's a compromise between trying to show some techniques and trying to avoid the audience getting bored and walking out which is very demoralising. Over the years some of us have tried some wacky things. Jamie Oliver rode on to the stage on a scooter and finished his last dish to a drum solo. Ainsley Harriott rushed on to the music of 'Bohemian Like You' by the Dandy Warhols. But all big openers end up with the chef frying sausages or fillets of fish shortly afterwards.

A couple of years ago, I did a tour of theatres first in New Zealand then in Australia, culminating in a show at the Opera House in Sydney. At one of them, we did a cunning false start: I failed to appear on stage. Instead, I was welcomed by the presenter, local TV journalist Mark Sainsbury, with a camera outside a strip club called the Mermaid which I swore I remembered in the sixties as being a fish and chip shop. I arrived on stage to laughter and applause – only to be cooking fish pie very soon afterwards.

The cookery school has been a source of great pride to me and out of it came an idea for a book not tied into a TV series but a comprehensive guide to preparing and cooking seafood, simply called *Seafood*. I must confess that I borrowed the idea of photographing the most important preparation and cooking techniques from a cookery series produced in the early seventies by *Life* Magazine and edited by Richard Olney, the only difference being that the *Life* books used black and white photos like a textbook whereas we made each colour shot atmospheric to give excitement to each phase of filleting a fish, shallow frying a Dover sole or making fish stock. *Seafood* won a James

Beard Award in the United States, prompting me to go on a short book tour there. Philadelphia, Chicago and New York – I hadn't been back there much since my Midnight Cowboy days in the sixties, and not being well-known in America, my book signings and cookery demos were sparsely attended. But I had the prize and there were just enough booksellers and chefs to tell me how much they liked my work to keep my ego ticking along nicely. I loved simply being there. Edgar Allan Poe's house and Rick's Philly steak sandwiches in Reading Terminal market in Philadelphia. Charlie Trotter doing a lunch of my dishes at his restaurant in Chicago. A tour of Frank Lloyd Wright's generous suburban houses, and getting ticked off at the Whole Foods Market in Columbus Circle in New York for taking a picture of their vegetable displays, there being nothing like it in the UK at the time. America was a great place after all.

# V

Following the success of *Seafood Odyssey*, David and I began to plan a second odyssey, this time taking in some much more remote areas where there was an extreme fishing element. Jill had an Icelandic friend called Ingrid and I rang her in Reykjavik. She'd seen some of my programmes and agreed that filming in Iceland would be rewarding. Brought up with my mother's enthusiasm for the Icelandic sagas, I sensed a rich seafood story among the rugged landscape of volcanoes and geezers, the ice and the mountains and the tough lives of those independent fishermen who had seen off our great British Navy in the cod wars of the early seventies. David and I had plans, too, of salmon fishing in Alaska, chasing the anchovy shoals in Chile and visiting the Tsukiji fish market in Tokyo. Maybe go out on a tuna fishing boat or do a matanza in Sicily where tuna are herded into a small pen made out of nets off the coast in May and June and slaughtered with long knives on poles. All this came to nothing: the BBC wanted us to stay in the UK. But early frustration soon gave way to enthusiasm for filming about my own waters.

*The Seafood Lovers' Guide to Great Britain and Ireland* came out of a reaction to what I had seen in *Seafood Odyssey*, all those lovely fish dishes that I had found all over the world, yet in the UK we didn't seem to share the same enthusiasm. My role in the programme was to travel round the coast of Britain and point out what was the best local fish and shellfish and also to identify where you could buy it and eat it whether in fish and chip shops, posh fish restaurants, raffish fish cafes, jolly beach kiosks or simple seafood shacks. I couldn't be too negative but the truth is that I was saddened by how few outlets of any kind there were in Britain. Nevertheless the fact that there was a dearth meant that when I did find somewhere good it was a time of celebration. The highlights were often the simplest. There was a tea room called the Shorehouse, for example, in Sutherland near Cape Wrath right up on the West of Scotland at a tiny harbour called Tarbet, where you can catch a small ferry to the nature reserve island of Handa Island. We ordered cups of tea and bread and butter and a great heap of boiled orange langoustines which they simply called prawns. The little ferry came and went and we sat outside happy with our good fortune at our almost secret find. These unbelievably delicious prawns were almost unknown. The majority of the catch in Scotland and Ireland goes to France and Spain.

Another delightful find was in West Mersea in Essex, a seafood shop simply called the Company Shed. We had lobster and oyster and a delicious piece of ray – washed down with a bottle of Chablis from the off-licence down the road. The fame of the West Mersea oysters dates back to Roman times; but the truth is that such a place as the Company Shed would not exist today were it not for someone like Heather Haward who opened it 25 years ago as a place to sell her husband Richard's oysters.

Running through *The Seafood Lovers' Guide* was an anxiety about overfishing. The dawning knowledge that our fish stocks are in danger is like trying to remember when you first realised that cigarettes caused lung cancer. When I first opened The Seafood Restaurant, crayfish – crawfish, or spiny lobsters as they are more correctly known – were plentiful and large. Within 15 years they were rare, and now if we get more than a couple a year I'd be surprised. The same applies to sea trout (which we call salmon peel). They used to arrive in the kitchen in the summer in hessian sacks. I'd empty the sacks on to a work bench; the fish would slither out covered in filmy green weed from the Camel estuary, some still alive. They came in so often that sometimes I wouldn't really want them but never said anything to Jim McOwen as he was too nice to refuse. He always wore a navy blue fisherman's sweater and had a nose of deep red and purple complexity. Sharp blue eyes. A little difficult to understand at times, but it's hard now to think of anyone more evocative of Old Padstow when all was good. These days, getting salmon peel is a special event.

David and I took a trip on a giant herring trawler from Peterhead, north of Aberdeen. We had been told to expect most of the crew to arrive in BMWs and Mercedes, so profitable was the fishing for large pelagic trawlers out of Peterhead and Fraserburgh. We had been invited by a skipper, Andrew Tait, to film on a seine net trawler, the *Chris Andra*, which would take us around Shetland. I described the ship as being not much smaller than a cross-Channel ferry. This was an exaggeration. But for someone used to the wooden fishing boats of Padstow, it was a fish killer. I was particularly impressed with the size of the otter boards. These are the two heavy boards which go either side of the mouth of a purse seine net, shaped so that they glide through the water turning away from the stern of the boat so keeping the net open. I'm fascinated by fishing gear, lobster pots and keep boxes, ropes, nets, chains and trawls, so after we boarded I was leaning over the aft rail, part admiring the eight-ton slabs of shaped steel above me but also doodling with my Psion organiser, when David grabbed me by the back of my jacket and pulled me away just as one of the steel boards broke loose and sliced through the space where my head had just been.

Even then I wasn't immediately aware of the danger, so in my own little world was I. I often don't seem to really notice what is going on around me which can lead to a certain clumsiness. Over the years David has made use of this in filming to good effect. Once – I think it was in *Taste of the Sea* – we had been filming a simple dish, a fillet of grey mullet cooked over charcoal with an extra-virgin olive oil dressing; just olive oil, garlic, a few chopped chillies, briefly soaked in white wine vinegar to take away the excess heat, and coarse sea salt. To mellow the slivers of garlic, I dropped them briefly into a pan of warm olive oil, added the chilli, put the fillets on a warm plate and surrounded the fish with the olive oil and chilli, and sprinkled it with the Maldon sea salt. I was in my element, a little over-confident, very proud to be using my charcoal barbecue on camera (no ordinary gas grill, the real thing). I was also pleased with the new Japanese mandolin I had acquired – a razor-sharp gadget – ideal for thinly slicing vegetables. But maybe not, in hindsight, ideal for slicing something as small as a clove of garlic. It had a safety holder which was too big for the garlic. But as I said to the camera while starting to slice the garlic with my fingers perilously close to the blade, you only cut yourself on one of these once.

It was almost as if David knew what was coming because, of course, I did cut myself on it. Hubris because I was too absorbed in the effortless simplicity of the dish actually to put any care into doing it.

I shouted, 'Fuck!'

David yelled at the cameraman: 'Julian! Why did you stop filming?'

'Rick's cut himself, there's blood everywhere.'

'You've got no journalistic sense,' David said in disgust. 'I knew Rick was going to do that. You should have kept filming.'

The next shot is of me slicing garlic with a thin knife and wearing a huge blue kitchen plaster. And the next voice-over says: 'If you just heard a clatter it was of a Japanese mandolin being thrown into the rubbish skip outside the back door.'

There have been a number of other incidents where my Inspector Clouseau clumsiness has made the filming all too painful. In the *Seafood Lovers' Guide*, we filmed a clam fisherman dredging for quahog clams in Southampton Water. Apparently the first clams were thrown overboard at the end of a Cunard voyage, which explains how they got there all the way from America. Now he also dredged up a cannonball encrusted with barnacles.

'How amazing,' I said to the camera. 'I'll just bang this on the gunwale to break off the barnacles.'

I did this not noticing in the excitement of filming that on the gunwale I had my other hand which I duly thumped.

I've been knocked over by a wave in Phuket, Thailand, doing a piece to camera walking along the water line with my trousers rolled up to my knees, holding my deck shoes and talking earnestly to the camera about the vibrancy of Thai cooking. I've burnt myself with hot olive oil filming cooking a paella. I have an almost pathetic enthusiasm when the cameras point at me: I want to be your friend. I'll jump off the boat in Sri Lanka into the water with the other fishermen to scare the fish into the back of the net. I'll swim in the Canal du Midi under the barge to help the skipper untangle some washing line from the propeller.

David uses my occasional lack of judgement to good effect. So it was very reassuring to know that when my awareness was impaired on the back of the *Chris Andra* he was there to save my life.

The quantity of herrings they caught on the *Chris Andra* is hard to believe. We discovered that the net they used was the size of a football pitch, that the haul was about 450 tons of fish and that, often, the haul is sold before it's landed, so accurate are the sensors in estimating its size. I did a piece right by a stainless steel channel with a blue and silver stream of live herrings flowing in an icy slurry down into hold. The sheer volume of fish shocked and excited me as the net was pulled in and began to tighten around the whole shoal. It looked like a zeppelin tied to the side of the ship rising and falling with the swell. I used the size of the catch as an example to ask the question 'Can we expect the oceans endlessly to produce such quantities?' It was, I think, a powerful piece but I didn't like doing it because the owners and crew had been very hospitable to us. Not only did they accommodate us in some style but they fed us remarkably well. Theirs wasn't the normal life on small trawlers – bunks with dirty blankets, a smell of diesel and cigarette smoke, and girlie mags everywhere. It was individual cabins and bowls of mini Mars Bars and Crunchies on the galley tables. They also arranged for us to transfer from the boat to another of their trawlers going back to Fraserburgh so we wouldn't have to do the five-day trip.

After the series came out, I had an aggrieved letter complaining that we had abused their hospitality. Since making the film, I'm no longer sure that such a massive fishing operation is so bad if the fishing is well controlled and restricted to a short season.

I was keen to spread my love of seafood yet at the same time worried that the world was running out of fish. Without admitting that most of what we like to do in life has a downside, I came to realise that it was OK to love seafood and to eat it, because the more people share this passion, the more they will be keen to preserve stocks and look after them wisely. I also recognised that we ought to become more familiar with less well-known species of seafood which are plentiful but under-used. Both points have turned out in a limited way to be true. There has been a much greater awareness of the fragility of fish stocks, and a proliferation of organisations dedicated to pointing us in the direction of 'safe' fish, notably the Marine Stewardship Council and the Marine Conservation Society. Films like *The End of the Line* have targeted the seemingly mindless overfishing of one species, the Blue Fin Tuna, and Hugh Fearnley-Whittingstall has laudably pointed out the inanity of throwing just-caught fish back dead into the sea because they don't meet fish quota requirements.

For a while my restaurants became a target for journalists who accused us of unsound practices because we put local cod on the menu at a time when many considered all cod in the British Isles to be endangered. Perhaps naively, I mentioned in a talk at the Cheltenham Literary Festival in 2008 that not all local stocks were under threat and pointed out that in the south west the fishermen were reporting very good landings of some species under threat including cod – so much so that the quota had actually been increased. Needless to say, the next day part of what I said appeared in the *Daily Mail*.

*Britain's top seafood chef has vowed to go on using endangered species of fish in his acclaimed restaurants despite warning of over-fishing.*

It reminded me of what I had learnt way back, editing the university newspaper: a news story has to be a story.

Shortage of fish has led to a greater awareness of previously lesser-known species. For one of these I think I can take some personal responsibility – the gurnard. Gurnards, when I was young, were bait for lobster pots. I started using them regularly in the 1980s following trips to Provence because I saw they were an important ingredient in bouillabaisse, as well as *bourride* and fish soup. All the books I read about bouillabaisse pointed out that the authentic version absolutely had to include *poissons de roches*. The French used rascasse whose heads gave the famous Provençale stew its unique flavour. I had only ever seen one rascasse-related fish at Newlyn Market, a scorpion fish, but gurnards we had a-plenty and gurnard belong to the family of *poisson de roche*. I started using them in my soups and stews and then created recipes for them. For the book *Seafood* I wrote a recipe for fried gurnard with sage. It was intended to go with a technique for skinning a whole gurnard. I simply fried the gurnard in butter, cleaned the pan, added more butter, sage leaves, garlic, lemon juice, salt and black pepper, and poured the instant sauce over the fried fish. Gurnard sales have been soaring ever since 2000 when *The Seafood Lovers' Guide* came out. They were less than 50p a kilo then; now in the summer months they can take as much as £14 a kilo, making their inflation in price a bit like property in Padstow.

I've now, after many more trips to the Mediterranean, identified the unique flavour of rascasse in a bouillabaisse. I think it's there in gunard too. If you cut up a gurnard's head and fry it with garlic and olive oil and a couple of tomatoes, you can smell a sunny oiliness much more appetising than that of mackerel or herring; a smell that takes me back to the bouillabaisse restaurant called L'Epuisette in Vallon des Auffes in Marseille where I filmed with my friend Simon Hopkinson in *French Odyssey*. You can't make a bouillabaisse out of any old fish. It has to be a rock fish, and what's more it has to have its head on. It adds that almost overpowering musty, oily taste – sort of off-putting – but in a bouillabaisse you need the warp and weft of a little bitterness. It's like shrimp paste – the ying with the yang – almost like an almost unpleasant perfume, but how you miss it when it's not there.

# VI

For our next series David and I planned a Food Lovers' Guide.
I wrote:

> *Just as I insist on the best and freshest fish, I do the same with meat,*
> *game, poultry, dairy produce and vegetables. I've always felt that*
> *the most important part about cooking good food is getting the best*
> *produce in the first place.*

However, Henrietta Green had already published a book with the
same title and the same intentions, and she was already irritated with
me for calling my previous book and series *The Seafood Lovers' Guide*.
I pointed out that the name had been invented by an American food
writer, Patricia Wells, who'd produced her *Food Lovers' Guide to Paris*
ages ago.

'That's not the point,' Henrietta said. 'It would have been polite
to have asked me.'

I could see where she was coming from. She had been
championing small producers for some time and running a series of
markets where they came to sell their stuff – and along comes me
with my TV following and I pick up her idea. Nevertheless, it was an
idea which could do with a lot more exposure.

Jane Root, the BBC controller, really saw the point of bringing
small producers to a bigger audience. Then a friend of David's,

Jane McKlusky, who was running West Country TV at the time, came up with the idea of *Food Heroes*. This was a perfect title for what I was trying to get across. I had long been a fan of the Slow Food Movement, founded in 1986 as a result of opposition to the opening of a McDonalds near the Spanish Steps in Rome. Like many, I felt the oppression of the spread of fast food, and the dismal unadventurousness of everything tasting alike, and the gradual loss of knowledge about cooking and the ability to tell ordinary from outstanding. We had even more of a task because we didn't have, in the British Isles, a tradition of small peasant producers like France, Italy and Spain. If we were to encourage the development of a culture of small producers of excellent food, in many cases we would have to start from scratch.

I have always had a mission to show people, not just at home but everywhere, that Britain is a place of really good-quality food. I've always wanted to dispel the idea that our cooking is bland and that our meat and vegetables are invariably overdone. I've always felt proud that in *Le Guide Culinaire*, Escoffier says that the best game in the world is the Scottish grouse. I think the best langoustine in the world comes from Scotland too; the best lobster and turbot comes from Cornwall; the best beef is the grass-fed beef that comes from my butcher, Warrens in Launceston. Making *Food Heroes* was a joy, mostly because it's no hardship to be paid to travel round our gorgeous country. Much of the filming was done in May and June. How special it is to be outdoors when the landscape blossoms and is transformed from a vista of bare branches, with a slight green tinge to it, into a canopy of sheer bright greenness where the sounds of early summer are almost muffled by the thickness of it. To travel in a Land Rover under skies pendulous with clouds interspersed with blue patches casting dappled light on the fields, to a beer festival at Tuckers Maltings in Newton Abbot to discuss the relative properties of fuggles and golden hops and the quality of Devon barley; or to be watching the shadows of clouds racing down the green Cambrian mountains and valleys at the source of the Severn in mid Wales on the way to visit a black beef farmer; or to drive over a humpback bridge over the River Test near Longparish in Hampshire, gazing briefly at the clear water below with river weeds wavering in the flow.

It was nights of finding wonderful pubs including the Bear Hotel in Crickhowell in Powys; and the Queens Head, a beamed and thatched pub near the village square in Billesdon near Claire Symington's Seldom Seen Farm in Leicestershire; and Crown Liquor Saloon just across from the Europa Hotel in Great Victoria St in Belfast, with its long red granite bar, carved wooden booths and exemplary pints of Guinness.

Before *Food Heroes*, I had viewed some British produce with ambivalence. The Australians have a phrase for my feelings – it's 'culinary cringe'. While I remained determined to prove that we had as good produce as anyone else, there were areas where I didn't even believe myself. One of these was cheese. Like most British people, I had become used to rectangular blocks of Cheddar and Leicester which cried out for the addition of a lot of pickles in a pub. Running a restaurant and having to try to put together a half-decent cheese board, I tended to rely on French cheeses.

Early on in our *Food Heroes* journeys we stayed overnight at a hotel in Tewkesbury where the restaurant manager was French. He reminded me of the taunting French guard in *Monty Python and the Holy Grail*. I asked him why there were no English cheeses on any menus in France and he said: 'Because we don't like them!' and I laughed. But it hurt because I didn't like a lot of them either, and I couldn't see the point of a tasteless British cheese.

That is, until I went to visit Ruth Kirkham and her son Graham at Goosnargh in Lancashire and tasted her cheese. It was no way bland. Complex and agricultural in flavour – by which I mean reminiscent of pasture and farmyards – her Lancashire cheese was matured for up to six months, and at each stage was stronger and more rewarding, in the same way as old red wine is. Similarly, in North Wales I discovered a light fragrant cows' milk cheese with far more character than I could ever have believed; it was a Caerphilly, a cheese I'd previously found too mild to bother with. No wonder that cheese makers are such interesting people – they are passionately committed. 'Blessed are the cheese makers' was a line David kept repeating from the film *Monty Python's Life of Brian*, slightly in jest and slightly in awe. He was amused by the fact that many of them were bossy women who were intimidating but admirable and full of character.

In Ireland, near Kilkenny, I asked a far-from-intimidating farmer's wife, Olivia Goodwillie, what was so special about her cows' milk Lavistown Cheese. We were sitting in Lavistown House at a large table in her completely un-modernised kitchen. It could have come straight out of Molly Kean's book on genteel, slightly impoverished Irish rural life, *Good Behaviour*. It was like the farmhouse kitchens you sometimes still see around Padstow, big central pine table, flagstones on the floor, a slatted wooden clothes drier above the range – often still coal fired – and once-upon-a-time hams hanging from the hooks in the ceiling. A door straight out to the farmyard and, next door, a proper larder – a long narrow dark room with floor to ceiling shelves on which were jars of homemade jams, pickles and chutney. 'I haven't a clue,' she said. 'It just happens.'

It was in no way a perplexing answer. You start with full-cream milk, add rennet and a yoghurt-type of culture ... and it just happens. No two batches of farmhouse cheese will ever taste exactly the same. Take the same recipe and make it at another farm and the cheese will taste subtly different. I realised it was like making wine and just as fascinating.

In Northamptonshire, we added Mrs King's Melton Mowbray Pork Pies at Cotgrave to our portfolio of food heroes. Three brothers, Paul, Neil and Ian Hartland, all dedicated rugby players, whose grandfather had bought the business from the eponymous Mrs King, made the pies every day. The hand-raised hot-water pastry was exemplary, the pork was all local and the jelly in the pies not crystals of gelatine but made by simmering the trotters with salt and spices to produce something as interesting to taste as the meat itself.

A bacon factory in Ayrshire, Ramsay's of Carluke, also springs to mind. Here they cooked us a breakfast of bacon butties to show that no liquid came out of the bacon when frying.

We did a blind taste test with a Women's Institute meeting at a pub in the New Forest, where we roasted a fresh free-range chicken and a cheap frozen supermarket one. Those WI members were not deceived, and the response was unanimously in favour of the free-range.

There was a wonderful saffron cake at a bakery near Callington in Cornwall. And an almost surreal experience visiting the rhubarb forcing sheds of E. Oldroyd and Sons near Wakefield. I talked to Janet Oldroyd, the High Priestess of Rhubarb, marvelling at the reverence with which she described varieties with names like Champagne and Timperley Early, which are forced at a tremendous rate. With a bit of cheating time-lapse photography, we filmed the rhubarb actually growing. But we were disappointed with ourselves in that we failed to realise that you can also *hear* it growing.

Of course, making any TV series includes disappointments and disasters. David is a believer in just getting on with it. From time to time, I get quite stroppy with him that we are even bothering to film things that I think are substandard, but he always says filming is like food gathering and that the edit suite is where the real programme is made. If I knew at the time that I was putting on my brave face that it was going to be dropped, I'd be very disconsolate, but of course I never do. Occasionally we get ourselves into a situation where we all know a story is never going to be used and – to avoid embarrassment – David calls for the strawberry filter, which is a code he uses to mean that the camera isn't running, though I carry on as if it is.

I must confess that as soon as we arrived at the house of a man rescuing battery hens from chicken factories, I thought the strawberry filter would be applied. I find mass-production in farming difficult to come to terms with. I was irritated when I filmed a fois gras farm in *French Odyssey* and had numerous letters of complaint about the shots of individuals force-feeding the fowls one by one. Restricting chickens in hundreds of thousands of tiny cages is cruel too, but no one seems to want to stand outside chicken batteries with placards like they do outside smart restaurants protesting against fois gras. When we got to the smallholding of the rescuer of battery hens there were chickens everywhere – not just in the garden but in the house, on the kitchen dressers, tops of cupboards, on the beds, everywhere. We filmed him in his back garden with a chicken on his head and another on his shoulder. I thought he was too eccentric to be a food hero in our series, but David, far from applying the strawberry filter, used just enough footage to highlight the good intentions and the humour and weirdness, without dwelling on the barminess of this house of chickens.

I also wondered whether a delightful young woman who had about ten outdoor sheds for chickens all laying blue eggs was a food hero. These days you can buy blue eggs in Waitrose but then to be able to buy free-range eggs with pale blue shells was exciting. The girl was passionate about her business. As we left filled with admiration for her dedication, we noticed a brand new BMW parked outside the house just as her husband was driving a Mercedes into the drive. We had assumed that her lifestyle was being maintained through blue-egg production, but having tried to work out how many blue eggs it takes to buy a shiny new BMW we weren't sure it wasn't more of a hobby than anything else.

There is no doubt, however, that Chalky was a hero, if not a food hero, in our series. This small family dog – a Jack Russell Terrier – had figured from time to time in the earlier programmes but in *Food Heroes* he stole the show. There I was, in my navy-blue Land Rover, driving across glorious skylines in Argyllshire or Suffolk, wearing a corduroy country sports jacket complete with leather patches on the elbows, and it was almost de rigueur that a dog would be sitting next to me in the passenger's seat – and there was Chalky.

Like Eddie in *Frasier*, his was the appearance that viewers were waiting for. The mere sight of David made him excited and animated. In his dog's brain he knew that David and the Land Rover meant that we were off on the road. Not just walks along Harlyn Beach but hopping over prickly stubble in September fields in Menheniott near Liskeard, out shooting pigeons and rabbit for pie, or squelching through salt marsh near Harlech, while we were talking to a lamb farmer. At Blenheim Palace he scampered across the park and peed near a sign saying 'Keep dogs off the grass'.

David was clever at getting artful shots. We were making a film about Cornish early potatoes with a spirited local girl who said that they sold their potatoes only within a 15-mile radius of Tintagel because 'You've got to have them as soon as they're dug to appreciate the best of them.' She said: 'The trouble with a new potato is it can go stale. By the time it's gone off the grading line and been pre-packed and delivered to the supermarket, it's no longer the same quality and flavour as having been dug here and having it on your table tonight.' While we were talking, David cut in a series of shots of Chalky trying to jump up from the ground on to the platform where I was standing with the potato baggers. There were too many people on the platform, so every time he tried to jump up, he couldn't, and each time he fell back, he gave a little growl. Finally someone got off and he hopped up, again with a little growl but this time of satisfaction. Paul Roberts added the growls later when they were doing voice-overs in the studio, but it was Chalky who gave the whole sequence an endearing spontaneity.

Chalky chased a rabbit around an old greenhouse filled with watering cans, rakes, potting trestles and cold frames, like one from a story by Beatrix Potter. Chalky crouched on rocks and peered over hedges looking at things. He seemed to know what I wanted. I had never bothered to train him but if I said 'sit' he would. He was a little star and he didn't know it. Even if he never learned how to bring sticks back when you threw one for him. Jack, my son, introduced me to his new springer spaniel puppy Bocca the other day. I threw an apple across the garden and Bocca brought it back. Chalky was too much his own man – or rather dog – to do that.

David, Bernard Hall and I used to take it in turns to have Chalky in our hotel room. Sometimes he got a bit restless and kept me awake. Every morning, he was up and ready for a walk before I was but on the whole he was no trouble. Of the three of us, Bernard probably looked after him best. David had a special relationship with Chalky but complained about him being noisy. David was the head of the pack when we were filming and it's not too fanciful to think that Chalky knew this and respected him. But not at home. David came round to dinner at Trevone once and we all got quite pissed and at one stage David lifted Chalky up on the table and moved his face right up to his saying what a great little dog he was. He must have invaded this 'great little dog's' personal space because he bit David on the nose, not at all badly, just a nip, but David was put out.

I think of Chalky in the series as some sort of exquisite paint in an artist's palette which David used – just a dab of light here and there to make the story come alive. That's David's skill, not just with Chalky but with the music he chooses and also manipulating me, I guess. He uses me to add personal observation and feeling to what we are seeing, but other times he uses my lack of awareness to make it funny. I'm thinking here of the time we smuggled Chalky into my hotel room in Edinburgh. It was a Thistle hotel and they had a policy of no pets. I don't doubt David had had a go at Arezoo about her oversight in not booking us into a hotel which welcomed dogs. She probably told him there was nowhere else. At some stage David might have said, 'Well, we'll just have to smuggle him in,' and then would have seen the humorous possibilities of filming the smuggling. I just didn't get it. I couldn't see that it would be funny, which is doubtless why I'm not a film director. David had Chalky popped into Bernard's blue overnight bag and he filmed him going up in the lift with his head poking out. Brilliantly on cue, Chalky chose to leap out of the bag in the corridor just *after* he passed a couple of security guys. What a dog he was!

In 2004, we began filming in France. I had fully intended to take Chalky. But the spontaneous nature of our style of filming means that we tend to leave organisation to the last minute. I hadn't appreciated that I couldn't micro-chip Chalky one day and take him on the ferry the next. Back then, it was necessary to get everything in order six months in advance. David made a virtue of this, and filmed me taking Chalky to St Merryn to the vet, who said (he'd been primed by me, of course) that he thought Chalky was too old to go. Well, Chalky *was* getting on a bit by then anyway, so David dreamed up a plot to send Chalky videos from France for him to watch back in Trevone. This cunning ruse kept Chalky in the show.

*French Odyssey* was the last time that Chalky took part in a cookery series; he was getting old. I made a couple of other programmes in Cornwall with him. One about John Betjeman who had spent many a contented holiday over the estuary from Padstow at Trebetherick, where he had written some of his best poetry celebrating the British seaside holiday. Betjeman's life in Cornwall was not all happy times, and Chalky was invaluable in that programme trotting along many a cliff path listening to my thoughts about some poem like 'Tregardock', where Betjeman compares the cliffs above the remote beach north of Port Isaac to the black vitriol of some journalist, who obviously didn't like his work.

> *Gigantic slithering shelves of slate*
> *In waiting awfulness appear*
> *Like journalism full of hate...*

Powerful stuff for me. Slippery cliffs in the autumn have a special resonance.

That was in 2005. The next year I made a programme about Daphne du Maurier's Cornwall. We filmed on Bodmin Moor and remembered an anecdote about how Daphne had got lost riding on the moor as a fog came down, and the setting for *Jamaica Inn* appeared to her out of the gloom that day. We also filmed around Fowey, where she had used local atmosphere and the beaches nearby for *Rebecca*. It was to be Chalky's last appearance. We took him to Money Penny Beach but he only managed a weak walk along the water's edge, stumbling a little as he went. I had said to David that I didn't think he would be up to it. He was partly blind and deaf by then and I'd almost lost him in Padstow Churchyard a couple of evenings earlier. That morning I picked him up and said to camera with sadness, 'he's not got long I'm afraid'. He died some months afterwards and I wrote this little obituary for him:

### *Chalky RIP*
### *August 1989 to 13 January 2007*

*Let's look on the bright side. Chalky, my family's dog, lived to 17. He was healthy and fit right up to the last six months and he had a wonderful life. He travelled all over the British Isles and Ireland, he nearly went to France, he got up to some mighty capers, leaping to bite a microphone, snarling at our cameraman so fiercely that we thought twice about using the film, fearing his shocking fangs would frighten children. He dispatched rats and caused consternation by doing the same with a rabbit or two. He was loved by my children. He swam and jumped on boats, he attacked crabs, ran rings round Alsatians and Border Collies, being much fiercer and never backing down, ever. He scampered over a duke's lawns and petrified me that he might bite the Prince of Wales (but he didn't). Most of all though, we knew him at home*

*as rather an unassuming, diffident dog who was never greedy,*
*pestered you a bit for walks, but not too much, and kept reasonably*
*quiet. But – my God! – he hated postmen. I don't know why. If he*
*couldn't get at them, he'd rip the letters to shreds.*

In truth, I'm very sad. He was loved by everyone. So many people, it's a source of puzzlement to me that he never knew how famous he was.

I know what Kipling wrote is thought a bit sentimental but it's actually true.

*There is sorrow enough in the natural way*
*From men and women to fill our day;*
*And when we are certain of sorrow in store,*
*Why do we always arrange for more?*
*Brothers and Sisters, I bid you beware*
*Of giving your heart to a dog to tear.*

*French Odyssey* was a success because the Canal du Midi is a work of art and the country through which it runs is a dream of rural beauty. I spoke in the programme of the peacefulness of a slow boat down the canal with the traffic rushing by on a nearby motorway. At the time, probably five kilometres out of Carcassonne, I remember thinking that this part of France was just the best, anywhere. The climate is completely agreeable; the food, apart from slightly too many *magrets de canard*, is lovely; the lifestyle restful and the people not arrogant in any way. Perhaps the traditional antipathy between French and English is only a Paris and northern France thing.

I don't know how long we could have gone on gliding through that green canopy with the yellow sunflower fields, vineyards, churches and

terracotta-roofed houses sliding by. Watching the programme with
Malcolm Ironton's music is mesmerising. It looks like a painting. Our
French odyssey was an impression of French country life so idealised
that it worked in the same sort of way as works by Monet and Seurat.
Like the art of the Impressionists, it represented yearning for the sort
of 'good life' depicted as modest rural reality which we all at some
point aspire to.

In fact, the life on the barge was not quite as idealistic as we
portrayed it. With one break for a week in the middle, we lived on
the water for eight weeks. It's a long time to be cooped up with five
others. The walls of our cabins were thin. I resorted to pushing one
of the twin mattresses against the wall adjoining the cabin of the
worst of the night-time snorers, David. The big problem, though,
was we weren't at all sensible with our alcohol intake. It was all too
easy. Normally, when filming, there is a lot of activity when we get
back after a shoot. For a start, we will often be checking into a new
hotel, which takes time, but, even if not, there will be unloading of
equipment and we don't necessarily come back to the hotel before
5.29 or (as David calls it) beer o'clock. In contrast, on the barges ,
the *Rosa* from Bordeaux to Toulouse and the *Anjodi* thereafter, we
didn't need to do much filming work at night, so every evening at
about 5.29 we'd assemble on what we called the poop deck which
was actually the fo'c'sle, all have a few beers followed by a few red
wines, then in very jolly mood climb down the companionway –
being careful not to bang my head on the ceiling going down to the
dining room (only once) where we'd drink a lot more wine with our
four-course meal.

And what meals, particularly on the *Rosa*, where Bernard, the
skipper, cooked for us. The French have a strict attitude to meals
and that's why most of them aren't seriously overweight. Fast food is

sadly getting a grip in France too, but there's still a culture of restraint in eating. The French – and particularly French women – don't get fat like me, because, unlike me, while writing these memoirs, they don't go to the fridge every 15 minutes to see if there's anything there which might be tasty. They eat only when they are sitting down for breakfast, lunch and dinner.

Bernard, we soon learnt, ran a very tight ship. The meals he cooked and served were extraordinarily formal, thus revealing the difference between the British and French attitude to food. Julie, the waitress/chambermaid on the *Rosa*, described a visit to a pen-friend in Grimsby as being very enjoyable, but peculiar in that the whole family seemed to be constantly watching TV and eating while they did so. Bernard's lunches and dinners were always four courses, always exquisite, always at a dining table, always taken at a leisurely pace and always just enough and no more. There is a French saying to the effect that one should always leave the table wanting more.

I did a little chat to the DV camera towards the end of the voyage, an inspired idea of David's: ten things we liked about France. Number one, of course, was the women – their style, their elegance in dress at whatever age – but number two was the simple fact that *everything* stops for lunch.

What Bernard cooked for us was not particularly unusual: artichokes with vinaigrette, sautéed eel with persillade, an onion tart, grilled *magret de canard* – the large duck breasts from birds reared for fois gras, with a faint flavour of that delectable luxury. It's not really a criticism to say he was pretty parsimonious too. It goes, I think, with a proper sense of economy in cooking. The first course was always tiny: a small quantity of soup, a thin slice of tart. On one occasion he produced a salad of sliced Quercy melons, Marmande tomatoes and cucumber with some crumbled *brebis*, a sheep's milk cheese – summer in Gascony on a plate. The next course would be a simple piece of fish or meat, again modest in size, followed every day by a choice of at least three cheeses, which Bernard would slice with the skill of a Japanese sashimi chef, and which he would deliver individually and with a running commentary, often of donnish anecdotes about the cheeses, such as the mould in the caves of Roquefort, the carrot juice which gave the extraordinary orange colour to Mimolette, or the fact that the word *crottins*, for the little disc-shaped goat's cheese, came from their resemblance to goat's droppings. The sweet would be maybe a *tarte aux pommes* from a *pâtisserie* near the canal or a crème caramel, again from a local shop.

Often the actual cooking on board would be just one course made by Bernard, but this is another thing so different in France – the availability in any nearby small town of shops that specialise in really good-quality cooked food.

But I'm not sure that in the average French household a big boozy lunch would be followed by a big formal dinner on the same day, every day, especially with yet more red wine. The net result of our indulgent regime was we seemed to be suffering permanently from hangovers and probably too much food, and this could make us rather grumpy with each other. David and I began to joke about a voyage into the heart of darkness. David had asked his best friend Bernard Hall to accompany us and make a video diary of the trip. David ominously called it 'Cabin Fever'. It was monumentally irritating, after having some row, normally with David, and having stomped off to my cabin, to have Bernard knock on the door and open it with camera pointing and say, 'Well, what you think of David at this moment?' My agent, Barbara Levy, heard about the planned extra programme and became extremely alarmed. Over lunch one day at Como Lario in Chelsea she explained that my viewers probably saw me as a nice person and would be shocked if they knew how bad-tempered I could be. I told David that I was un-keen on 'Cabin Fever', but he just said 'Trust me'. He meant that I was to trust him not to include any awful bits; for example, calling him a string of four-letter words, which I certainly wouldn't have liked repeated on film. In the event 'Cabin Fever' was a success. We always used to say that going on filming trips was like going on holiday and, even during memorable holidays, you fall out with your family. My father once filmed my older sister Janey and her best friend Penny having a row in the Scilly Isles, and all you can see is them kicking each other. It's funny because we all know what it's like to be very, very cross.

The truth of it all was that while making *French Odyssey*, we were having the time of our lives and the odd little tiff just made it better. All of us would jump at the opportunity to do a trip like that again. Who knows, maybe we will.

On *French Odyssey*, David had somehow imbued our barge with a sense of a journey, by gradually building up my excitement as we got ever closer to the Mediterranean. He kept me on my toes with references to sunnier climes and comments on the changing landscape after the appearance of olive trees and citrus groves. In Marseille, after eating the bouillabaisse with my friend Simon Hopkinson, we steamed out of the mouth of the Rhône past Port-Saint-Louis into the Mediterranean Sea, with me saying, 'I just want to keep going.' After we'd finished the piece to camera and had turned round and were making our way back to Port-Saint-Louis, David suddenly suggested that I should jump overboard and literally keep going by swimming furiously out to sea. Naturally, wanting to please, I was keen to do just that. I like a swim very much anyway. Fortunately I noticed a large piece of wood whizzing at speed on the outgoing flow of the river and I suddenly realised that by the time they'd turned round to pick me up I would have been miles out to sea.

*Mediterranean Escapes* sort of flowed on from *French Odyssey*. It started on a ferry going from Marseille to Corsica, and continued to numerous islands, ports and beaches. We covered a vast area with diverse cuisines, and tried linking them through flavours such as olives, olive oils, grapes, tomatoes, garlic and fish; we also tried looking at the Mediterranean as the centre of Western civilisation. But I think if you were to classify the TV series as music albums you'd say *French Odyssey* was *Sgt. Pepper's Lonely Hearts Club Band* and *Mediterranean Escapes* was *The White Album*.

I was able to put many more Mediterranean dishes on my menus in Padstow than had been the case with dishes derived from *French Odyssey*. And my food memories were exotic: baklava made with fresh green pistachio nuts, grouper cooked with charcoal. Fabulous, warm, freshly-made hummus, served in a scruffy cafe in Tarsus, St Paul's birthplace, topped with sizzling hot oil and chilli. In Morocco, at the blue city of Chefchaouen in the Rif mountains, I was given a cookery lesson in how to make a perfect lamb tagine with apricots and prunes.

The next series, *Far Eastern Odyssey*, continued the flush of new and exciting recipes for my restaurants. I decided that the combination of hot, salty, sweet and sour was the glorious assault on the senses which we all really craved. The heat from chilli is perhaps an essential part of what makes food satisfying. Maybe not as much chilli as you get in south-east Asia, though. The first two or three days in the orient were habitually accompanied by a definite ache in the stomach caused by the amount of chilli I was taking on board but, once I had become used to it, I found that the combination of plenty of rice, a small amount of protein, plenty of vegetables and a lot of spice was healthy. You feel that your body is responding with joy to what you are giving it. I'm no dietitian but I think that reverence for food is a simple way to ensure that you will live a long time in good health.

I was conscious that I was finding dishes that I could easily put on the Padstow menu. Charming little Thai, Cambodian or Vietnamese salads with maybe some prawns, rice noodles, coriander, mint, chilli, lime, palm sugar and fish sauce. Or slices of raw beef with green mango or papaya shredded and tossed with a spicy dressing plus some texture from roasted rice or cashew nuts or crisped onions.

We went to a fishing village on the banks of Tonle Sap Lake near Siam Riep in Cambodia, and found ourselves in a haze of wood smoke: everywhere the fishermen's wives and children had spread hundreds of thousands of little fish from the lake on trestles and were salting, drying and smoking them in the sun. It was the dry season, so the water levels happened to be low but all the houses were on stilts three to four metres high. We climbed up the rickety stairs to the living room of the aunt of our guide and watched as she prepared a salad, comfortably cross-legged on the floor; the floorboards were set with gaps and the water with which she scrupulously washed her preparation dishes poured through them to the ground far below. Even at the time I was thinking that I could easily adapt her dish: crispy smoked fish shredded in a fiery salad which was fragrant and fresh-tasting too. I managed to get near to the original taste by drying out hot smoked mackerel.

In Bali we visited a Swiss chef called Heinz Von Holzen who was running a cookery school and restaurant called Bumbu Bali at Nusa Dua. We had lunch at his restaurant and then filmed him making a seafood stew using just local seafood and the local spice mix called bumbu Bali which is basically just a pounding of fresh vegetables, herbs and rhizomes, i.e. galangal, turmeric, ginger with chillies, garlic, shallots, lemon grass with some local candlenuts, shrimp paste, fresh nutmeg, vegetable oil and lime juice. The resulting paste he simply fried then added coconut milk and poached some fish (prawns and squid) in the fragrant stock. He said that his Indonesian food is totally authentic but added that, unfortunately, it is rare to find it made as faithfully as he does. He also pointed out that he added some Swiss precision to the process and that what he achieved with this dish was an exact cooking of the seafood so that it was perfectly tender and juicy.

When filming in Bangkok, I met up with my friend David Thompson. In the mid-Nineties he'd had a restaurant in Sydney, called Darley St Thai. I had been astonished by the subtlety of the Thai food he was cooking, accustomed as I was then only to green chicken curry and hot and sour prawn soup, *tom yung gung*. David Thompson used a variety of textures. Crunch from chopped nuts and roasted rice; crispness from green mango shreds, shallots, deep-fried fish skin; tantalising smoky flavours from palm sugar and tea-infused fish. There were little parcels of spiced fish or meat wrapped in leaves, satisfying spicy jungle curries. Now I met him again at the Or Tor Kor Market where he cooked a yellow curry with prawns and lotus shoots. Like Heinz, he seemed to have discovered a wealth of authentic recipes almost forgotten by most Thais. During our walk through the market he bought a couple of fatty preserved pork sausages, deep red and spicy, and a handful of bird's-eye chillies, and explained that if you eat one with the other the fat of the sausage coats your mouth and stops the chilli burning. Pointless, you might think – but the subtlety of the ensuing heat is a pleasure in its own right.

So enthusiastic was I about meeting David Thompson again that I was moved to quote G. K. Chesterton. We had been talking about the scents in the markets and how we ought to educate our sense of smell. I was inspired by the fragrances of red, yellow and green curries, Thai holy basil, different varieties of salted fish, shrimp paste, fish sauce.

> *They haven't got no noses,*
> *The fallen sons of Eve;*
> *Even the smell of roses*
> *Is not what they supposes;*

David looked at me through the camera lens and said, 'What is he on?'

I often wonder what I'm on. I guess a bit of a roll. Since *Far Eastern Odyssey*, David Pritchard and I have made a series in Spain which gave me the confidence to create recipes which, though based on Spanish methods, have been changed to reflect my own taste in food. There's a recipe from Navarra, for example, where I've taken a *cordero al chillindrón*, slow-braised lamb with red peppers – a dish loved by Ernest Hemingway – and much increased the amount of pimenton picante in it because I can't get enough smoked paprika, so much the flavour of Spain to me. My recipe is almost the Spanish equivalent of a curry.

About ten years ago, David chose to film a short sequence in Cornwall and, as luck would have it, selected the fatal cliff near Polventon. It was early summer. There was the pink thrift beneath my feet and the blue sea below. I was to read a poem by Douglas Dunn about a dish I was going to cook.

*Consider please this dish of ratatouille.*
*Neither will it invade Afghanistan*
*Or boycott the Olympic Games in a huff.*

David noted my lack of élan, and later he asked me why I'd seemed curiously out of sorts. I explained. Why on earth hadn't I told him, he asked. I said I hadn't wanted to influence his choice of site. 'Prepare this stew of love, and ask for more,' ran the poem. How could I shatter that idea on a beautiful morning? If I could sit there and not show it maybe it would help me.

These days, I don't only do cookery TV, I indulge other interests such as music and literature, often linked to food. I've mentioned John Betjeman and Daphne du Maurier. I did another programme on the often luxurious cookery of nineteenth-century Italy and the operas of Rossini, Puccini and Verdi. I tried to suggest that these composers who all loved their food were, if not directly influenced in their opera writing, at least filled with a wish to embrace life in their work with the same passionate enthusiasm.

It was David Pritchard, of course, who linked my love of the blues of the southern American states with food. We went to Mississippi to talk to people about blues and southern fried catfish. He arranged for me to interview BB King. We travelled to Indianola, Mississippi, where the great man had grown up, and waited outside in 100-degree heat for him to show up on a tour bus. He was due to play at a blues festival named after him. Eventually, the bus drew up – but he didn't get out. We waited some more in the heat while he took an afternoon nap in his special bedroom at the back of the bus. Finally, he was helped down the bus steps and into a wheelchair.

After all that anticipation, I just blurted out, 'Mr King, are you looking forward to some good food?'

He answered with dignity, 'I look forward to coming home every year. If I had the time, I'd stay here for five or six weeks.'

'But you love the Delta food, don't you?'

He patted his stomach. 'You don't have to ask that.'

He mentioned how many friends he had in London, and then he was wheeled off.

David had told me to ask whether the food in his childhood in Mississippi had been influential in shaping the blues music for which he was famous. What a terrible question, I was thinking at the time. In the programme, we had set out to draw some correlation between the local food and the blues. A bit like asking The Stones if fish and chips had been an influence on their early music. I only mention that because I happened to be in the fish and chip shop in Chipping Norton when I first heard The Rolling Stones. 'Come On' was on the jukebox. I'm certain fish and chips didn't influence them but the memory lingers on for me.

I've just finished making a new series in India. India presents a dilemma. I suspect that I am not alone in feeling pity and horror – fear even – at the sheer pressure of people, the slums, the poverty, the beggars, the smells, the cruelty to animals, the dust. How can you be enthusiastic about anything in a continent of such hardship? How can you even think of food when you can see all around such hunger? Even after three months of filming, I can't begin to answer these questions. I can only say that India casts its spell of magic. It's not that your heart becomes hardened; it's that you realise that you can only change some things, small things – you can't change the vast picture – and that you should meanwhile open up to all the things that are wonderful about India. Enjoy the humour, the colours, the sensuality, the history, the beauty, the variety, the laughter. And above all, enjoy the food – the unbelievable food – of India. Half the programmes have been shown and the feedback is very positive. People say I seem to have been enjoying myself. Indeed I was.

# PART FIVE
## Back to Australia

I was 50 when I first met Sarah Burns. It was August 1997 and I had been contacted by Carolyn Lockhart, the then editor of *Australian Gourmet Traveller*, who asked me if I would be interested in coming to Australia to be the foreign judge of an annual competition they were running with the aim of finding the best restaurant in Australia. Carolyn came to Padstow with her husband Bob, and I got on very well with them, as indeed I do with most Australians. Today, importing someone from outside Australia to do the judging would be strange, but I still think it was a good idea as it removed any suggestions of favouritism. It didn't take me long to make up my mind. Business-class flights and three weeks eating food which I'd become very enthusiastic about and drinking wines which I really enjoyed … what's not to like? Sarah Burns was the publicity manager of *Gourmet Traveller*. I spoke to her on the phone about arrangements. She was breezy and had an abrupt sense of humour which I thought I understood.

On Malaysia Airlines they gave me satays, skewers of beef and chicken, with masses of sweet lumpy peanut sauce with a tantalising taint of shrimp paste. I poked my cheeks with the pointed skewers as I gnawed off the spicy chunks of meat, and I ended up scooping up the delicious sauce with the skewers like chopsticks and dropping it down my shirt. Later I had *nasi lemak* for breakfast – coconut rice with fried anchovies, peanuts and sliced boiled eggs and a curry sauce – still, in my opinion, the best of airline food available anywhere. The smell of the jasmine rice is the scent of south-east Asia to me.

Landing in Sydney, I was met by Carolyn Lockhart at about 6 a.m. I arrived at the Sheraton in Elizabeth Street overlooking Hyde Park on a brilliantly bright winter's morning and made my way to the swimming pool on the top floor of the hotel. I swam with young businessmen, like those working out in the gym next door. I was moving on to a better life. I had slept a lot on the plane but the time difference seemed to make my brain work faster and thereby take in more.

'See you in the morning at quarter to eight and don't be late,' Sarah Burns said, when I met her.

I wasn't sure whether she was serious or not.

The next morning I wasn't late. I started talking to Sarah on the flight to Brisbane. Her father, Tony, lived in a small village in Sumatra and had just confronted a tiger in his garden. Her mother had died when she was eight, and Tony had never got over it. She had a brother, Anthony, a sister, Samantha, and two half-sisters, Georgina and Annabelle, and a stepmother called Janine and a step-grandmother called Betty who appeared to be an enormous influence in her life. Her father had left Australia to help his brother Keith in a coal-mining venture in Indonesia but he had never come home.

The family had originally had huge houses in Sydney and Melbourne. Her stories were funny. One was about her uncle, Kevin, who had been delivered to school as a five-year-old by the chauffeur, decided he didn't like it, and got a taxi home by himself and hadn't been required to go back till he was eight. I couldn't help but be attracted to her tales of the eccentric behaviour of her large family which had perhaps had more than its fair share of ups and downs. I told her about my family, which was not without a certain flamboyance too. It was an extraordinary conversation; it was as if I was talking to someone I already knew.

She told me I could call her Sas, and confessed that she had had no idea who I was before she'd been asked to publicise the tour; in fact, they'd wanted Simon Hopkinson but he couldn't do it. Great!

We got to the Hilton at Brisbane and she took me to lunch at a restaurant called Two Small Rooms. I've come to enjoy the way that the Australians have of making a title romantic just by sticking to the bare bones of it. The most charming example of this to me is a winery in the Mornington Peninsula called Ten Minutes by Tractor, referring to the fact that it's a ten-minute tractor ride from one vineyard to the other. Two Small Rooms was just two small rooms of a single-storey 'Queenslander' house. These are single-storey wooden houses with corrugated iron roofs, verandas and wooden floors on stilts to let the air circulate and keep the building cool and allow for water to flow in a downpour – of which there are plenty in Brisbane. I looked at the menu and chose Jack's mud crab omelette. There again was that use of the prosaic which ends up being anything but. A plump omelette filled with the white meat of the mud crab which comes from the mangrove swamps of Queensland. It was served with stir-fried veg flavoured with lime, chilli, garlic, palm sugar, fish sauce, mint and coriander. It was everything I was coming to love about Australia: a fluffy omelette, great crab, exciting Asian flavours. I put the recipe in *Seafood Odyssey*. Jack's memory lives on in his omelette of choice.

After lunch Sas went shopping and I went for a swim in the hotel pool outside on the ninth floor, this time in the cooling late afternoon air, office blocks all around, and the bright colours as the shadows grew darker. That evening we went to the first of the restaurants I had to judge. My fellow guests were a local freelance journalist called Jan Power and a Catholic priest from South Brisbane, Peter Dillon.

The conversation was lively, the food not so good. Indeed I was rather worried that if this was to be the standard on the trip I was in for an embarrassing time. I had escalope of kangaroo with a cream and Marsala sauce which I didn't enjoy. The problem with kangaroo is that it's really lean meat, leaner even than veal, and even with a creamy sauce, it tasted tough and dry. I've never got quite used to eating kangaroo because it reminds me of my days back in Deepwell – the railway camp near Alice Springs drinking billy tea in a caravan with a kangaroo hunter. I don't feel any compunction about eating animals but the disdain with which this man spoke about the 'vermin' which were kangaroos and his enthusiasm for dispatching them in large quantities was depressing. He had blood under his fingernails. When he described the stink of disembowelling them, I felt sorry for the kangaroos, remembering a tender D.H. Lawrence poem:

*Delicate mother Kangaroo*
*Sitting up there rabbit-wise, but huge, plump-weighted,*
*And lifting her beautiful slender face, oh! So much more*
*Gently and finely lined than a rabbit's, or than a hare's,*
*Lifting her face to nibble at a round white peppermint drop*
*Which she loves, sensitive mother Kangaroo.*
*Her sensitive, long, pure-bred face.*
*Her full antipodal eyes, so dark,*
*So big and quiet and remote, having watched so many*
*Empty dawns in silent Australia.*

Not unnaturally, with native game on the menu, conversation turned to anecdotes of eating wallabies, goannas, crocodiles and emus. Jan Power told about going to a very serious aboriginal meeting in the Flinders Ranges in South Australia. Lunch was a piece of burnt meat of indeterminate origin. She asked the chief what it was and was told echidna. 'That's interesting,' she said. 'I haven't eaten echidna before. Where did you catch it?'

'I scraped it off the road this morning; it hadn't been dead more than a couple of hours.'

It was one of those evenings when the awfulness of the food only served to improve the spikiness of the conversation. Not only was Jan Power full of robust humour but Peter Dillon was the sort of priest you dream of meeting but so rarely do, in other words, religious but with a sense of humour, very widely read, nicely dressed conservatively (herringbone jacket, English-university professor look), the sort of person you would trust to help you through a difficult time. Sas, I had discovered within the first half-hour of meeting her, was a Catholic. I suddenly wanted to be one too.

The second of our restaurants was called E'cco which means 'here it is' in Italian. It was one of those perfect restaurant evenings which occur only occasionally. One of the other judges was a cookery writer called Jacki Passmore. It helped that I had already got one of her books on Thai cooking and admired her recipes. I ordered a wine called MadFish Premium White. On the label it had an aboriginal painting of a turtle with fish swimming around it. The wine was a blend of Chardonnay and Sauvignon Blanc. It seemed to sum up everything I was enjoying about Australia. The first course was some soft white crab meat with parsley, tomato and linguine pasta with a little olive oil and chilli. I took both this dish and the MadFish back to Padstow. Crab linguine has become common everywhere now, but it's too often overcooked and over-handled, with too much stuff added. I make it by carefully warming some olive oil and gently sweating a little chopped garlic, then adding skinned, deseeded and chopped tomatoes, a pinch of chilli, salt, pepper and parsley. Then I very carefully fold in crab meat so as not to break it up and heat it only enough just to warm the crab through. I pile the sauce on to just-cooked linguine. The cooking of Philip Johnson, the chef at E'cco, was like that, an instinctive understanding of the innate simplicity of Italian cooking.

I had no means of knowing that night that E'cco would be my choice of the best restaurant in Australia – there were so many more to visit in Perth, Adelaide, Hobart, Melbourne and Sydney – but one of the things that was clear to me was that it was a restaurant in balance with the capabilities of its staff and also serving the food that its customers wanted to eat. The Australians have a love of Italian food. Certainly the climate is more like Italy than the 'old country' and I think they sense that Italian cuisine is more appropriate. Philip had worked in London as well as Australia and, like me, has a joy in finding great raw materials and cooking them simply.

In Fraser's restaurant in Perth, I was introduced to the delight of pearl meat. This is the muscle that opens and closes the plate-sized shells of the pearl oyster. I always scrape out and eat the same meat in our own oysters but it's only tiny. With these it's about the size of a scallop; it's tough, like abalone, but if it's thinly sliced and seared, marinated with lime juice or braised slowly, it is of a similar taste and quality. But memories of Perth are more tied up with Sas than eating the excellent food at Fraser's.

We flew in from Brisbane, arriving in the early afternoon, and she rang my room in the Hyatt and asked me if I'd like to go to Cottesloe Beach. For her, it was mid-winter, so she was rather surprised that I wanted to swim. The water temperature was about 18 degrees, warm by my standards. I swam for over an hour and when I got back to where she was lying reading in the sun in a yellow swimming costume, she was actually a bit worried about me. I learnt later she'd been on the phone to one of her friends saying I was a bit of an idiot. I'd gone swimming a long way out in 'shark city'.

As I walked up to her, I took in long tanned legs. I wasn't yet interested in her physically. She was tall and blonde. I was a bit intimidated because she wore glamorous clothes. She also wore glasses which added to the somewhat icy demeanour she seemed to have. But talking to her was easy and delightful. She had a sense of humour and knew lots of chefs. The year before she had travelled with Robert Carrier and had got on well with him. He called her Duchess and she used to go to his room and read with him. I was slightly in awe of someone who could behave so naturally with someone so famous in my world.

When I came back from my swim she ticked me off about swimming out so far.

'It's a dangerous beach for sharks.'

'Nice of you to tell me now,' I said.

We moved to a pub on the beach called The Cottesloe Hotel which was filled with surfers and the sort of people you would find in a Newquay pub; the Australians call them bogans. She seemed a bit embarrassed that the main pub on such an iconic beach was filled with very ordinary people. I said it was absolutely what I liked and I had two schooners of Swan lager to celebrate. Later we went into Freemantle to see a mutual friend, Ian Parmenter, an English TV producer who had made a name for himself in front of the camera with a long-running Australian television show called *Consuming Passions*. That night we ate at the Indiana Tea House back at Cottesloe Beach. I found myself telling Sas much more about my life. Possibly a bit too much.

The next day was a Sunday and a trip to Rottnest Island had been organised with a local wine writer called Peter Forrestal. I first met Peter on the jetty going out to the boat. He seemed to be carrying an inordinate amount of wine and provisions for what I gathered were only seven of us going on the boat for one night – two cases of wine and a couple of insulated Eskys of food and wine plus some other boxes with more food – all this fetching and carrying along the rocking planks accompanied by his beagle, Munch. Peter was short and square and was looking after the provisions with seriousness. He reminded me of Badger in *The Wind in the Willows*. I took to him immediately and we've been friends ever since. He had left a message via Sas to ask if there was anything I would like to be taken on board to cook that evening, and I suggested squid. At the time I was keen on stir frying squid in olive oil with a touch of garlic, chilli and roasted red peppers, so I cooked that. Everyone seemed to enjoy it. Peter cooked some abalone and Mike, the boat owner, did some steaks and a couple of large salads. Peter had brought some wines from Margaret River, a Pierrot Chardonnay as well as some more Chardonnay from the 1995 Art Series from Leeuwin Estate. There was also some Sauvignon Semillon from his friend Vanya Cullen at Cullen's Winery and a bottle of old Moss Wood Cabernet from another friend, plus some vintage Bollinger for Sas, who drank only champagne.

We motored over to Rottnest, dropped anchor and ate and drank late into the night. All that evening I was conscious of Sas not talking to me. I felt I was being ignored. It seemed something had changed from the night before when perhaps too much had been said. I felt that somehow I had crossed a line of propriety.

The next morning we awoke in Rottnest Harbour to discover that Princess Diana had died. I wonder if there is a special kinship between you and the people you are with when some dreadful news is announced. I remembered the same sort of slice of time and place with the assassination of Kennedy; I'd just arrived to play a rugby match at Sedbergh School in Cumbria. This time I was sitting in the stern of a boat in bright sunshine feeling slightly anxious about Sas.

The next day, back in Perth, she was back to her normal abrupt breeziness. We flew to Adelaide and ate a test dinner at a restaurant in the Hilton Hotel called the Grange where a Malaysian-Chinese chef called Chiung Liew was cooking a fusion of Malaysian and European flavours.

We talked and talked, first in the restaurant and then in the hotel bar. The night at the Indiana Tea Rooms in Perth was being repeated but this time with a fatal sense of concentration on everything she said, the sparkle in her blue eyes and every movement of her body. It was like the space ship at the beginning of *2001, A Space Odyssey*, locked into the gravitational pull of the giant circular space station, gradually assuming the rotation of the wheel in space and being guided, inexorably, into its heart.

The next morning we went for lunch in McLaren Vale, a wine-growing region just outside Adelaide. I was feeling a mixture of dread and elation. I had crossed a border into another land.

Looking from the terrace of the Veranda Restaurant at d'Arenberg Winery, down the valley to the rows of budding vines and the low hills behind in the early spring sun, and feeling so utterly filled with the knowledge that, for better or worse, nothing would ever be the same again …

Whenever I feel depressed about how much trouble and pain I've caused, I go back there in my mind and I'm filled with such a sense of the acute clarity of that morning, that it's no longer a question of right and wrong. It had to be.

There was something about Sas that I couldn't forget. Her cheerful Aussie directness, her way of summing things up in a few witty words, her love of books, her enthusiasm for life. I met her father, Tony, who was over from Sumatra for his first visit to Sydney in 15 years. Like his daughter, it was almost as if I'd known him all my life. I've often told her that meeting him sealed it for me. It felt almost like I'd come home. It was too much to wrap up as a bit of 'what-goes-on-tour-stays-on-tour'.

⌒

Before long I was talking David into another TV series with the BBC. Why not a seafood odyssey? Why not visit all the places I'd been before? In the back of my mind, I knew I'd make a big part of the new series in Australia. And so it turned out. Sas visited England before we started filming, and the next time I saw her was in Noosa, where of course I'd got her the job of fixer on the Australian leg of our film. I kept ringing her from Goa, when we filmed there, and then from a resort hotel in Hua Hin in Thailand, where I realised I was in love with her. For the next four years, I tried to see her whenever I could, but at one stage we were apart for two years. All the time, I was desperately inventing reasons to fly to Australia. Tours, food festivals … I accepted them all, grasping at every opportunity. Nobody guessed. I hid it from everyone.

In 2002 I moved out of the family house in Trevone. It was the year I made *Food Heroes* and the series shows me setting out in the Land Rover with Chalky from a bungalow overlooking the Camel river. The same year, Edward married his girlfriend Kate. I went to the wedding feeling like an outcast. Yet it was enchanting. Edward and his friends made extraordinary speeches and his best man, Russell, wrote a touching poem which he read out loud instead of giving a speech.

Jill and I divorced in 2007. We still run the business together and she now has a successful interior design business as well.

My long-distance love between England and Australia has been hard. Sas can't yet move permanently to England because her children are at school in Australia. We flit from one side of the world to the other like time-travellers. But we have a rule that we must never be apart for more than four weeks. I feel – and so does Sas – that it is worth every single air mile.

In Cornwall, I don't go out much and miss Sas dreadfully. The best part of the week is going to The Cornish Arms for two pints with Johnny Walter, my brother-in-law Chris, and a couple of old friends, Chris Rowe and Hugo Woolley. We go for just an hour and each of us drinks two pints, except for Chris who prefers gin and tonic and Hugo who always has Famous Grouse with water from his own Famous Grouse jug which is behind the bar. We are as boring as men who have known each other for ever can be, and I love it. I think it partly alleviates the restlessness of living half in Australia and half in Cornwall. I guess with me, I don't want to go gentle into that good night.

There was criticism about my choice when I finally announced in Sydney who had won the Australian Gourmet Traveller accolade. By then I'd been to most of the great and good restaurants of the time in Australia, and had especially enjoyed the Rockpool in Sydney and Jacques Reymond in Melbourne. But I stuck to the brief, which was to reward the restaurant that was greater than the sum of its parts and, as such, a contribution to human happiness. It was a hard choice because Australian restaurants are very good, and it's difficult when you're eating delicious food night after night to stay objective, but in the end it's your choice. I'm pleased to note that Philip Johnson has gone on to keep the faith with his restaurant E'cco: he hasn't expanded. Sure, he runs a cookery school now as well as the restaurant, but he's still in Brisbane cooking lovely food.

I'm still in Padstow – dividing my time between Australia and Cornwall. I don't cook as much as I used to but I still dream up recipes for all my restaurants and all my cookery books. I pass my ideas on to my son Jack who runs our development kitchen where he tests recipes, checks on existing dishes for consistency and works out how best to cook everything for large numbers. He's becoming increasingly good, too, at copying his old man and doing television which makes me very proud. Jack's never lost for words.

Charles is working in London for a wine company called The Vintner which suddenly seems to be getting more and more of our business. We've got the three restaurants in Padstow and two fish and chip shops, one in Padstow and one in Falmouth, and now we own my beloved old pub, the Cornish Arms in St Merryn.

Apart from missing Sas, what journalists call Padstein is a source of great satisfaction to me. I live in a cottage just up the hill from all the restaurants, so I can walk into all the kitchens in a couple of minutes. I work with our executive chef, David Sharland, and the head chefs, Stephane Delorme at The Seafood, Paul Harwood at St Petroc's Bistro and Luke Taylor at the Cornish Arms. Today we employ 290 people all the year round, and up to 400 in the summer months. Over the years, my sons, nephews and nieces have all done time in the business. Edward and Jack must have been about 14 when I had them washing dishes – an early and brutal reminder of the realities of restaurant work. My brother John's wife Clare – who will always have a place in my heart because she was so welcoming to Sas – sent her daughter Kate to learn the ropes at St Petroc's. Kate is a doctor now. William and Polly, John's two older children from his marriage to Fanny, are now respectively high up in BT and a teacher in Oxford, but they also put in their hours. Molly, Henrietta and my brother-in-law Phil's daughter, was once a waitress at The Seafood in the vacations from drama school. She may have decided to be an actress after teenage dramas with her father and mother. How girls change after 20. Julius, son of my sister Janey and Shaun, used to work with me in the kitchen at The Seafood – and I still feel bad about how tough I was on him all those years ago. Now he's Judge Jules, the famous DJ. His brother Samuel was a very popular presence in The Seafood; he now has a pub in London. In fact the restaurant was a focal point for my family in the early days. My mother, naturally, was a tireless supporter but I always used to feel a little sorry for her when she came with the children, my nieces and nephews including William and Polly, Julius and Samuel and my brother Jeremy and his wife Jenny's children, Anthony and Frances, because she was always on tenterhooks that they wouldn't behave or that something would go wrong; she never seemed to be able to enjoy it as much as I'd wanted. But they all did behave and loved it, still do. Henrietta and Phil's daughter Rosie – grown up and a psychologist now – will still stop to tell me how much those visits to The Seafood Restaurant meant to her.

Lucy – Clare and John's other daughter, now an artist – gave me one of her paintings, which depicts her boyfriend Hammy holding up a cod on the quay while Lucy climbs over the harbour wall in a bikini. She said it was inspired by the Padstow of her childhood and her memories of The Seafood Restaurant.

*

And now I've got Sas. Sas is sunny and Aussie. She doesn't see the world, like me, a bit gloomily. Her friends get ill and die just like everyone else's but she mourns for them and gets over it and remembers them with great love. I used to feel ten years younger when I got off that plane in Sydney, now it's 20 years younger.

Ever since the days of the search for the best restaurant in Australia I've been aware that Sas has a much brisker and more efficient attitude to business matters than me. At that time, after an early radio interview in Adelaide, I came out of the studio thinking I'd been marvellous and said to her,

'How was I?'

'Don't worry, I'll tell you if you're terrible.'

So we've taken on a restaurant together on the south coast of New South Wales at Mollymook called Rick Stein at Bannisters. Our business partner, Peter Cosgrove, owns Bannisters Hotel which is right on the sea. I look after the food, and Sas looks after promoting it and keeping a friendly eye on everything when I'm away. Mollymook is like Padstow. They are both holiday places where the same families come back year after year and the seafood is good. I found an enthusiastic fish merchant called Lucky in Ulladulla, which is the town with a fishing harbour next door to Mollymook. I cooked fish for Sas and her family every year, learning what was local and excellent. For me, cooking with snapper, kingfish, tuna, blue-eye trevally and leatherjacket was a fascinating change from cod, monkfish and turbot. The local estuary prawns, the squid which they call calamari, abalone and oysters were for me, as Sas says, like being a kid in a lolly shop. I found a supply of sea urchins and a local lobster fisherman called Chiller, so named because he keeps his lobsters in chilled sea water in tanks in his garage. The menu I devised for Mollymook is very similar to Padstow's. Same dishes, different fishes.

Sas was divorced in 2003. Her children, Zach and Olivia, were much younger at the time of the break-up than my children. I've been in their lives since they were too young to remember, and I strive to be a good stepdad to them.

It took me seven years to propose to Sas, which I did sitting in a rented car next to a rubbish bin outside a computer shop in Puglia in southern Italy. It all came out in a rush. I didn't even know I was going to say it. And afterwards, typically, I was anxious about what I'd done. But I needn't have worried. We were married in 2011, and I've loved every minute of it since. The wedding was at a register office in Sydney. We told no one – not her children, nor mine. In other words, we eloped.

Subsequently, we threw parties both in London and in Mollymook – and called them our elopement celebrations. At both parties, I found myself very emotional because it had been a hard time for many reasons but I felt that everyone was, at last, pleased for us. After so many difficult years, I could quote Mrs Patrick Campbell, 'Wedlock is the deep, deep peace of the double bed after the hurly-burly of the chaise-longue.'

⁓

These days, I swim whenever I can. It stems from a growing realisation that we all ought to take some sort of exercise. I was walking with Sas through Hyde Park early one morning when we saw a number of gentlemen – generally rather elderly like myself – swimming among the ducks and swans. Sas said, 'Why don't you do that, Ricky? It'd be good for you.' I started to swim in the summer months – and in the warmth of Mollymook. But now I swim right through the year. The colder it is in Cornish waters, the more scared I am of the extreme shock and the vulnerability of a warm human body in a vast freezing sea. But I am driven to seek affirmation of being alive, and I relish the feeling of ruddy good health afterwards.

Last summer, near high tide, something drove me to swim from Mother Ivy's Beach across to the cove on Trevose Head where my father died. As I swam closer, I became increasingly uneasy; the waves seemed bigger, the sea deeper and darker. I almost felt I had to turn back. There's no path down from the top, and I remembered that they had to launch the lifeboat to recover his body from the sea so there would be no easy way out.

But as I got to the strip of sand still left from the incoming tide, I realised that the cliff looks different from below. From above it's a perilous drop. I couldn't tell the exact spot where – a lifetime ago – he had dashed himself on to the rocks. It all looked much less threatening. I started to relax. Was this really the fatal spot? Maybe I had started to realise that it no longer matters exactly what happened.

# AFTERWORD

I'm driving down to Mollymook with Sas and Zach and Olivia. It's a great time: we are going on holiday. We always stop at the McDonald's in Albion Park. I order a Grand Angus Burger. Zach says he doesn't want anything. He doesn't approve of McDonald's. He's 16 and very serious. But at the last minute he too orders a Grand Angus. I know that the reason Zach has relented is because it's traditional. Once a year we have McDonald's, once a year he says no, and always he changes his mind and says yes.

As we resume the journey going south I say, 'It's much better driving to Mollymook these days because Olivia's not being sick all the time.'

'Yes Olivia,' says Zach, teasing her. 'We were always having to stop on the freeway.'

I catch her in the rear-view mirror looking a bit embarrassed: she's cross and beautiful.

'I was always sick in the car when I was little,' I say.

My son Jack used to call these times his 'black and white feeling'. Special times. Times like family Sunday lunch at Trevone.

I'm very lucky. Zach and me and Olivia get on very well. They came to Edward's Finals sculpture exhibition of the work he'd done at the City and Guilds College in Kennington in London last summer. Charles came too, and Henrietta and her husband Philip, and William my nephew, and our good friend Anita who we were lucky to see as she was going crazy working for a company selling merchandise at the Olympic Village. It was a precious time for me. I was very attracted to Edward's work, which included a perfect sphere in blue-black Cornish granite with a teardrop design hand-carved and an alphabet, which I bought there and then. His wife Kate couldn't come as she was looking after my grandson, Hugh, who is the most beautiful and perfectly formed baby I've ever seen. It was a moment to realise that my children and stepchildren like each other. Sas really gets my family. We come from the same sort of background which, I guess, was what attracted me when I first met her. She also has a sympathetic understanding of people and I'm happy that she's started to write. She gets on well with the staff at Bannisters and, above all, she understands and likes chefs who, she realises, are often difficult but underneath are creative people with good hearts. She persuaded me to write this book and may or may not admire what I'm writing now. She's a little controlling of me, which I like. She's always been loved and confident and can afford to share it around.

# ACKNOWLEDGEMENTS

I would like to thank my wife Sas for her tireless support during the writing of this; without her it wouldn't have happened. Thanks to Penny Hoare, who assisted me in turning a draft which rambled a little into something much more organised. Thanks to Fiona MacIntyre, Managing Director of Ebury Publishing, for supporting this book before I had written a word; our initial discussion was in the Hilton Hotel at Paddington station, formerly the Great Western Hotel, in whose basement I had my first kitchen experiences as a raw teenager.

I love the look of the cover, and thanks for this is due to David Eldridge.

After the process of editing, a lot of people, whom I would have loved to have mentioned and acknowledged, have, of necessity, been sadly left out. Friends, relatives, colleagues, staff of The Seafood Restaurant – past and present – you know who you are, and I hope that you all realise how very much you have meant to me.

And lastly, I love to show off with where I wrote this. My cottage in Padstow; Neutral Bay in Sydney; my holiday house in Mollymook, NSW, Australia; my flat in Chelsea, London; Il Convento di Santa Maria Marittima, Puglia, Italy; the Malabar House Cochin, Kerala, India; The Dylan Hotel, Amsterdam; The Ritz Hotel, London and my friends Tim and Nicky's house in St Tropez.

# ABOUT THE AUTHOR

Rick Stein is a well-loved and respected chef, TV presenter and author who has produced an array of award-winning books and television series, including *Rick Stein's Seafood*, *Seafood Lover's Guide*, *Taste of the Sea*, *Food Heroes*, *French Odyssey*, *Mediterranean Escapes*, *Coast to Coast* and *Far Eastern Odyssey*. All of his books and programmes show a commitment to good-quality produce, sustainable fishing and good husbandry.

Rick owns four restaurants, a delicatessen, a patisserie, a seafood cookery school and forty guest bedrooms in the small fishing port of Padstow, Cornwall. In 2003, Rick was awarded an OBE for services to West Country Tourism. He divides his time between Padstow and Australia, which he regards as his second home.